D1508922

CHILD DEVELOPMENT WITHIN CULTURALLY STRUCTURED ENVIRONMENTS

Social Co-construction and Environmental Guidance in Development

Volume 2

Edited by

Jaan Valsiner
University of North Carolina at Chapel Hill

ABLEX PUBLISHING CORPORATION
NORWOOD, NEW JERSEY

Printed in the United States of America

Library of Congress Cataloging-in-Publication Data

Social co-construction and environmental guidance in
    development.

    (Child development within culturally structured
environments ; v. 2)
        Bibliography: p.
        Includes index.
        1. Children and adults. 2. Social interaction
in children. 3. Cognition in children. 4. Culture—
Psychological aspects. 5. Environmental psychology.
6. Developmental psychology. I. Valsiner, Jaan.
II. Series.
BF723.A33C48   vol. 2   303.3′2s   88-6364
ISBN 0-89391-488-6   [303.3′23]

Ablex Publishing Corporation
355 Chestnut Street
Norwood, New Jersey 07648

Contents

List of Contributors

Eve Brotman Band, Clinical Psychology Program, Department of Psychology, University of North Carolina at Chapel Hill, Chapel Hill, N.C. 27514.

Norris B. Johnson, Department of Anthropology, University of North Carolina at Chapel Hill, Chapel Hill, N.C. 27514.

Thomas Kindermann, Graduate School of Education and Human Development, University of Rochester, Rochester, N.Y. 14627.

Cynthia Lightfoot, Developmental Psychology Program, Department of Psychology, University of North Carolina at Chapel Hill, Chapel Hill, N.C. 27514.

Julie Ann Robinson, Department of Psychology, LaTrobe University, Bundoora, Victoria 3083, Australia.

Ellen Skinner, Max-Planck-Institut fur Bildungsforschrung, Lentzallee 94, D-1000 Berlin(W.) 33, Federal Republic of Germany.

Jaan Valsiner, Developmental Psychology Program, Department of Psychology, University of North Carolina at Chapel Hill, Chapel Hill, N.C. 27514.

Frederick Verdonick, Institute for Gerontology and Department of Developmental Psychology, University of Michigan, Ann Arbor, Mi. 48105.

Lucien T. Winegar, Department of Psychology, Randolph-Macon College, Ashland, VA.

Uwe Zänker, Department of Education, Fachhochschule Düsseldorf, Dusseldorf, Federal Republic of Germany.

PART ONE

Culturally Structured Environments for Children: Canalization of Child Development

INTRODUCTION: BASIC IDEAS IN CONSTRUCTIVIST THEORIZING

Contributions to Part One of this second volume of *Child Development within Culturally Structured Environments* outline different approaches to the understanding of the *constructive* nature of child development. Such approaches have been rare in developmental psychology. The constructivist approach presumes recognition of the active nature of the social construction of child development, on both sides—that of the developing child, and of its caregivers. It becomes also necessary to recognize that novel outcomes may result from the social construction of child development. That recognition has had limited popularity in the social sciences of the past (see Epilogue of this volume).

The three chapters in Part One attempt to advance co-constructivist theorizing in different ways. Lucien T. Winegar (Chapter 1) extends our theoretical understanding of the mechanisms by which adults "influence" children's actions, and through which children trigger adults' actions. His co-constructivist theory starts from the assumption of children's and adults' active role in canalizing one another's development on the background of particular environmental contexts. The "constraints" that interaction partners set upon one another's actions are seen as the means by which the process of co-construction takes place. By constraining, the interactants lead one another towards "progressive empowerment" of their actions within environment. There is a basic asymmetry in adult–child interaction, paralleling that of "expert"—"novice" role distinction. Winegar's empirical observations illustrate the applicability of his theoretical thinking to child–adult transaction in everyday environmental contexts. He describes ways in which preschool teachers organize the activity of a group of 3- to 4-year-old children during a snacktime in the preschool.

In Chapter 2, Cynthia Lightfoot provides an analysis of a largely forgotten aspect of Piaget's developmental theory of equilibration—that of the interdependence of cognitive schemata and their affective counterparts. Her extension of Piaget's theory in the direction of viewing the parental role in guiding the process of progressive equilibration (or at times-towards purposefully enhanced disequilibration) integrates the children's development of sensori-motor schemes with its affective and interactional contexts. Lightfoot presents a longitudinal description of how a young infant first learns to locomote over a step in the home environment, using assistance of the parents. Subsequently, that skill temporarily dissipates, as the parents' reduce their assistance to the child who is seen to have mastered the basic locomotion skill. The skill reappears later as a new form of means–ends connection, again with the social support for this development on parents' side.

Thomas Kindermann and Ellen Skinner (Chapter 3) deal with contextual embeddedness of toddlers' development through analyzing the *developmental tasks* shared by the caregiver and the child at any given age. The developmental tasks are viewed as settings for joint action that organize children's development through assisting them in learning new skills. Different cultural belief systems, as well as families within the same cultural group, may differ in *what* is considered to be a "developmental task." However, Kindermann and Skinner argue that, once a given objective is construed as a developmental task, its structure minimizes interfamily and intercultural variability in *how* that developmental task is accomplished—in comparison with such variability either before, or after, that task gets accomplished ontogenetically. Developmental tasks are thus focal moments of relevance for child development within culturally organized environments, which play directive (canalizing) role in the life of the developing child.

CHAPTER 1

Children's Emerging Understanding of Social Events: Co-Construction and Social Process*

Lucien T. Winegar

Department of Psychology
Randolph-Macon College
Ashland, Virginia

Much as children's early contacts with the physical world are viewed as fundamental in theories of cognitive development, early interpersonal encounters provide occasions for acting, feeling, and thinking which are fundamental to the development of children's social understanding. Both the physical and social environment provide information for performance that organizes and constrains children's action. Similarly, just as children's levels of sensori-motor development structure their exploratory manipulation of objects, children's levels of social under-standing constrain their choice of action during social encounters and limit information that they can extract from exchanges with social partners. Further, social others provide additional constraining of chil-dren's actions, perceptions, and representations in efforts to channel children toward appropriate social functioning. Through these processes,

---

* The research reported in this chapter was supported in part by a Faculty Research Grant from Haverford College. Portions of this chapter were presented in a different form at the 16th Annual Meeting of the Jean Piaget Society, May 1986, Philadelphia, PA.

I would like to thank the children and teachers who participated in this study, and Polly Stephens for her assistance in data collection. The ideas expressed in this chapter have benefited greatly from my discussions with Robert H. Wozniak, K. Ann Renninger, F.F. Strayer, and, especially, Jaan Valsiner. Finally, I am grateful to Renée Cardone for her support and encouragement during the writing of this chapter.

children's understanding of their social world emerges from their interaction with others in everyday contexts.

Some of the processes through which children's understanding of mutual conventions and commonly occurring events emerges from their interaction with others in social contexts are detailed in this chapter. Children's understanding of events and conventions is described as a co-constructed relation between the environment and the child. The relevant external environment for the development of this understanding includes information provided by the physical surroundings, including cultural artifacts, and constraints on performance provided by social partners. Also of particular importance are the child's current general level of understanding and his or her past experience in the same and similar events.

The intent here is not to suggest the existence of adult influences on children's performance. Rather, it is assumed that such influences exist, and an attempt is made to describe some aspects of the nature of these influences. This description proceeds from the metatheoretical assumption that children's understanding of their world, as reflected by their performance in it, need not be considered as following from solely structural changes in their knowledge, but rather can also be fruitfully construed in terms of social transactions which characterize members of social groups.

Specifically, two general questions are addressed in this chapter: (a) What is the nature of children's action in, and understanding of, the everyday events in which they participate? and (b) What are some of the characteristics of the social processes through which adults provide information and direction to channel children toward socially appropriate actions and subsequent understanding? Toward these questions, a discussion of two interrelated aspects of adult–child interaction in commonly occurring social events is directed. First, the nature of children's understanding of social procedures and conventions is discussed. It is proposed that children's understanding of social events may be considered as co-constructed knowledge. As part of this metatheoretical claim, both intra- and interpersonal definitions of co-construction are developed. Second, a theoretical description of the nature of constraining tactics used by adults to support and enable children's action in accordance with social conventions is presented. Further, changes that occur in these adult tactics as children assume greater responsibility for self-regulation within social settings are examined. The co-constructed nature of children's understanding of events, and the social processes which support the development of this understanding, are illustrated by empirical findings from an observational study in which the interaction between teachers and preschool children was observed during snacktime.

CO-CONSTRUCTION AND SOCIAL PROCESS WITHIN SOCIAL EVENTS

Co-Construction

Most discussions of children's understanding of social events have posited the existence of knowledge structures which enable appropriate action in given social contexts (e.g., Nelson, 1981). Such an approach is exemplified in the "script" construct (Schank & Abelson, 1977) which has been employed to account for appropriate behavior in repetitive, routine social interactions. A script is a schema which specifies information about actions, procedures, and contingencies in a particular context. Its elements are organized as a predictive, cohesive unit. This unit consists of a sequence of actions which are linked both causally and temporally and are oriented toward a goal. Thus, scripts are proposed as "representations" of the world.

There are two distinct but related uses of the term *representation* (Mandler, 1983). First, representation is used as a synonym for knowledge. In this usage, representation refers both to content of knowledge and organization of knowledge. It is this use of the term that is most akin to Piaget's (1951) "representation in the broad sense."[1] Alternatively, representation is used to refer to words, images, or other symbols that stand for some aspect of the world or some aspect of a person's knowledge of that world. This use of representation as referent or expression of knowledge is similar to Piaget's "representation in the narrow sense."

Perhaps nowhere is the blurring of these two meanings of representation better illustrated than in the study of social event knowledge in preschool children, which has proceeded from within a script framework. The majority of studies in this area employ interviews to collect children's statements about events (Nelson, 1986). These statements are then subjected to linguistic analyses, and the organization and content of children's language about social events is taken to be representative of the organization and content of chilren's knowledge of the events (Fivush, 1984).

There are several potential problems with this approach. First, the

---

[1] Note, however, that Piaget would not use a single term to refer to both structure and content of knowledge (see Sigel, 1983, for a comparison of Piagetian and schema-based approaches to knowledge).

use of an interview procedure entails the assessment of children's knowledge of an event in a situation that is far removed and has very different demands and expectations than the situations in which children experience events and in which it would be appropriate for them to express their understanding. What children say in the context of an interview may be very different from what they may actually do while within the social event in question. Thus, children's verbal reports obtained through interviews reflect as much the demands and structure of the interview setting as they do the demands and structure of the event itself or children's knowledge of the event.

Second, in using language as the sole measure of children's understanding, much of the research guided by script theory appears to assume a direct structural relationship between representation as knowledge and representation as expression of knowledge. This is especially the case in those studies of children's event representations, in which the structure and content of children's language about events is interpreted as reflecting the structure and content of children's knowledge of the same event. Such use of language to assess knowledge seems to be especially questionable when investigating the understanding of young children. Children's proficiency with the formal aspects of language in verbal interview may result in their appearing formally competent in structural aspects of social event knowledge (e.g., temporal and causal order) when no corresponding action competence exists. That is, children may say more than they know. Paradoxically, children's ignorance of the linguistic referents for content aspects of a social structure or action may result in their appearing less competent than might be indicated by their action. That is, they may know more than they can say.

Thus, many investigations of children's event knowledge guided by the "script" construct have tended to ignore influences of social context on both the development and expression of children's understanding. At least as importantly, these investigations have also failed to consider that language, though it may reflect some aspects of knowledge, need not reproduce the structural characteristics of the underlying knowledge it expresses.

In contrast, it is possible to investigate children's understanding of social events proceeding from the premise that language, and other psychological processes, are better viewed as "signs" of knowledge rather than structurally isomorphic representations of knowledge (Winegar, 1986a). This premise is characteristic of a co-constructive metatheory (Wozniak, 1983, 1986). Under such an approach, "experience, symbolic discourse and action are *co*-constructions that arise (in the here and now) *in* the interaction of mental structures and mental acts with physical/social objects and events and (ontogenetically) *from* the interaction of mind with physical/social reality" (Wozniak, 1986, p. 41; emphasis in original).

From such a metatheoretical stance, psychological processes such as perception, language, and action are all expressions of underlying knowledge. Knowledge is expressed through these three processes, but the structure of perception, language, and action are not assumed to directly reproduce the structure of the knowledge being expressed. Further, the metatheoretical perspective of co-constructivism emphasizes that knowledge is an active co-construction arising from current knowledge and environmental information. In this way, contextual influences on the expression of knowledge are explicitly considered.

Moving from a metatheoretical level to a theoretical level, children's understanding can be described as a system of knowledge and value that is both canalized through, and provides structure for, children's perceptions, representations, and actions. When viewed from such a perspective, children's performance in social settings is best conceptualized, not as caused only by knowledge structures in the children's heads, but, in addition, as supported both by the organization of information in the physical environment and by social processes within cultural environments.

A co-constructive approach recognizes the co-contributions of environment and individual to the development of knowledge. More importantly for the current discussion, recent attempts to combine a co-constructive approach and a discussion of social structure (Winegar & Renninger, 1985) provide a theoretical foundation for explorations of the development and organization of children's understanding of social events. This theoretical foundation is based, not on the assumption of direct structural similarity between knowledge and symbolic discourse, but rather on the assumption of co-contributions of environment and individual to expressions of knowledge. In the social environment, it is the expert's acting *as if* the novice has gained (or will gain) information that in fact enables the novice to acquire such information. By placing understanding and its development within processes of social interchange, such a metatheory emphasizes the fundamental role of social interaction in the ascription of meaning by individuals.

Thus, social events are co-constructed in two senses. First, participants' understanding of the event is an active co-construction arising from the participants' current levels of understanding and information provided by the environment. Participants do not simply take in information as offered by the physical and social environment, but rather *construct* meaning out of both this information and their understanding gained from previous experience. In this sense, understanding of events is an *intra*individual co-construction of information in the world and knowledge/value of the participants. It is this intra-individual aspect of co-construction which is usually discussed in most presentations of a co-constructive metatheory (e.g., Wozniak, 1983, 1986).

However, there is a second sense in which understanding may be considered to be co-constructed. Much as active integration of current level of understanding and information in the environment gives rise to co-constructed knowledge, interaction between individuals gives rise to co-constructed understanding. Joint action of individuals objectifies their knowledge through its expression in language and action. When individuals express their understanding through their language or action, the meaning of these expressions, and hence the social value of the knowledge underlying such expressions, is derived from the relation of one individual's actions to the actions of others. Individuals' actions do not have meaning in isolation; actions acquire meaning in their relation to complementary actions of others. Actions of individuals in and of themselves do not constitute social events; events are social interactions that are negotiated and interpreted between participants. Participants do not follow pre-established "scripts" for performance; rather, they jointly *construct* the organization and social meaning of the activity. In this sense, social procedures, conventions, and events are *inter*individual co-constructions of social organization. It is this interindividual sense of co-construction that is often referred to as intersubjectivity (e.g., Newson & Newson, 1975; Rommetveit, 1979), and is beginning to be expressed in discussions of social construc*tion*ism (e.g., Gergen, 1985, in press).

Information does not flow unaltered from the environment to reside as knowledge structures in children's heads. Neither does knowledge map directly onto action without adjustment for contextual differences. To emphasize this orientation, then, it may be meaningful to speak of children's understanding of social activity rather than of their event representations or knowledge. From this perspective, social events are best characterized, not as preplanned, well-scripted series of procedures, but rather as co-constructed social transactions. This perspective is reflected in the use of the phrase *social organization* rather than *social structure*.

Social Process

Theoretical and empirical work in developmental psychology has begun to focus on the role played by more competent others in the development of children's knowledge. Originally guided by Piaget's (1962) discussion of "contradiction," and later by Vygotsky's (1978) description of "zone of proximal development" and Hunt's (1961) proposal of "optimal mismatch," others have begun to investigate the role of adults and more competent peers on the development of a variety of children's abilities (e.g., Bearison, 1986; Doise, Mugny, & Perrot-Clermont, 1975; Greenfield, 1984; Rogoff, 1982; Wertsch, 1984). Specific abilities of interest have included conservation ability, logical reasoning, language development, and categorization performance. All such studies have reported clear (if occasionally contradictory; cf. Winegar, 1986b) evidence for the influence of expert others on children's developing abilities.

It has been proposed that social partners and social situations provide constraints on action that channel children toward socially appropriate understanding of their cultural environment (Winegar & Renninger, 1985; Valsiner, 1984, 1987). *Constraints* are defined as boundary conditions within which some actions of the child are promoted and others are discouraged. Social others, especially parents and teachers, employ a variety of strategies in constraining children's action. Examples of social constraining include tactics such as employing social labels and directing perception through highlighting particular aspects of the environment and ignoring others (Feurstein, 1980), and asking questions which distance children's representations (Sigel & Cocking, 1977). Further, social partners appear to make adjustment in their constraining activity that are often quite intricate and usually outside of reflective awareness. These adjustments in constraining tend toward a lessening of adult-provided constraint as the child increasingly demonstrates self-regulation of his or her own actions. As such, they can be considered as a kind of instructional "code switching" (Berko Gleason, 1973; Shatz & Gelman, 1973). It is partially through the guidance provided by the constraining actions of adults that children's understanding of their world develops.

The complementary relation between an adult's or other "expert's" decreasing organization of task demands and a child's or other "novice's" increasing responsibility for task performance can be described in terms of *differential constraining/progressive empowerment* (Renninger & Winegar, 1985a; Winegar & Renninger, 1985). When engaged in teaching/learning activities, experts employ a variety of methods to provide constraints on a novice's language, perception, and action and so channel the novice's development along socially acceptable lines. This provision of constraints by experts can be observed in both formal and informal learning situations. The term *differential constraining* refers to experts' tendency to adjust, usually unreflectively, both the amount and type of constraint they provide in relation to their perception and expectation of novice performance. Such constraining is "differential" since experts alter both the form and degree of constraining they provide as the novice exhibits increasing responsibility for acceptable performance. The term *progressive empowerment* refers to the increasing responsibility for performance of socially acceptable action demonstrated by the developing novice. Novices internalize constraints initially provided by the expert and so become increasingly "self-constraining." Increased responsibility for performance assumed by the novice in turn necessitates further adjustments on the part of the expert. The terms differential constraining/progressive empowerment thus describe complementary aspects of a social process in which experts provide direction and support for novice's performance, which simultaneously enables a novice to complete an immediate action and develop further understanding of the activity.

So defined, the notion of differential constraining/progressive empowerment is similar to *scaffolding*. Both processes differ from *shaping* in that the former entail the completion by a novice (usually a child) of the whole action (albeit with expert [adult] support) rather than successive approximations of it (Greenfield, 1984). However differential constraining/progressive empowerment differs from scaffolding in two important ways. First, unlike early descriptions of scaffolding (e.g., Bruner, 1972), the use of the term differential constraining recognizes that expert performance in an interaction is not held constant, but rather is continually readjusted in relation to the expert's expectations and perceptions of novice ability. Experts vary their degree and type of constraining in relation to the difficulty and goal of the desired activity, a practice recognized by later discussions of scaffolding (Wood, 1980). Further, the use of the term progressive empowerment recognizes that expert support for novice performance not only enables the novice to perform the current action, but that so doing also supports the novice's future independent action in the same and similar settings. Through this social process, expert supports may themselves become internalized and so subsequently be employed by the novice.

Thus, differential constraining of information by experts supports progressive empowerment of novices. All instances of empowerment include some degree of each of the following: (a) accomplishment of immediate action, (a) enablement of future actions of the same type, (c) more general learning with the possibility of transfer, and (d) learning and internalization of metacognitive and social strategies. Instances of empowerment most often involve sacrificing the most efficient accomplishment of the immediate action for the enablement of future actions of the same type. It is for this reason that the social process of differential constraining/progressive empowerment is usually observed in relationships in which the primary goals are teaching and learning rather than production (see Wertsch, Minick, & Arns, 1984, for a discussion of the goals of social interactions in terms of "activity").

This last point suggests that there exists a hierarchy of goals for the expert and a hierarchy of actions to be learned by the novice. Experts tend to reflectively consider those goals higher in this hierarchy. Experts also are more likely to anticipate alternative actions that may be exhibited by novices as they begin to learn actions higher in this hierarchy. This can be seen in experts' responses to novices' actions which are either initiated or anticipated. Experts are initially more likely to be preemptive with those alternatives actions by novices that are higher in the hierarchy, and more reactive with those aspects lower in the hierarchy. As novices take more responsibility for the first actions of greater importance, experts may become preemptive on the previously less important aspects of the event. In subsequent exchanges, experts may act in preemptive ways with the actions of novices that have occurred previously, and remain reactive with previously unencountered actions.[2]

Although the concept of differential constraining/progressive empowerment previously has been applied to mother–child discourse and teacher–student interaction on cognitive and academic tasks (Renninger & Winegar, 1985b), it can be observed in other social activities as well. When defined generically, experts take many forms, as do novices. Such is the case in therapist–client relationships, at least as construed from several theoretical approaches (Haley, 1976). In many activities, experience leads to a shift in regulation of action from primarily an expert responsibility to primarily a novice responsibility. However, at either extreme of responsibility there remain environmental conditions which continue to provide both definition of, and support for, acceptable action. Such supporting environmental conditions include cultural artifacts provided in different settings, observation of others in the same setting, and the ready reminders of others in response to perceived violations of appropriate action.

The co-constructed nature of children's interaction and understanding, and the social process of differential constraining/progressive empowerment, can be illustrated by observations from the naturally occurring preschool event—snacktime.

TEACHERS AND CHILDREN AT SNACKTIME

Eighteen children (31 to 57 months) and their teachers were observed interacting as a group during the preschool event of "snacktime."

---

[2] In a specific setting, i.e., mother–child interaction in a store, Holden (1983) refers to similar strategies as *proactive* and *reactive,* respectively.

Seventeen of the children had not attended preschool previously. One child had attended the same preschool the previous year although with different teachers. The three teachers were all new to the preschool although one had previous preschool teaching experience. Teacher direction and child performance during this event were observed and recorded daily for the first 3 weeks of school, twice a week for the remainder of the year, and again daily for the week immediately after Christmas break. Observations from the first eight weeks of school will be presented here.

In the preschool observed, snacktime occurred each day, after children had been in school for about an hour and a half. Snacktime followed a period of free play, and children were required to put away the toys used in play before taking a seat at the snack table. Children chose their own seats in chairs at low tables of appropriate height for children of this age. The teacher or teachers usually directed and observed the activity while standing and moving around the table. Often, toward the end of snacktime, a teacher would seat herself at the table with children who were not yet finished eating. On occasion, especially during the first few days of school, parents and siblings were present during snacktime. Though siblings often ventured into the snack area and were offered food or drink, parents generally kept their distance, standing off to the side and on rare occasions making comments to their own children in support of the teachers' directions.

At the beginning of snacktime a pitcher of water and a pitcher of juice were placed on the table. Children were provided with paper cups for their drink and usually with napkins that were used both for wiping faces and hands and as plates for food. The food available for snack varied from day to day. It included a variety of crackers and fruits and, occasionally, baked goods such as muffins, pancakes, or banana bread, either made by the children at school or brought by a parent and child from home to share with the group. Children ate almost all foods using their fingers. Eating utensils were observed only twice, once when children spread peanut butter on bananas using a communal knife, and once when children ate hot apple crisp with individual spoons. Occasionally, a metal bowl was put on the table to be used to discard unwanted or inedible pieces of food such as orange rinds, seeds and muffin papers. Children were responsible for cleaning up after themselves by discarding used cups and napkins in a large trash can on one side of the room. After snacktime children were encouraged to use the bathroom. Snacktime was usually followed by either outside play or circle time.

The first several days of the new school year provided an opportunity for the observation of the initial development of rules and conventions in this setting. The first 3 days of the year were used for orientation for teachers, parents, and children. The class of 18 children was divided into three approximately equal groups, and each group attended school on one of three orientation days. Parents and occasionally siblings were present on the day of their child's orientation. In this way there were three "first days of school" on which to observe teachers and children and the formation of conventional procedures.

Co-Construction of Snacktime

Since considering knowledge as a co-construction is a metatheoretical assumption, it is not itself directly testable. Nevertheless, several observations of teachers' and children's interaction during snacktime suggest that it is a meaningful and heuristic description of the nature of their understanding. The co-constructed nature of the teacher's and children's understanding of snacktime is illustrated both in the general evolution of the snacktime event over time and in specific episodes occurring during this event.

The seating arrangement and general procedure for snacktime underwent a gradual evolution over the first 2 months of school. During the first 3 weeks of school, six children were seated at the table at a time, one on each end and two on each side. When more than six children were present on a school day, as they were after the first 3 days of school, the remaining children waited for a seat to be vacated by a finishing child and then took that child's place at the table. Initially, extra children waited in the same room where snacktime was held. The teacher designated a long bench on one side of the room as a "waiting bench," and a rocking horse as the "waiting horse," where children were expected to wait their turn. However, waiting children were quite impatient, and this arrangement proved unsatisfactory. At the end of the second week, waiting children were kept occupied in an adjacent room and were allowed into the snack room only when a seat became vacant. At the beginning of the fourth week, two tables were combined to make a slightly larger table at which seven children could eat snack at a one time. The rest of the children continued to remain in the adjacent room until a seat was available. In the seventh week this larger table was used with an additional table seating four children so that 11 children could eat at once. Later in the seventh week a third table also was used at snacktime, thus allowing all children to eat simultaneously.

The teachers' co-constructed understanding of snacktime can be seen in the evolution of snacktime over the first 8 weeks of school. The teachers start with a plan for snacktime that initially works very well.

However, changes in the number of children at snacktime disrupts this initial plan. The procedures and conventions of snacktime then undergo a series of changes until the teachers again reach a satisfactory solution. These changes in snacktime further highlight what a difficult task it is for children to perceive the invariants in social interaction. As this example illustrates, children must constantly see past daily fluctuations and variations in procedures if they are to discover what in fact are the defining features of a particular social event. Thus, again we see the influence of contextual variables on children's understanding of social events.

Several specific examples of teacher–child interaction during snacktime further illustrate the co-constructed nature of the participants' understanding of the snacktime event. In the first two episodes the influence of children's understanding of language and conventional event procedures on their actions in the setting of interest can be seen.

Episode 1: Cracker Passing. At the beginning of snacktime, as children are sitting down, one child is passing cups to other children by taking one cup at a time off a stack and handing the rest to the other children. The teacher says, "Can you pass the cups around so that everyone has one? Thanks."

About a minute later, the teacher, while helping one child pour juice, says to a different child, "How 'bout if you start the crackers? Can you take one and pass it to everyone? Can you pass the basket around . . ."

The child responds by taking packages of crackers out of the basket and passing packages of crackers to each child rather than passing the basket of crackers.

The teacher looks up and adds, ". . . or pass the packs?"

Episode 2: Bubble Blowing. Teacher is sitting at table with five children who are having their snack.

The child to teacher's right blow bubbles in his cup of water. He looks at the teacher, who isn't looking in his direction. The child looks around at the other children also seated at the table.

The child again blows bubbles in his water. Pauses. He looks at the teacher, who is still looking away. The child says to the teacher, "Watch." The child again blows bubbles in his juice.

Teacher says, "Ah, a bubble blower. How 'bout if you just drink the water. Can you just drink it?"

The child again blows bubbles in his drink (while the teacher is watching).

The teacher leans over and whispers to the child, "Just drink the water. Just drink it?"

The child continues to blow bubbles in his drink. He laughs and looks at the other children at the table, who also begin to laugh.

A second child blows bubbles in her drink as the teacher is repeating to the first child, "How 'bout if you just drink the water?"

The teacher turns and takes a long look at the second child.

All children at the table laugh.

The teacher says something inaudible to the second child.

The parent of the second child says, "Bad form. That's not good at all."

A third child blows bubbles in his drink.

The teacher more sternly begins to say to third child, "How 'bout . . ." then, looking around at all children, continues, "let's not blow bubbles. That's not good because sometimes you could choke and that wouldn't be very good."

These examples suggest that children's understanding in this event are also co-constructed. Teachers and children brought to the activity expectations and understanding gained from other settings and from interaction with others both generally and in similar events. In the first example, the child passing the crackers understands the teacher's instructions as requiring the passing of individual packages of crackers. This understanding may have arisen because of the child's observation of a previous passing episode or because of the teacher's phrasing of the directions (or both). In either case, the child's action of passing crackers reflects both her previous understanding and the information provided in the immediate setting.

In the second example, the child who initially blows bubbles in his drink seems to have some understanding that such behavior is not permissible or at least will get an adult's attention. This is suggested by his visual and subsequent verbal referencing of the teacher. When the teacher first responds to his actions only with acknowledgement ("Ah, a bubble blower.") and mild correction ("How 'bout if you just drink the water?"), he, and apparently two other children as well, take this as a sign that they are committing no major violation of the rules (or are successful in gaining the teacher's attention). Only after the bubble blowing escalates does the teacher's admonishments to stop similarly escalate.

In the snacktime setting, teachers are not simply transferring procedures about the day's activity. They provide information and constraints on children's perception, language, and action. However, children interpret such information and constraints and so co-determine the expression of their understanding of the event. Thus, the children's (and the teacher's) perceptions, language, and action are all co-constructed in the interaction of their knowledge with the physical and social environment.

The procedures and conventions of the event are also interindividually co-constructed. That is, both the teacher and the children begin and participate in the event with only general expectations of what is to happen and what limits there are on behavior. Further, they are both willing to adjust procedures (within limits) as circumstances dictate. This can be seen in the two examples reported above. In the cracker passing episode, the teacher adjusts her verbal instructions to include the passing method of the child. In the bubble blowing episode, the teacher initially treats the incident as minor and progressively admonishes the children's actions only when they escalate.

An episode from the first few days of school further illustrates both the intra- and interindividual sense of co-construction.

Episode 3: Grape Counting. Teacher passes basket of grapes to each child, instructing and helping each to count three grapes. After all children have gotten their grapes, the teacher notices that one child does not have enough. The teacher instructs the child to take an additional grape by saying, "I think you need to have another one. You only have two. Can you take another one?"

Child takes one more grape and then another and another. Teacher notices. "Can you count three? How many do you have there?"

Child (who has four grapes) counts, "One, two, three, four, five."

Teacher says, "I think you have four. Can you put one back in the basket?"

Child pauses, then shakes head "no."

Teacher shakes head in imitation of child and then says, "Can you give everyone another grape so they can all have four?"

In this episode the influence of the child's current level of cognitive ability on one aspect of the procedures of snacktime is illustrated. The child seems to understand that part of what you sometimes do at snacktime is to count out items, often food or cups, and so readily engages in that activity. However, since the child is not yet proficient at counting, the desired end of this counting procedure from the teacher's point of view (probably to have the children practice counting and to ensure that all children get an equal portion of food) does not appear to be understood. The child's shaking her head "no" is as much an indication that she doesn't understand the counting procedure (and therefore how many grapes she has or is supposed to have) as it is a refusal to comply with the teacher's instructions.

In this episode we also see the interindividual co-construction of social conventions during snacktime. Here, the teacher alters her previously established limit of three grapes per child in response to the child's reluctance to return an extra grape to the basket. While, in the cracker passing episode reported above, the teacher adjusts her instructions to include the child's method of passing, in this grape counting episode the teacher adjusts her previously established limit of three grapes to include the number of grapes the child has taken. Further, this adjustment in limit, though made in response to a single child's action, is applied to all children at the table. So the child is instructed to ". . . give everyone another grape so they can all have four."

Thus, the procedures and conventions of snacktime are both intra- and interindividually co-constructed. Children's (and teachers') understanding of snacktime as a social event arises from their general level of understanding, previous experience in this and with similar events, and information provided by the physical and social environment in which the event occurs. Children's and teacher's participation in snacktime involves not only the completion of the actions of the event, but also the negotiation of procedures and conventions as applied both to immediate experience and to future occasions.

Social Process During Snacktime

In order to assess the nature and change in teachers' directing of the snacktime activity, teachers' statements directed toward the children during this activity were coded for degree of directiveness. All statements made by teachers toward children during snacktime were coded into one of the following four categories: directive statements, nondirective statements, informative statements, and socializing statements. *Directive statements* were those that made a direct request for children's behavior or change in behavior. Examples of directive statements include "Sit down in your chair," "Just take one cracker," and "Can you ask him to pass the juice?" While some statements may appear grammatically to be questions, they were coded as directive statements since they were not intended to elicit a verbal response from the child but rather a compliance response. Examples include "Can you just drink your juice?" and "Will you pass the cups?" In contrast, *nondirective statements* were statements made by teachers that supported a child's performance but did not make a direct request for the change. Examples include "Who remembers what we do after we finish our snack?" "I like the way you asked to have the juice passed," and "Can you pour your juice by yourself?" This category also included statements that offered children legitimate choices of behavior. Examples include "Would you like more crackers or are you finished?" "When you're finished go sit on the rug unless you have to go to the bathroom," and "Here's a seat for you." *Informative statements* provided information for performance or interpretation of an occurrence. Examples include "We are only having three grapes today" and "That is somebody else's chair." Finally, *socializing statements* were social pleasantries that did not require compliance on the part of the child. Included in this category were inquiries about the child's state or feelings, and statements of information that do not support or suggest performance. Examples include "Would you like apple juice or water?" "Do you like orange juice?" "Would you like another cracker?" and "Are you feeling better now?"

Since teachers often repeated and/or rephrased a statement, a series of statements on the same topic or with the same apparent intent were not coded separately but rather as a single unit. For example, the series of statements "Just drink your juice. I want you to drink your juice" was coded once as a directive statement. The only exception to this rule was allowed when two or more different categories of statements were included in a single series of statements. In that case, each category was coded as occurring once. Thus, the example "Take a cup. You only need one cup" was coded twice, once as a directive statement and once as an informative statement.

Frequencies and proportion of type of teacher's statements during snacktime during the first 4 weeks of school are shown in Table 1. As can be seen, the proportion of the total number of teacher statements that are directive declines over this period of time. On the first few days of school, about half of the teachers' statements are in this category. By the fourth week the proportion of directive statements make up less than a third of teachers' total statements. In contrast, the proportion of teacher statements classified as nondirective shows an increase during the same time span. During the first 2 weeks of school, nondirective statements comprise less than 20% of total teacher statements. By the fourth week the proportion of nondirective statements approaches 30% of total teacher statements.

These observations of changes in teachers directing style over the first 4 weeks of school suggest some aspects of the social processes through which children come to participate in the snacktime event in socially acceptable ways. During the first 2 weeks of school, the largest proportion of teachers' instructions were aimed at accomplishing the basic acts of the event, developing children's self-sufficiency and directing transition times. Generally, teachers' constraining of children's actions in this event proceeded from direct tuition, in the first 2½ weeks, to, in later observations, giving praise for notable performance and asking children to restate rules. After the 2 weeks, the majority of teachers' statements at snacktime provided information and supported child performance rather than directed children's behavior. After this

Table 1. Number and Proportion of Teacher Statement Type by Day[a]

			Statement Type		
	Directive	Nondirective	Informative	Socializing	Total
Day 1					
Number	44	8	15	23	90
Proportion[b]	.49	.09	.17	.26	
Day 2					
Number	38	12	18	8	76
Proportion	.50	.16	.24	.11	
Day 3					
Number	56	19	12	26	113
Proportion	.50	.17	.11	.23	
Day 4					
Number	27	10	15	12	64
Proportion	.42	.16	.23	.19	
Day 5					
Number	60	26	37	19	142
Proportion	.42	.18	.26	.13	
Day 6					
Number	57	21	53	13	144
Proportion	.40	.15	.37	.09	
Day 7					
Number	55	33	20	28	136
Proportion	.40	.24	.15	.21	
Day 8					
Number	32	24	20	15	91
Proportion	.35	.26	.22	.16	
Day 9					
Number	67	36	26	37	166
Proportion	.40	.22	.16	.22	
Day 10					
Number	38	28	15	13	94
Proportion	.40	.30	.16	.14	
Day 11					
Number	20	17	21	17	75
Proportion	.27	.23	.28	.23	
Day 12					
Number	30	19	27	14	90
Proportion	.33	.21	.30	.16	
Day 14					
Number	38	31	32	16	117
Proportion	.32	.26	.27	.14	
Day 15					
Number	24	22	30	2	78
Proportion	.31	.28	.38	.03	

[a] Snacktime was not observed on the thirteenth day.
[b] All proportions do not sum to 1.00, due to rounding.

time, usually only violations of rules by children or changes to the general routine resulted in directing statements by teachers.

A specific example further illustrates this change in the teacher's style of direction. During the first day of school, the teacher instructed the children in pouring pitchers of drink in the following manner: Teacher holds up two pitchers of liquid and says, "Today we have apple juice and water. This pitcher has apple juice and the pitcher with the red mark has water." Teacher asks a child which he would like to drink. The teacher then sets the appropriate pitcher next to the child's right hand. She then says, "Okay, hold the pitcher in one hand and your cup in the other." Teacher helps child by guiding his hands with hers, then says, "That's good."

In contrast, several days later the teacher's style of instruction and degree of assistance is quite different. For example, on the sixth day the pouring of drinks goes as follows: Teacher gets two pitchers of liquid and, holding up one of them, says, "Who remembers what is in the pitcher that has the red mark on it?" Holds up pitcher with red mark and repeats, "What's in this one?" After a pause, several children respond, "Water!" Teacher replies, "Water! And we have orange juice. We have orange juice today." Pitchers are passed around to the children. Each, in turn, pours his or her own drink, holding the pitcher in one hand and the cup in the other. The teacher, who is passing out grapes to each child, watches the children pour and occasionally expedites the passing of the pitchers. On occasion she comments on the pouring, for example, asking a child, "Can you pour your juice by yourself?" but at no time does she provide assistance for the act of pouring. Later in snacktime a child asks, "Can you help me pour?" The teacher stands behind the child, watching the child and lightly guiding the child's hands while the child pours the liquid. When completed, the teacher says, "You did a very nice job."

Two days later children are observed pouring their own juice while the teacher is not present. On this eighth day of school, three children are sitting at the snack table prior to the start of snacktime. Though pitchers of drink and cups are on the table, no teacher is present. In turn, the children each pour their own juice; each holds the pitcher in the right hand and steadies the cup with the left. The pouring is accomplished without incident and before the teacher returns.

This change in teachers' methods illustrates the increasing responsibility for action that is given by teachers and assumed by children during experience in this event. Initially, teachers provided well-defined, publicly announced, often before-the-fact supports for particular action. They start the school year by explicitly stating rules and closely monitoring children's compliance—a kind of "here's what we're going to do" approach. As children and teachers gain experience in the event and familiarity with its conventions, the role of the teacher changes and her support for proper action takes another form. So, by the sixth day the teacher is asking children to restate rules rather than stating them herself, and is correcting action which violates previously established conventions. At this stage, the teacher's support for particular action is less a public statement of general rules and more a correction of a particular instance of rule violation by a child—a kind of "don't do what you just did" approach.

As these examples illustrate, the social process of differential constraining/progressive empowerment can be observed in the snacktime setting as well as in more formal teaching situations. With experience, there is a shift in regulation of behavior from primarily a teacher responsibility to primarily a child responsibility. At either extreme of responsibility, however, there remain environmental conditions which continue to provide both definition of, and support for, acceptable action. This can be seen in the pouring example reported above. The teacher's constraining of the children's action is different in the second episode from the first. Initially, the teacher guided the children through the action physically and verbally; later, she relies on verbal guidance only. The pitcher is still placed next to the child's right hand, however, and, in so doing, the teacher provides environmental support for the child's manipulation of the pitcher. Further, the teacher forgoes the most immediately efficient method of distributing drinks (pouring the juice herself) and adopts a less efficient method (having the children's awkwardly pour their own with much assistance and supervision) and, in doing so, eventually enables independent pouring by the children themselves.

Just as in instances of differential constraining/progressive empowerment in academic settings, at snacktime the teacher's initial provision of a greater degree of support for the child's pouring, which is later progressively lessened, enables more than just the child's learning of the general pouring task. Teachers' support for the child's performance enables the child to (a) complete the immediate action of pouring the juice from the pitcher without spills, (b) learn to pour the pitcher properly in this setting, (c) practice a pouring skill that can be applied elsewhere, and (d) experience a process of learning that may support the development of future understanding. While the successful completion of the pouring action (a) is the primary goal and the skill at which the child shows immediate improvement (b), learning for transfer (c) and learning to learn (d) are aspects of the empowerment process which are supported by the teacher's adjustment of her level of guidance. Thus, the social process of differential constraining/progressive empowerment also enables the development of understanding that the child can apply in unsupported situations or in reflection upon previously supported situations and so discover and create understanding different from that originally supported in the specific interaction.

In many interactions between teacher and children successful accomplishment of a specific action and learning of the general action is the primary goal. This appears to be the case in the pitcher pouring episodes. The teacher's adjustments are made in support of the child's eventual independent use of the pitcher; there appears to be only secondary concern for their influence on pouring in other settings and no concern for their influence on metacognitive processes. However, in addition to helping children learn the procedural rules of the event, teachers also used snacktime to direct children's learning in other ways. Teachers used snacktime as an opportunity to have children practice cognitive skills by incorporating activities such as counting grapes and cups, and by supporting children's planning activities (e.g., "First I'm going to have water and then I'm going to drink juice"). Also during this time, teachers introduced social rules regulating peer interaction (e.g., not knowing it is someone else's is an acceptable reason to take another's chair), encouraged children to be polite and attentive to others (e.g., by passing food or cups, saying "please"), and practice self-control (e.g., by placing limits on amount of food consumed, waiting for all children to be served before beginning). In many of these episodes the transfer or metacognitive aspects of empowerment are often more important than the successful completion of the immediate action or the learning of that action generally.

An episode illustrates this change in importance. Often, children would have both crackers and grapes for snack. On these occasions the teacher would pass around a basket of grapes and have each child count out three grapes for him or herself. The teacher would assist each child by counting with them to three. In these episodes, the primary goal was not to have children get food for themselves, but rather to practice counting, a skill that had greater application outside the snacktime setting. This claim is supported by the observation that, when children had only grapes for snack, and therefore were allowed 10 grapes each, the teacher herself counted out 10 grapes for each child. Whether the teacher did this because she perceived counting to 10 to be too difficult a task for 3-year-old children, or simply to expedite the distribution of grapes (or both), is not clear. However, it does suggest that, when doing so did not entail a great cost, she was willing to sacrifice quick distribution of food for the opportunity to have children practice counting.

This suggests that there exists a hierarchy of goals in the event for both teacher and children. Teachers are primarily preemptive with those goals of the event that they have previously encountered or considered, and reactive to those actions by children that the teacher may not have thought about ahead of time. In subsequent episodes, teachers may act in preemptive ways with actions that have arisen previously and remain reactive with previously unencountered actions. Further, there appear to be a hierarchy of actions in the event to be learned for both teacher and children. Teachers are initially more likely to be preemptive with those aspects higher on the list, and more reactive with those aspects lower on the list. As children take more responsibility for the first actions of greater importance, teachers may become preemptive on the previously less important aspects of the event.

An example of a change from reactive to preemptive can be seen in an examination of the teacher's instructions concerning the ending of snacktime over the first 3 days of school. On the first day, the teacher instructs the children to throw their trash in the trash can (the ending action of snacktime) only after the first child has finished eating and has gotten out of her seat. This instruction is repeated and elaborated for the next child finished (". . .and if you have juice left you can throw it in the sink"). However, the next activity (sitting in a circle in the other room and meeting our new friends) is not mentioned until all the children but one have gotten out of their seats, thrown their trash away, and are milling around waiting for the next activity. On the second day of school the teacher mentions the final activity of snacktime (throwing trash away) before the children have finished eating and while all children are still seated at the table. The next activity (circle time in the next room) is not mentioned until after two children have thrown away their trash and have gotten up from the table. On the third day, the teacher simultaneously instructs children in the final action of snacktime and informs them of the next activity ("When you're finished, throw your trash in the orange trash can and then go sit in the other room so that we can all see who our new friends are"). Further, this instruction and information is provided and repeated while all children are still seated at the table.

In this example, the teacher instructions for both the last action of snacktime (throwing away trash) and the next activity (circle time) were initially reactive; both were first mentioned in response to actions of the children. On the second day, the teacher acts in a preemptive way with the last action of snacktime by instructing children to throw their trash before any of the children are ready to do so. However, she remains reactive with the next activity and does not mention it until several children have already left the table. On the third day the teacher uses a preemptive strategy for both the last action of snacktime and the next activity. Further, she combines the two into a single statement, thus marking the transition from one activity to the next.

Since these examples occurred during the first 3 days of school, during which different children were in attendance, the change in the teacher's instructions appears to reflect change in her own understanding of the event rather than changes in the children's action. This suggests that snacktime is not a tightly constructed, preplanned event for the teacher. Rather, she seems to come to the event with more of an outline of what is to happen and continually adjusts her interaction with the children as they and circumstances dictate. This again suggests that, rather than being construed as cognitive "scripts" which are played out by individual agents, snacktime and other social events may be considered as social transactions that, though influenced by past experience, are continually and actively co-constructed by interdependent participants.

SUMMARY AND CONCLUSIONS

The intra- and interindividual co-constructive nature of understanding and social process of differential constraining/progressive empowerment have been discussed as they apply to the naturally occurring and unobtrusively observed preschool event of snacktime. This study illustrates processes of socialization that occur in daily settings and suggests the existence of complementary capabilities in children and processes in social interaction that support the child's developing understanding of social events.

Children's and teachers' understanding of snacktime can be described as co-constructed both intraindividually and interindividually. In an intraindividual sense, snacktime participants' action in, and understanding of, the event is an active co-construction of their knowledge gained from past experience in the event and information provided by the physical and social environment. In an interindividual sense, snacktime is a negotiated interaction between its participants. Thus, each participant's understanding of the event is expressed during the event and is meaningful in terms of its articulation with the interdependent actions of others.

During snacktime, in which children participate in a daily preschool routine, we can observe some processes which adults use to organize children's behavior in naturally occurring social events. Teacher strategies include explicit instruction, modeling, and praise. Strategies are adjusted with time and as children assume more responsibility for regulation of their own behavior. While, initially, teachers devote much of their time and energy at snacktime to explicitly instructing children in the rules and conventions of the event, with experience children assume greater responsibility for their behavior. In complement, teachers spend less time in explicit instruction and, instead, correct violations and socialize with the children.

When viewed from the theoretical perspective proposed at the beginning of this chapter, these observations from snacktime suggest that children bring to social interactions a capacity for rapid acquisition of temporal and casual relations that constitute social events. At least as importantly, children also bring to social interactions a sensitivity to constraints on perception, representation, and action placed by social others, and rely on such social constraining to highlight relevant aspects of social exchange and so lead to understanding. The organization of the interaction within which knowledge is acquired, i.e., differential constraining of possible action by expert adult in complement with progressive empowerment of novice child, suggests a process of social constraining within which understanding of events develops.

REFERENCES

Bearison, D. (1986). Transactional cognition in context: New models of social understanding. In D. Bearison & H. Zimiles (Eds.), *Thought and emotion: Developmental perspectives* (pp. 129–146). Hillsdale, NJ: Erlbaum.

Berko Gleason, J. (1973). Code switching in children's language. In T.E. Moore (Ed.), *Cognitive development and the development of language* (pp. 159–168). New York: Academic Press.

Bruner, J. (1978). Learning how to do things with words. In J. Bruner & A. Garton (Eds.), *Human growth and development* (pp. 62–84). Oxford, England: Oxford University Press.

Doise, W., Mugny, G., & Perrot-Clermont, A. -N. (1975). Social interaction and the development of cognitive operations. *European Journal of Social Psychology, 5,* 367–383.

Feurstein, R. (1980). *Instrumental enrichment: An intervention program for cognitive modifiability.* Baltimore, MD: University Park Press.

Fivush, R. (1984). Learning about school: The development of kindergarteners' school scripts. *Child Development, 55,* 1697–1709.

Gergen, K.J. (1985). The social constructionist movement in modern psychology. *American Psychologist, 40,* 266–275.

Gergen, K.J. (in press). If persons are texts. In S.B. Messeri, L.A. Sassi, & R.L. Wollfolk (Eds.), *Hermeneutics and psychological theory,* New Brunswick, NJ: Rutgers University Press.

Greenfield, P.M. (1984). A theory of the teacher in the learning activities of everyday life. In B. Rogoff & J. Lave (Eds.), *Everyday cognition: Its development in social context* (pp. 117–138). Cambridge, MA: Harvard University Press.

Haley, J. (1976). *Problem-solving therapy: New strategies for effective family therapy.* San Francisco, CA: Jossey-Bass.

Holden, G. (1983). Avoiding conflict: Mothers as tacticians in the supermarket. *Child Development, 54,* 233–240.

Hunt, J. McV. (1961). *Intelligence and experience.* New York: Ronald Press.

Mandler, J.M. (1983). Representation. In J.H. Flavell & E.M. Markman (Eds.), *Handbook of child psychology: Vol. 3. Cognitive development* (3rd ed., pp. 420–494). New York: Wiley & Sons.

Nelson, K. (1981). Social cognition in a script framework. In J.H. Flavell & L. Ross (Eds.), *Social cognitive development: Frontiers and possible futures* (pp. 97–118). New York: Cambridge University Press.

Nelson, K. (1986). *Event knowledge: Structure and function in development.* Hillsdale, NJ: Erlbaum.

Newson, J., & Newson, E. (1975). Intersubjectivity and the transmission of culture: On the social origins of symbolic functioning. *Bulletin of British Psychology-Social, 28,* 437–446.

Piaget, J. (1951). *Play, dreams and imitation in childhood.* New York: Norton.

Piaget, J. (1962). *The language and thought of the child.* New York: Meridian.

Renninger, K.A., & Winegar, L.T. (1985a). Emergent organization in expert–novice relationships. *Genetic Epistemologist, 14,* 14–20.

Renninger, K.A., & Winegar, L.T. (1985b, August). *Teacher-student interaction: Differential constraining/progressive empowerment.* Paper presented at the 93rd Annual Convention, American Psychological Association, Los Angeles.

Rogoff, B. (1982). Integrating context and cognitive development. In M.E. Lamb & A.L. Brown (Eds.), *Advances in developmental psychology* (Vol. 2, pp. 125–170). Hillsdale, NJ: Erlbaum.

Rommetveit, R. (1979). On the Architecture of intersubjectivity. In R. Rommetveit & R. Blakar (Eds.), *Studies of language, thought and verbal communication* (pp. 93–108). New York: Academic Press.

Schank, R.C. & Abelson, R.H. (1977). *Scripts, plans, goals and understanding: An inquiry into human knowledge structures.* Hillsdale, NJ: Erlbaum.

Shatz, M., & Gelman, R. (1973). The development of communication skills: Modifications in the speech of young children as a function of listener. *Monographs of the Society for Research in Child Development, 152,* (Serial No. 152, No. 2), 1–38.

Sigel, I.E. (1983). Cognitive development is structural and transformational— therefore variant. In L.S. Liben (Ed.), *Piaget and the foundations of knowledge* (pp. 125–140). Hillsdale, NJ: Erlbaum.

Sigel, I.E., & Cocking, R.R. (1977). Cognition and communication: A dialectical paradigm for development. In M. Lewis & L.A. Rosenblum (Eds.), *In-*

teraction, conversation, and the development of language (pp. 207–226). New York: Wiley & Sons.

Valsiner, J. (1984). Construction of the zone of proximal development in adult–child joint action: The socialization of mealtimes. In B. Rogoff & J.V. Wertsch (Eds.), *Children's learning in the "zone of proximal development"* (pp. 65–76). San Francisco, CA: Jossey-Bass.

Valsiner, J. (1987). *Culture and the development of children's action: A cultural-historical theory of developmental psychology.* New York: Wiley & Sons.

Vygotsky, L.S. (1978). *Mind in society: The development of higher psychological processes.* Cambridge, MA: Harvard University Press.

Wertsch, J.V., (1984). The zone of proximal development: Some conceptual ideas. In B. Rogoff & J.V. Wertsch (Eds.), *Children's learning in the "zone of proximal development"* (pp. 7–18). San Francisco, CA: Jossey-Bass.

Wertsch, J.V., Minick, N., & Arns, F.J. (1984). The creation of context in joint problem-solving. In B. Rogoff & J. Lave (Eds.), *Everyday cognition: Its development in social context* (pp. 151–171). Cambridge, MA: Harvard University Press.

Winegar, L.T. (1986a). Social event experience and young children's action, language and memory. Manuscript submitted for publication.

Winegar, L.T. (1986b). *Theoretical considerations in research with experts and novices.* Manuscript submitted for publication.

Winegar, L.T., & Renninger, K.A. (1985, April). *Social influence on knowledge: Structural constraint and procedural constraining.* Paper presented at the meeting of the Society for Research in Child Development, Toronto, Canada.

Wood, D.J. (1980). Teaching the young child: Some relations between social interaction, language, and thought. In D.R. Olson (Ed.), *The social foundations of language and thought* (pp. 280–296). New York: Norton.

Wozniak, R.H. (1983). Is a genetic epistemology of psychology possible? *Cahiers de la fondation archives Jean Piaget, Numero 4,* 323–347.

Wozniak, R.H. (1986). Notes toward a co-constructive theory of the emotion/cognition relationship. In D. Bearison & H. Zimiles, (Eds.), *,Thought and emotion: Developmental perspectives* (pp. 40–64). Hillsdale, NJ: Erlbaum.

CHAPTER 2

The Social Construction of Cognitive Conflict: A Place for Affect

Cynthia Lightfoot

Department of Psychology
University of North Carolina

Developmental psychology appears to be experiencing a new wave of scientific action intended to integrate individuals and their environments. Thus far, action taken in this direction has not gone smoothly. The primary obstacle is met at the moment the problem is stated: Questions of how to wed individuals and environments presuppose a vision of initial separation. Mainstream methods of data collection and analysis are, indeed, focused on illuminating relationships which hold between individual and environmental variables (see Valsiner, 1987, and Ignjatovic-Savic et al., this volume). Admittedly, psychologists are moving away from dualistic conceptions of individuals and environments. This is particularly true for psychologists interested in relationships between individuals and their social environments. It is sometimes difficult, however, to transcend the historically given; and although there is now widespread acceptance of perspectives which claim an essential interdependence between organisms and environments, research methodologies continue to undermine important conceptual advances. A case in point is Piaget's theory of genetic epistemology, at the foundation of which lies the assumption of organism–environment interdependence. In practice, however, Piaget focused on endogeneous processes and the development of internal structures of thought. Hence, his theory is often described as individualistic.

The aim of this essay is to consider the individual–environment relationship, and the implications it has for understanding another difficult relationship—that between affect and cognition. The work was inspired by a fortuitous event: An infant was being videotaped for a longitudinal study of the development of creeping. In the course of the investigation, she learned to locomote over a 5-inch step which separated two rooms of her home. However, after becoming quite competent in ascending and descending the step, she became fearful of locomoting over it. It was only after a period of coaxing and various degrees of assistance that she was able to move beyond the immobilizing effects of both wanting and not wanting to cross over the step. This developmentally rich event raised questions about the relationship between affect and sensorimotor developments, the nature of the conflict, and the role of the social environment as a regulator of conflict. This essay dwells on these issues, and draws upon Piaget's notion of disequilibration and his ideas regarding the relationship between affect and intelligence. The general goal was to describe the structural interdependence between children and their social environments. Although Piagetian theory was found to fall short of this mark, some of the difficulties were redressed by Valsiner's individual-socioecological perspective on development. It was argued that the relationship between affect and cognition could be profitably studied within a research paradigm which views the organism–environment relationship as a co-constructed totality. The extent to which this exercise proved successful was evaluated according to its usefulness in illuminating the empirical material which inspired it.

THE ROLE OF CONFLICT IN DEVELOPMENT

In developmental research, methods are often employed which introduce obstacles to overcome, or stress the system in such a way as to halt or slow down the natural flow of developmental events. In this way, we gain insight into the functioning, organization, and transformation of the systems of interest. The method is pervasive: Infants are separated from their mothers and introduced to unfamiliar adults (e.g., Ainsworth & Wittig, 1969); they are habituated to particular stimuli and then presented with discrepancies (e.g., Super, Kagan, Morrison, Haith, & Weifenbach, 1972); young children are given contradictory or ambiguous events (e.g., Bugental, Kaswan, & Love, 1970; Robinson & Robinson, 1982), and moral dilemmas (e.g., Kohlberg, 1969). In general, subjects are given problems meant to be solved over time, rather than immediately or automatically, in order to slow down the process and make it more amenable to investigation.

Methods of the sort described here implicitly or explicitly assume that conflict has systemic consequences for the thought and action of the child. However, these consequences are not always theoretically integrated into the overall research paradigm. Paradoxically, there are also theoretical arguments which maintain that conflict acts as a general mechanism of development, and that ontogenesis proceeds by way of successfully resolving conflicts encountered during earlier developmental periods. The paradox lies in the fact that these theoretical ideas are not often translated into empirical questions. There are noteworthy exceptions. One is Walker's (1983) work on the induction of stage transitions in moral reasoning. In this case, development was facilitated by presenting children with moral arguments which were reasoned at levels higher than those which the children were capable of producing. It was argued that conflict induced by a clash between the child's own organizational capacities, on the one hand, and the structural organization of the experimental intervention, on the other, led to the acquisition of higher forms of reasoning. The second example consists of experiments carried out by Inhelder, Sinclair, & Bovet (described in Inhelder, Sinclair, & Bovet, 1974), in which children received training in conserving quantity. It was found that the success of the training varied considerably as a function of the children's initial cognitive levels. Children whose cognitive levels were substantially below that which is necessary for understanding conservation did not benefit from the training experiences. In contrast, children whose initial cognitive levels put them on the brink of spontaneously understanding the concept of conservation were found to progress as a consequence of the training. Both Walker and the Geneva group interpreted their findings in terms of Piaget's theory of disequilibration.

Studies of this nature address theoretical issues regarding the role of conflict in development. Disequilibration, or conflict, is thought to act as a general mechanism of development: Clashes between the mental structures of the child and the external structures of the environment are ultimately resolved and induce developmentally more complex internal structures. The general assumption is that the child acts to hold conflict in abeyance. Conditions under which conflict remains unresolved, or is exacerbated rather than resolved, are rarely examined, nor are their developmental consequences. This is also true, as we will see below, of Piaget's notion of disequilibration.

Conflict and Disequilibria

Piaget maintains that development proceeds according to internal structural changes brought about by disequilibrations to existing structures which then become equilibrated at higher, more complex levels. Although Piagetian theory is most widely known for the concept of structural disequilibria, in his later works he undertook systematic studies of functional disequilibria (Piaget, 1980). These he defined as incomplete compensations between the affirmative characteristics of an action, and its negative effects. Incomplete compensations are manifested at all stages of cognitive development (sensorimotor through formal operations), although the form in which they are expressed varies in relation to the subject's particular stage of development.

A crucial issue for Piaget concerned the nature of the initial disequilibration. He claimed that it arose from the spontaneous tendency of every action to direct itself toward a positive, affirmative goal:

> Contradiction stems from the fact that the subject, being centered on the goal or arrival point of the actions because they are positive values, ignores the concomitant negations, subtractions, or negative factors. (1980, p. 300)

In this way, Piaget viewed the affirmative characteristics of every action as primary to its negative characteristics. Negation, in contrast, was described as the product of secondary developments that resulted from a disturbance to the initial positive action. The affirmative and negative characteristics of action were therefore seen as developmentally asymmetrical:

> We indeed observe a systematic disequilibrium favoring affirmations, constituting the more natural and spontaneous behavioral reactions, over negations, which, being much more difficult to construct and handle, invariably lag behind affirmations until one reaches operatory levels. In particular, for a long time the subject completely fails to perceive that every action must necessarily and intrinsically entail a negative aspect (moving away from the starting point and destroying the initial state) as well as a positive one (moving toward the goal and producing a final state) accompanied by a transfer which entails a sort of initial subtraction (taking something away at the start) as well as the final addition (adding at the arrival point). (p. 295)

An example corresponding to the sensorimotor level of intelligence would be a case in which a baby attempts to draw a long object horizontally between the vertical bars of a crib. The positive characteristic of the action is seen in the child's attempt to draw the object through the bars, and the bars produce the negative effect which must be compensated by the child. In this respect, the positive and negative elements of the child's action must be brought into relation, and coordinated with each other. Piaget maintained that this takes place through the double process of internalization and relativization: internalization resulting from the child's constructive processes, and relativization resulting from the consequent complexity in the child's manner of assimilating information. That is, the child's endogeneous constructive efforts result in a complex schema in which the positive and negative characteristics of the action are systematized and coordinated. The epistemological consequence consists of a new way of assimilating exogeneous data such that the positive and negative aspects are relativized within the broader, more inclusive mental schema. This developmental process is represented in Figure 1. Here, the child's initial and internal schema *A* acts to assimilate event *B* (which may be of internal or external origin). *B* provides perturbations to *A*, reflecting unsuccessful assimilation. This leads to the child's construction of the negative aspects of *A* in relation to *B*, such that the negative aspects are internalized and both *A* and *B* are relativized to the more inclusive schema *A'*. The path of development is thus observed to spiral outward.

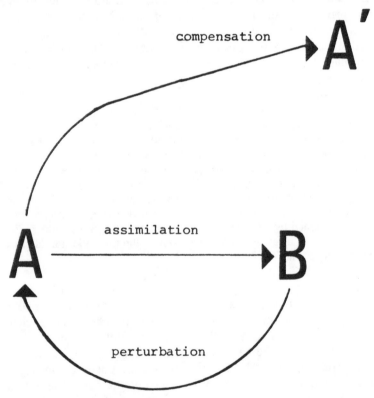

Figure 1. The coordination of affirmation and negation.

This may be illustrated with the crib example given above: A represents the child's initial action schema of drawing objects toward the body. B represents negative effects brought about by the enactment of the scheme on an object which resists assimilation. In this case the negative effects are induced externally, by the position of the crib bars. A condition of disequilibration is said to exist due to the initial action scheme's inability to compensate between the positive effect (drawing the object toward the body) and negative effect (resistance from the bars) of the child's action. The result of compensating between affirmations and negations is A', in which the negative effects are internalized, and the negative and positive effects are relativized with respect to one another. Figure 2 is provided to help conceptualize the double process of internalization and relativization proposed by Piaget.

This figure illustrates the initial asymmetry between the structure of the child's action and the attributes of the object which the child attempts to assimilate. The asymmetry between the positive characteristics of the child's action on the object and the negative effects (provided by the crib bars) results in a perturbation. The child, in one or several more attempts, may ultimately compensate the negative and positive effects in a way that simultaneously "conserves" the original structure of action, and also modifies the action relative to the object's attributes. Hence, what was initially accomplished on the plane of action is transformed and becomes internal.

At the level of sensorimotor intelligence, the negative characteristics of action are directed at removing obstacles to positive goals. All action is subordinated to the pursuit of the positive goal involved. Action schemes are thus assimilatory in nature: They are used to satisfy particular needs, and they are conferred with positive properties to the extent that they result in need satisfaction.

The idea that action schemes, as means to a positive goals, take on value relative to the value of the goals has been elaborated by Piaget in a monograph on the relationship between intelligence and affectivity (1981). As is true of his discussion of incomplete compensation at the sensorimotor level (in contrast to the other developmental levels; see Piaget, 1980), his ideas regarding the relationship between affect and intelligence have been theoretically but not empirically validated. It will be seen, however, that his theoretical analyses may usefully contribute to the explanation of the empirical material presented below.

PIAGET'S THEORY OF AFFECT AND INTELLIGENCE

Piaget (1981) developed his most comprehensive argument regarding the relationship between affect and cognition in a monograph devoted

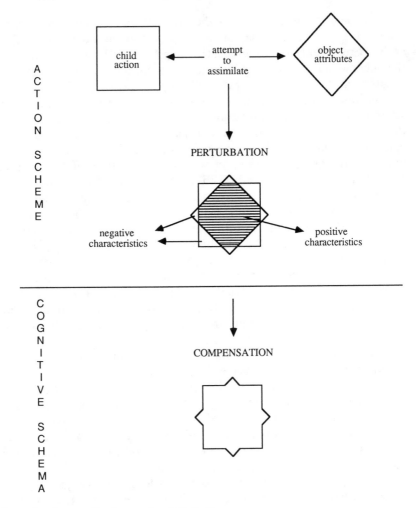

Figure 2.   Internalization and relativization.

to the topic. His basic premises, however, are present in earlier writings. In *The Psychology of the Child* (1969), for example, he described behavior as comprising two separate, interdependent aspects; one cognitive and structured, the other affective and energetic (p. 21). Likewise, in *Play, Dreams and Imitation in Childhood* (1962), he argued that "affectivity regulates the energetics of the action while intelligence provides the technique" (p. 206). The structure—energetic distinction constitutes his first premise.

The second premise concerns the constructive nature of both aspects. The term *constructive* is used by Piaget to express how knowledge and its development represents a confrontation between existing interpretive frameworks and external reality. *Object knowledge,* broadly defined, is not construed as directly available to the subject, but rather results from the endogeneous processes of assimilation and accomodation. These processes function to simultaneouly organize external reality and reorganize the internal, interpretive frameworks. The dual aspect of intelligence and affectivity is captured in the following statement taken from *The Child and Reality* (1973): "To assimilate an object to a scheme is therefore simultaneously to tend to satisfy a need and to confer on the action a cognitive structure" (p. 71). Piaget's constructivistic focus led him to define both affective and cognitive experience according to endogeneous criteria.

These two premises, the structure–energetic distinction, and the endogeneous, constructive nature of experience, will be apparent in the following presentation of Piaget's argument. And, in the form outlined by Piaget, they will also be found inadequate for characterizing the developmental nature of the affect–intelligence relationship. However, in conjunction with theoretical ideas developed by Valsiner, Piaget's analysis suggests interesting paths for investigation.

Structure and Energetics: Interdependent Systems

Piaget began his analysis by describing two systems which are functionally interdependent and which develop in parallel. The affective system constitutes the energy source on which the functioning of intelligence depends; it serves a regulatory function. The cognitive system, on the other hand, is distinguished by its structural nature. Piaget clearly had in mind a functional and dialectical coordination of separate, although interdependent, systems:

> In our view, it is dangerous to start off by dissociating behavior into two aspects, affective and cognitive, and then to make one the cause of the other. Understanding is no more the cause of affectivity than affectivity is the cause of understanding. Energetics cannot generate structure nor structures create energy. Failure to understand the concomitant indissociability and fundamental heterogeneity of cognition and affectivity leads to paradoxical explanations. (Piaget, 1981, p. 25)

Although the affective system does not generate or modify structures of thought, with ontogenetic development, feelings may become structurally organized by the cognitive system. Piaget argued that structural organization is unique to cognitive systems, which may be affectively regulated, but not affectively generated or modified. To support this contention, he appealed to a distinction between open and closed systems. For Piaget, the affective system was considered an open system, that is, in an exchange relationship with the environment. In contrast, the defining feature of cognitive structures is their closure.

The most stable and closed structures are observed in the logico-mathematical structures characteristic of formal operational reasoning. Transformations within closed structures do not go beyond the boundaries of the system, but always lead to other internal elements. The series of whole numbers, for example, is generated by particular transformations (addition, subtraction, etc.) which form a closed system. The transformations never result in anything beyond the series of whole numbers. The system is internally regulated, atemporal, and context-free. Open systems, on the other hand, are characterized by openness towards the environment. They are regulated by feedback, and are temporally and context bound. Systems of this sort include linguistic, sociological, and psychological structures. Although they are characteristically open, they strive for closure due to threats from the environment (food, sex, cognitive stimulation, etc.). Closure, however, is ultimately unobtainable. Piaget also made this point with respect to the relationship between affect and intelligence when he insisted that the closure of cognitive systems does not imply developmental completion:

> One system can always be integrated into a more general system later. . . . The closure of a structure designates, therefore, a completeness or stability which is at least provisional but which may be toppled at some later time as the system moves toward a broader and more stable equilibrium. In contrast, energetics are always open. Finally, we should remark that cognitive systems are more or less structured and are, therefore, more or less closed depending on their level of development. Because of this they are more or less profoundly penetrated by affectivity according to the level under consideration. (Piaget, 1981, p. 11)

Both systems are considered to develop and transform in the course of ontogeny. Therefore, Piaget argued for comparing cognitive structures and affective systems which are contemporaneously present at particular points in the life history of the individual. He spoke of a term-by-term correspondence between the two systems. Piaget has described these interconnected systems and traced their corresponding developments from the instinctual reflexes and drives present at birth, to their developmental conclusions in abstract logical reasoning and feelings for collective ideals. From the beginning, then, structure and energetics stand in functional correspondence to one another. In the young infant, for example, structure is observed in the coordination of reflexes into systems that are capable of satisfying the particular needs which energize them.

Piaget organized his analysis of the affect–cognition relationship into two broad developmental periods, distinguished according to the presence or absence of verbal language. The first period, marked by an absence of language, was described as *nonsocialized*. It encompassed sensorimotor intelligence in the cognitive sphere, and intraindividual feelings, or feelings that accompany the subject's own action, in the affective sphere. This period gives way to the second, *socialized*, period, in which the cognitive sphere is characterized by verbal intelligence, and affective life is characterized by interpersonal exchanges between people. Each period is composed of three successive stages, and Piaget described the corresponding affective and intellectual developments of each. In the context of the interests at hand, the third stage, the final stage of the first period, is particularly important. In addition to its relevance to the empirical data presented below, this stage is also crucial to Piaget's theoretical analysis because it marks the period in which the affective system becomes differentiated into energetics and values. As we will see, this subsystem distinction allowed Piaget to describe affect and cognition as simultaneously distinct (according to his energetic–structure distinction), yet also isomorphic (according to the intellectualization of affect into value heirarchies). His argument regarding the relationship between affect and intelligence thus hinges on his analysis of the differentiation of the affective system into energetics and values.

Energetics, Values, and Interest

During the final stage of sensorimotor intelligence (which corresponds to the fourth, fifth, and sixth sensorimotor substages as usually described by Piaget), the child becomes capable of distinguishing between means and ends. The means for achieving particular goals become differentiated from the goals themselves. Later, the child also becomes capable of combining previously acquired actions in order to attain particular goals. These are, however, cognitive achievements. On the affective plane, the child begins to form a hierarchy of values with respect to goal attainment:

> In the context of intentional action, certain objects, without interest in themselves, take on interest in relation to other objects which are valued. In other words, the value of the means is determined in relation to the value of a particular goal, and labile heirarchies of values arise from activity of this sort. (Piaget, 1981, p. 26)

In his analysis of affective life, Piaget drew extensively from the ideas of Janet, Claparede, and Lewin. Piaget's interpretation of their works will be presented, but certain elaborations (i.e., summations from the original texts) were considered necessary for the sake of clarity.

Pierre Janet developed a theory of behavioral regulations in which he distinguished between "primary" and "secondary" actions (see Janet, 1921). Primary actions were cognitive in nature. Secondary actions, in contrast, were of affective origin. They functioned to regulate primary actions, that is, to increase or decrease the force of behavior, and finally to terminate it. The affective system of secondary actions thus served an energetic purpose.

Janet's theoretical analyses were targeted on the affective system. They are outlined in Figure 3.

Janet argued that activation regulations mobilize forces for action. These forces may be experienced as effort, which induces continued

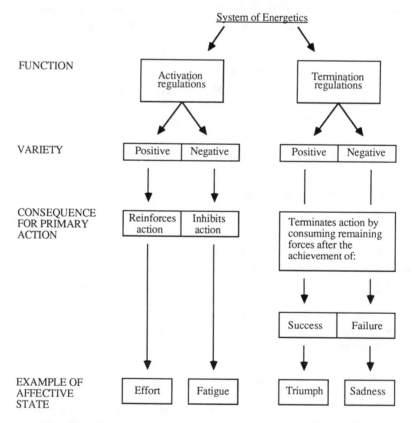

Figure 3. Janet's affective action system.

action and consumes energy, or fatigue, which depresses activity and conserves energy. The termination regulations depend on the perceived consequences of these actions (e.g., success or failure) and are represented by feelings (e.g., triumph or sadness) which act to consume residual forces. For example, sadness might occur upon the termination of an unsuccessful action, and would have the effect of consuming the unused forces of effort. According to Janet, all action strives to maintain an affective equilibrium, a balance between the cost of the means needed to achieve a goal and the value of the goal itself. The value of the goal is determined by the subsequent savings of energy. In this way, certain actions may be costly at a given point in time, but would be cost effective in the long run. An example would be a child's initial efforts to walk. At this point, crawling may be a more effective action in terms of energy expenditure. According to Janet's analysis, however, the additional effort made by the child in the context of learning to walk may be interpreted in terms of future energy savings: Once walking becomes developed and well coordinated, it is often a more efficient way of locomoting. Affective equilibrium was therefore conceptualized in terms of an economy of action.

Piaget (1981) generally agreed with Janet's analysis, although he rejected Janet's principle of the economy of action. Arguing that Janet's theory does not adequately account for activity that has no apparent goal other than mastery, Piaget proposed a distinction be made between the cost of an action and the value of that action. He claimed that, "a costly action may be preferred to one that costs less but that the subject also values less" (Piaget, 1981, p. 31). This contrasts with Janet's proposition that costly actions are justified, not because they may be more valued, but because they are actually less costly in the long run. Piaget therefore argued that the affective system is not limited to energetics, but also includes aspects of valuation. He proposed that the affective system was composed of two distinct subsystems, energetics and valuation. Initially fused, these two subsystems become differentiated during the sensorimotor period.

The energetic aspect of the affective system constitutes an internal regulation of energy which corresponds to the individual's particular needs at specific points in time. In contrast, the valuation aspect refers to the individual's evaluation of previously successful or unsuccessful activities as they relate to the object perceived as capable of need satisfaction. These evaluations result in modifications to the value conferred upon the object by the individual. So the energetic aspect is essentially quantitative (i.e., governs the amount of energy expended, and thus determines the intensity of feelings) and a function of the current need state of the individual, while the valuative aspect is essentially qualitative (i.e., determines object choice) and a function of the individual's history of activity.

Borrowing from Claparede's analysis of the role of interest in regulating energy, Piaget claimed that interest was the mechanism which functionally united the two subsystems. In this light, interest was viewed as the motivational aspect of cognitive schemes: An object is perceived as interesting if it can be integrated into a scheme. Once activated (by an external object, or internal stimulation, e.g., hunger), if the scheme does not succeed (e.g., in finding food), a perturbation occurs which is subjectively experienced as need (Vuyk, 1981). Thus, interest constituted the relationship between the need and the object capable of need satisfaction. Need was taken as evidence for the disequilibration of structures. Re-equilibration was established by need satisfaction, the result of structural functioning. According to Piaget (1981):

> The elementary interests found in children are linked to fundamental organic needs. They are progressively interwoven into complex systems as the child grows up. Much later they will be intellectualized and become scales of values. (p. 34)

Piaget's distinction between the two subsystems of energetics and valuation corresponds to Claparede's two meanings of interest. One of these referred to the energetic function of interest: Interesting objects liberated energy, while disinteresting objects inhibited energy expenditure. The second meaning referred to the content of interest: Object choice was a function of specific needs. To assist his elaboration of the relationship between needs and interests, Piaget made use of Kurt Lewin's field theory (1951).

Lewin maintained that behavior (B) and its development depended upon the state of the person (P) and the environment (E), as represented by the equation: $B=F(P,E)$. P and E were defined as a single constellation of interdependent factors which Lewin termed the *life space*. Accordingly, he determined that "the task of explaining behavior then becomes identical with (1) finding a scientific representation of the life space and (2) determining the function (F) which links the behavior to the life space" (Lewin, 1951, p. 240). The structure of the life space was expressed in topological terms and thought to determine the *locomotions* (i.e., actions) possible at any given time. The specific course of action undertaken depended on the combination of certain psychological *forces*. Forces were held to be determined on the basis of the individual's need state and the nature of the goal items contained in the life space. In addition, Lewin maintained that these forces could be described in terms of valences; need state and goal item forces could have positive (attractive) or negative (repulsive) valences.

An important aspect of Lewin's field theory concerned the way in which need, force, and cognitive structure were related. Needs were viewed as hierarchically organized, and responsible for organizing behavior. They were also described as being closely related to valences: An increase in the intensity of a need increased the positive valence of particular activities (or goals), and simultaneously increased the negative valence of other activities. The combination of forces acting simultaneously constituted the *resultant force*. Lewin summarized the relationship between force and cognitive structure in the following way:

> Whenever a resultant force (different from zero) exists, there is either a locomotion in the direction of that force or a change in cognitive structure equivalent to this locomotion. The reverse also holds: whenever a locomotion or change of structure exists, resultant forces exist in that direction. (Lewin, 1951, p. 256)

That Piaget found Lewin's ideas appealing in terms of a structure–energetic distinction is clear from the discussion above. The structure of the total field, according to Lewin's analysis, provided certain action possibilites. The valence of particular actions, on the other hand, determined the specific action undertaken.

Drawing upon the ideas presented above, Piaget claimed that obstacles to need satisfaction resulted in disequilibration (Piaget, 1981). Need was here defined in terms of the attractive force of valued objects. Barriers that might intervene between the individual and the valued object constituted a negative force. The opposition between these two forces resulted in disequilibrium, which was subjectively experienced as tension. The individual was thought to then act in ways to reduce the tension, and thus resolve the conflict. The particular actions attempted were accompanied by corresponding feelings. In addition, Lewin demonstrated in his experiments that previous success or failure vis-a-vis tension reduction modified the value placed on subsequent tasks as evidenced by changes in subjects' levels of aspiration. The dual functions of the current state of affairs (with respect to need) and previous experiences (with respect to valuation) are emphasized in a summary statement about the two subsystems of energetics and valuation:

> Even more characteristic of this stage (of sensorimotor intelligence), however, is the appearance of a value system which is not just a matter of the economy of action but which has to do with its finality. This

value system determines the energies employed in action. It was extracted not just from current behavior but also from behaviors that have come before . . . Value, we said, is difficult to define at the stage considered here. An object or person has value vis-a-vis the subject's action. In a sense then, values *enrich* action. This may be in terms of force, but more than anything else, it is a functional enrichment in that valued objects or people provide the subject with new goals. (Piaget, 1981, pp. 42–43)

Piaget did, indeed, have difficulty defining what he had in mind when he spoke of value at the level of sensorimotor intelligence. However, it is not hard to imagine that he would concur with the following passage taken from Lewin. Here Lewin described the developmental nature of *aspiration:*

To a child of six months, lying on his stomach and trying to reach a rattle, it seems to make no difference whether he finally reaches the rattle as the result of his own effort or whether the rattle is brought within his reach by someone else. The child will be satisfied both ways. A child of three, trying to jump down from the third step may refuse help. He will not be content unless he has reached certain results by his own effort. The very young child seems to know only satisfaction and dissatisfaction but not success and failure. In other words, he has needs and goals but not yet a level of aspiration. (Lewin, 1951, p. 285)

In transposing this onto Piaget's framework, we could say that the older child may be distinguished from the younger on the basis of a value hierarchy. In the example provided by Lewin, the older child's independent activity had become part of the goal (Lewin, 1951), and this goal was more highly valued than a goal which did not include independent activity.

To capsulize Piaget's analysis of the affect–cognition connection, we may return to the two basic premises presented in the introduction to his work. Piaget viewed affect and cognition as two separate, though interdependent systems. This was based on the premise that cognitive functions were closed, structured systems while affective functions, in contrast, were open, energetic systems. It was argued that the energetic system, specifically the subsystem of valuation, may become structured into hierarchies, but that this represented an intervention of cognitive origin. Piaget's second premise concerned the constructive nature of both systems. Object attributes and values were each viewed as being enriched by endogeneous, constructive processes. These processes were thought to act in ways which conserve previously acquired affective and cognitive developments, yet also provide for their modification. Hence, both systems may be conceptualized as developing in a spiral fashion which reflects their fundamental historicity and modification through ongoing interactions with the environment.

Some Difficulties with Piaget's Analysis

As foreshadowed in the introduction, there are certain ambiguities regarding Piaget's structure–energetic distinction. These ambiguities will be found to converge on issues intimately tied to Piaget's version of structural development and the role allocated to the environment in contributing to this development. Specifically, Piaget's constructivistic epistemology has elevated individual cognitive processes to a primary position in mediating between the subject and the environment. This has had significant and problematic consequences for his analysis of the affect–cognition relationship.

The first area of difficulty concerns the structure–energetic distinction which Piaget consistently and emphatically defended. As discussed above, structure was reserved for cognitive functions, which were characterized as closed systems. Piaget's insistence on the closed nature of cognitive structures has been criticized as paradoxical in light of his constructivistic focus:

> The paradoxicality of Piaget's developmental theory is embedded in the conjunction of his emphasis on organism's active role in interaction with the environment on the one hand, and the preferred status alotted in his epistemology to context-free logico-mathematical structures, on the other. (Valsiner, 1985, p. 83; emphasis in original)

It is clear that Piaget did not intend structural closure to imply developmental stasis. Indeed, he has made explicit attempts to capture the dynamic nature of cognitive structures. One attempt is found in this passage taken from *Biology and Knowledge:*

> The material or dynamic elements of a structure with cyclic order we shall call $A, B, C, . . ., Z$, and the material or energetic elements necessary for their maintenance, $A', B', C', . . . Z'$. We shall then have the following figure, the sign X representing the interaction of the terms of the first range with those of the second, and the sign→ representing the end point of these interactions:
>
> $$(A \times A') \rightarrow (B \times B') \rightarrow (C \times C') \rightarrow . . .$$
> $$(Z \times Z') \rightarrow (A \times A') \rightarrow \text{ETC.}$$
>
> In a case like this we are confronted by a closed cycle qua cycle, which expresses the permanent reconstitution of the elements $A, B, C, . . . Z, A,$ and which is characteristic of the organism; but each interaction

$(A \times A')$, $(B \times B')$, etc., at the same time represents an opening into the environment as a source of aliment. (Piaget, 1971, p. 156)

This passage expresses Piaget's desire to formalize the open *and* closed aspects of structures. On the basis of the analysis above, we might describe him as successful. There are, however, two important problems. The first concerns the way in which Piaget has embedded structures within a larger structural system. In the context of the passage above, Piaget intended $A, B, C, \ldots Z$ to represent elements of a cognitive sort. $A', B', C' \ldots Z'$, on the other hand, were intended to represent energetic elements. The larger structural system is thus open to the environment by virtue of its energetic elements. However, the opening of the cognitive elements themselves is uncertain. It may be that the interation (X) terms were meant to provide opportunities for exchanges with the environment. However, the nature of these interactions was not defined, nor were the conditions of their functioning specified (see Broughton, 1981, for a discussion of other ambiguities inherent in Piaget's interactionism). What is implied in Piaget's attempt to integrate the open and closed aspects of structures is that the energetic elements constitute the source of exchange between organism and environment. The opening is described as "a source of aliment." However, placed in the broader context of his theory of assimilation and accomodation, we have reason to believe that Piaget would be unhappy with this interpretation.

The second difficulty with the attempt to reconcile open and closed structural properties is closely related to the first: In this example, the energetic is included as an element of the total structure. However, this is at odds with most of Piaget's other discussions of the af-fect–intelligence relationship, which describe energetics as open systems lacking structure. If, on the other hand, the energetic elements are construed as simple "tag-alongs," which function to maintain the cognitive elements and insure need satisfaction, Piaget's allusion to distinct types of energetic elements (each corresponding to a distinct type of cognitive element, eg. $A \times A'$) becomes obscure. Once again, we are confronted with the elusive interaction term: What is the basis of association between the distinct cognitive elements and their corresponding energetic elements? In his monograph on intelligence and affect, Piaget suggested that this association may be explained by the subsystem of valuation, in which the energetic system becomes "intellectualized." The problem with this solution is apparent in his definition of *interest*, which is meant to reference the subsystem of valuation. As we saw above, the organism ascribes interest to objects which it is capable of assimilating to existing schemes. This introduces the difficulty of specifying what mechanism may be held accountable for "recognizing" object properties permissive of assimilation. The mechanism's system of origin, affective or intellectual, is another open question which is not addressed in Piaget's analysis.

In summary, Piaget's distinction between structure and energetics collapses at several places in his analysis of the relationship between affect and cognition. In addition, the valuation subsystem proposed to retain the dialectical interdependence of affect and cognition ultimately led to the imposition of cognition onto affect—a relationship of dependence rather than interdependence.

Piaget's Structuralism: Active Organism and Passive Environment

The problems encountered with Piaget's analysis may be traced to his conception of the organism–environment relationship. His interest in the development of internal structures and disregard for the organization of the environment has been criticized in many circles. Piaget has been rightfully recognized for playing a critical role in understanding the active nature of the developing child. There is increasing concern, however, that an adequate account of developmental processes requires an equally detailed analysis of the active nature of the child's environment (see Grossen & Perret-Clermont, 1984; Perret-Clermont & Schubauer-Leoni, 1981). The notion that children and their environments play mutually supportive roles in structuring and restructuring transactions is understated in Piagetian theory. This, indeed, reflects his individualistic orientation. It is therefore not surprising that Piaget entirely neglected the role of affect as having communicative value with social consequences. He claimed that affect had no place in structural generation or modification. On the other hand, it would be hard to argue against the idea (or the sea of empirical data supporting the idea) that expressions of affect generously contribute to the organization and reorganization of child–environment interchanges. Piaget was not naive to the proposal that the child constituted a part of the "total field" (consider his admiration for Lewin's field theory, as discussed above). The crucial question, however, concerns the relationship between structured interchanges within the total field, and the development of the child. This question cannot be systematically addressed within Piaget's theoretical frame of reference because it excludes the purposeful actions of others who contribute to the organization of the child's environment (Valsiner, 1987). An alternative to this frame of reference, which allows us to retain Piaget's emphasis on the constructive nature of development, and also consider the role of others in contributing to that development, is provided by Valsiner.

VALSINER'S INDIVIDUAL-SOCIOECOLOGICAL FRAME OF REFERENCE

Valsiner's theoretical system is premised on the understanding that development takes place within culturally structured environments jointly organized by the activities of children and the people around them (Valsiner, 1985a, 1987). The total social system is an open system, and thus subject to developmental change. Change is defined in terms of structural transformations which take place within the child (ontogenetically) and between the child and the environment (microgenetically). Valsiner claimed that both children and their environments are at all times culturally seated and structured. Individuals in the child's life are thought to organize and regulate interchanges between child and environment according to culturally given systems of meaning. The child's internalization of these cultural meaning systems constitutes the product of development. Internalization, however, does not produce exact copies of the meaning systems enacted by others. Instead, these meaning systems are constructed according to the child's own developmental history. Thus, development is always a *personal* construction, and in this sense, unique to each individual, although it shares many features with broader cultural systems.

Central to Valsiner's thesis is the concept of *canalization,* which he proposed as a general mechanism of development. Canalization was defined as a set of structured constraints which function to limit and promote the child's activities and developmental possibilities. Constraint structures are determined by the child's current developmental status, ongoing behavior, and "purposefully acting participants who take the child's current developmental state into account" (Valsiner, 1987, p. 85). Previous child–environment interactions are thought to canalize subsequent developments, which in turn influence the structural transformation of child–environment transactions.

In order to elaborate the canalization of development, Valsiner proposed a system composed of three mechanisms: the zone of free movement; the zone of promoted action; and the zone of proximal development. These three mechanisms were considered to act in concert in the determination of development. The zone of free movement (ZFM) restricts the child's access to particular areas of the environment, objects within these areas, and ways of acting on the objects. According to Valsiner, "as a result of development the child learns to set up ZFMs in his personal thinking and feeling—the ZFMs become internalized" (Valsiner, 1987, p. 97). Internalization was construed as a social construction to the extent that it issues from interactions between the child and the cultural meaning systems enacted by individuals in the child's environment. The counterpart to the inhibitory function of the ZFM is the zone of promoted action (ZPA), which refers to specific areas, objects, and ways of acting on objects that exist within a given ZFA and are actively promoted by individuals in the child's environment. Valsiner described the interplay between the ZFM and ZPA as follows:

> The two types of zone-concepts—zones of free movement and zones of promoted action—work jointly as the mechanisms by which canalization of children's development is organized. This applies equally to the development of children's actions and thinking. In the first years of life, the joint work of the ZFM/ZPA system is easily observable in naturalistic settings. Later during the childhood, however, some of the functioning of that complex becomes rarely observable as a result of children's internalization of the control over their own actions and thinking. (Valsiner, 1987, p. 101)

The ZFM and ZPA represent the way in which the child's social environment canalizes development by structuring and restructuring child–environment interactions. The dependence on cultural meaning systems is an essential feature of the ZFM/ZPA complex; cultural knowledge provides caregivers with guidelines for canalizing the child's action and development. However, the relevance of the ZFM and ZPA for future development is intimately tied to the child's current developmental capabilities (in contrast to others' *perceptions* of the child's capabilities). This is represented by the third mechanism in Valsiner's system, the zone of proximal development (ZPD).

Originally defined by Vygotsky as "the distance between the actual developmental level as determined by independent problem solving and the level of potential development as determined through problem solving under adult guidance or in collaboration with more capable peers" (Vygotsky, 1978, p. 86), Valsiner has integrated the ZPD into his overall system as a mechanism that links the ZFM and ZPA, and determines their potential impact on the course of development:

> It is the ZPD that organizes the child's psychological development on the ontogenetic plane. It moves the ZFM/ZPA complex along a trajectory of ontogenetic transformation. At every developmental period, the ZFM/ZPA complex is being transformed into a new state under the demands of the given context on the one hand, and in accordance with the ZPD on the other (Valsiner, 1987, p. 112).

Thus, the ZFM/ZPA complex constitutes a microgenetic construction which attains ontogenetic relevance as a consequence of the functioning of the ZPD.

The implications of the ZPD for determining the developmental relevance of the constraint system as it is structured by the caregivers may be enumerated as follows (Valsiner, 1987, pp. 108–109):

1. Under conditions in which the ZPA and ZPD do not overlap, the efforts of others to promote the child's actions will not be successful.
2. Maximum developmental effects will be obtained under conditions in which the ZPA and ZPD overlap.
3. The "interests" of the child at any particular point in time will influence the specific content of the ZFM, ZPA and ZPD (i.e. specific areas of the environment, objects within these areas, and ways of interacting with the objects).

Valsiner has examined his theoretical system in several different contexts, including children's mealtimes (Valsiner, 1984a, 1987) and climbing activities (Valsiner, 1984b; Valsiner & Mackie, 1985b). In an extensive examination of how children's mealtimes are culturally and historically organized, it was argued that mealtimes provide an excellent illustration of the interplay between the ZFM, ZPA, and ZPD. The ZFMs of all infants and toddlers are narrowed and delimited for the purpose of organizing mealtimes. For example, young children may be restrained in infant seats or high chairs. Once certain feeding goals have been achieved, the boundaries of the ZFMs may be restructured and more broadly defined. Valsiner provided an example of a mother attempting to spoon-feed her child "just one more bite" of cottage cheese (Valsiner, 1987, pp. 190–191). Initially, this took the form of the mother chasing the baby's mouth around with the spoon, apparently waiting for the child to stop flailing his arms and legs, turning his head from side to side, and to open his mouth. This failed, yet the mother's goal remained, so she further narrowed the child's ZFM by restraining the child's hand movements. Still this was not sufficient, so the mother took hold of the child's face and forced the child to accept the food. Thus, the ZFM was narrowed once more, and the child's action possibilities were reduced to swallowing the food or spitting it back out. (In this case, the child did the latter.)

The ZPA is also regulated in mealtime contexts. It was proposed that parental organization of the ZPA functions to promote mastery of specific activities in which the child has already demonstrated a certain degree of competence. Valsiner described the ZPA as a structure which "canalizes the child's own motivation to act, whereas the ZFMs canalize the actions themselves without an emphasis on the child's wishes or will" (Valsiner, 1987, p. 192). An example would be a child who, having demonstrated the ability to spoon-feed independently, reverts to finger feeding. The caregiver might then structure the ZPA simply by drawing the childs's attention to the spoon (e.g., placing the spoon in the child's hand, or telling the child to use it). In this way, the ZPA represents a "suggestion" proffered by the parent, and does not entail any inherent "obligation" on the part of the child.

In contrast to the ZPA and ZFM, both of which function to canalize the child's existing abilities, the ZPD is the mechanism responsible for the development of novel actions. This begins by organizing narrow ZFMs which become reorganized and more broadly defined as the child gains increasing control over the new activity. Valsiner provided an illustration of a child learning to use a spoon (1987, pp. 192–193): Initially, the adult controls the entire action. When the baby begins to grab at the spoon, or when the adult considers it appropriate to begin teaching the child how to use it, the adult gradually transfers control to the child. For example, the child will be encouraged to hold the spoon while the parent retains control over its movement from bowl to mouth. In this way, the adult organizes action within the child's zone of proximal development, yet maintains the overall structure of the feeding session. The child gradually internalizes the actions promoted by the caregiver, and ultimately, the entire structure of the mealtime context as it pertains to spoon feeding.

PIAGET AND VALSINER: SHARED PROCESSES, DIFFERENT STRUCTURAL PROPERTIES

The theoretical system proposed by Valsiner shares several features with Piaget's theory. Both theorists conceptualize mental life as structured, define development in terms of structural transformation, and view the child as an active participant in the developmental process. There are, however, important differences which center on different views of the nature of child–environment relationships.

The Contribution of Others

Perhaps the most obvious difference concerns the role accorded to other individuals in influencing the course of the child's development. Piaget and Valsiner both claimed that mental structures and their transformations resulted from child–environment transactions. Valsiner, however, placed a great deal of emphasis on the contribution of caregivers in regulating the child's interactions. This emphasis is apparent in his discussion of the ZFM/ZPA complex, which defines how caregivers limit and encourage specific interactions, and also in his discussion of the ZPD, in which developmental competence is defined in terms of children's abilities to reach problem solutions with the assistance of others, when they would be unable to do so independently.

It is important to realize that the difference between Valsiner and Piaget on the issue of caregiver contributions goes beyond one of emphasis. It is not the case that caregiver actions, as described by Valsiner, simply provide the child with content to assimilate and accommodate according to existing mental structures, as might be argued by Piaget. Instead, the caregiver and child act jointly to establish structured interactions, which are subsequently internalized by the child: "the temporary nature of the external structure of action constraints is transformed into a cognitive internal structure of constraints" (Valsiner, 1987, p. 113). Thus, compared to Piaget, Valsiner's thoughts on the organization of child–environment relationships allow a higher degree of specificity regarding the formation and transformation of mental structures. We noted above, for example, that Piaget's definition of "interest" was problematic. Specifically, it was never made clear what mechanism might be held responsible for "recognizing" objects, or object properties, that could be assimilated to existing schemes. Valsiner's system, on the other hand, provides clues as to how this might take place.

The Development of Interest

According to Valsiner, cultural meaning systems, which are themselves highly structured, provide guidelines for the organization of the ZFM/ZPA complex; they influence the specific interactions that a child is likely to have with the environment, and, as a consequence of internalization, they also contribute to endogeneous mental structures. From this perspective, "interest" may be thought to constitute the internalization of the ZPA. Indeed, Valsiner claimed that the ZPA canalizes the child's *motivation* to act. It is not the case, however, that the structures internalized are mirror images of the actions promoted (cf. Vygotsky's, 1962, analysis of "inner speech" as an internalized although modified version of vocal speech). Nor is it the case that internalization of the ZPA takes place in an all-or-none fashion. Instead, the internalization of the ZPA may be extended in time, and according to Valsiner, is a function of the child's zone of proximal development. Given that the ZPA is organized according to cultural meaning systems and the child's ongoing activity, it is reasonable to suppose that the child's interest also functions to canalize the actions promoted by the caregiver. Thus, "interest" is a joint function of the caregiver's enactment of cultural meaning systems and the child's ZPD.

In other words, cognitive structures represent the internalization of culturally mediated interactions with culturally relevant objects. "Interest," then, is not endogeneously determined but socially constructed according to previous internalizations and subsequent interactions organized by the ZFM/ZPA.

Equilibration and Disequilibration: Structural Assumptions

Another difference between Piaget and Valsiner, which again circles back to their different perspectives on the nature of child–environment relationships, concerns the pervasiveness of *structure*. Again, we are faced with surface similarities that belie underlying differences. Both Piaget and Valsiner concerned themselves with the formation and transformation of mental structures. Piaget considered structure, on one level, to be an ontogenetic affair. The mental life of the young child was less structured than that of the older child; the period of formal operations was construed as qualitatively more structured compared to less mature developmental periods. On another level, Piaget described development in terms of cycles of structural equilibration, disequilibration and re-equilibration. Disequilibration, from this vantage point, constitutes a type of structural chaos.

In general, Valsiner favored Piaget's notion of increasing equilibration, and indeed incorporated it into his own theoretical system. However, he rejected Piaget's position on increasing structuralization, a position which reflected Piaget's ideas regarding developmental tendencies toward system closure. Instead, Valsiner attempted to integrate Piaget's ideas in a way which would maintain the open-system nature of development. To this end, he incorporated the notion of increasing disequilibration from Prigogine (1976), which is meant to describe the amplification of disequilibration that accompanies any structural transformation. Hence, disequilibration is considered the rule rather than the exception.

Valsiner admitted that, in one sense, the difference between Piaget's increasing equilibration and Prigogine's increasing disequilibration is similar to the difference between a glass of water that is half full and one that is half empty (Valsiner, 1987, p. 58). He argued, however, that each maintains very different assumptions with respect to the openness and context dependency of the developing organism. Piaget's notion of increasing equilibration, in the service of increasing structuralization, suggests that interiorized knowledge tends towards closure and becomes context-free. Increasing disequilibration, in contrast, implies irrevocable openness and context dependency.

THE SOCIAL CONSTRUCTION OF DISEQUILIBRATION

Implicated in Valsiner's analysis, although not dealt with specifically, is the idea that disequilibration is expressed in the organization of child–environment transactions. Given that mental structures constitute the internalization of external action structures (according to the ZFM/ZFA and the ZPD), and given that disequilibration accompanies structural transformation, it follows that disequilibration extends beyond the internal machinations of the child's thought processes. It must be the case that disequilibration is constituted in the caregiver's organization of the ZFM/ZPA, as well as in the child's ZPD. As such, it is necessarily manifested in child–environment transactions.

The idea that disequilibration is relevant to the structural organization of child–environment interchanges is central to Piaget's description of the child as actively constructing reality. However, viewing the child–environment relationship as a unified and structured totality organized according to the ZFM/ZPA and ZPD, presents a somewhat different picture of structural genesis and transformation. Actions within the zone of proximal development presuppose disequilibrations between the child's current endogeneous structure of action and structures of action organized between the child and more capable individuals. In this respect, disequilibration is a function of ontogeny. On the other hand, the specific actions promoted by others within the child's ZPD (e.g., overlap between the ZPA and ZPD) necessarily encourage disequilibration to the extent that the ZPA promotes mastery of activities in which the child has already demonstrated *some* competence. So, in the same way that the caregiver canalizes the child's action and development, and in this way induces disequilibrations, the child canalizes the action of the caregiver, and induces disequilibrations of the "total field." That is, caregiver organizations of the ZPA which contribute to disequilibrations represent overlaps between the ZPA and the ZPD. The child's actions provide clues about whether disequilibrations have taken place, and the caregiver may reorganize the ZPA accordingly. The structural properties of the child–environment relationship, which are internalized over time, are thus socially constructed; both child and environment actively participate in the developmental process.

This analysis of disequilibration as a property of child–environment transactions does not challenge Piaget's original formulation of the process. It does, however, invite questions regarding the contributions of purposeful individuals who organize the child's environment in ways that encourage disequilibration and ontogenetic movement. These questions are also raised in the context of the training studies conducted by Walker and by the Geneva group. In this case, situations were constructed to induce disequilibrations, but only the developmental outcomes were examined. The intention of the work presented here is to redress the implicit, but underdeveloped, thesis regarding the child as embedded within the "total field."

Implications for Affect and Intelligence

The perspective outlined above casts a different light on the relationship between affect and intelligence as originally outlined by Piaget. In introducing his work on the relationship between them, Piaget wrote the following:

> We propose to show that even if affectivity can cause behavior, even if it is constantly involved in the functioning of intelligence, and even if it can speed up or slow down intellectual development, it nevertheless does not, itself, generate structures of behavior and does not modify the structures in whose functioning it intervenes. (Piaget, 1981, p. 6)

In contrast to Piaget's position, the analysis above would indicate that expressions of affect may significantly alter the organization of child–environment interactions and, accordingly, the child's intellectual development. Expressions of emotion, drives, will, or interest (Piaget considered differences between them only a matter of degree), would depend on previous developments (i.e., internalizations of ZFM/ZPA's according to the child's ZPD), and would have consequences for the caregiver's ongoing and future organizations of the ZFM/ZPA complex. This may be particularly relevant during periods of disequilibration accompanying structural transformations. The child's intellectual and affective responses to the caregiver's organizational efforts may express the degree of overlap between actions promoted by the caregiver and the child's zone of proximal development. In this way, the child's responses would function to align the ZFM/ZPA complex with the ZPD, and promote increasing disequilibration and structural transformation.

TO CLIMB AND NOT TO CLIMB

This section was intended to examine a naturally occurring event in light of the theoretical ideas presented above. The event seemed particularly relevant to the issues at hand due to the obvious presence of conflict expressed in the child's action, and the social regulation of conflict. Indeed, as mentioned in the introduction to this essay, the event described below initiated efforts to present a systematic account of the relationship between affect and cognition, and the implications this relationship has for the process of disequilibration. From a global standpoint, the goal was to present this account in a way that would preserve the interdependence of the child–environment relationship as emphasized in the works of Piaget and Valsiner. The local concern was to analyze the conditions under which a child resolved an apparent conflict of both wanting and not wanting to climb over a step. This task was given direction by the theoretical arguments presented above concerning the nature of disequilibration, and its affective and cognitive manifestations in child–environment transactions.

The Context and Goals of the Investigation

A child was videotaped at weekly or biweekly intervals between the ages of 25 and 38 weeks. During this time, she developed the ability to independently locomote up and down a 5-in step which separated two rooms of her home. After becoming quite facile in step-climbing, she exhibited reluctance and distress when enticed to climb down the step (cf., Campos, Hiatt, Ramsay, Henderson, & Svejda, 1978, for similar examples of this developmental shift). After a period of time, and by 38 weeks of age, she was once again able to independently locomote over the step.

Of particular interest was the interval bounded by the child's initial expression of conflict, and the resolution of the conflict. The typical setting during this interval was as follows: The child would be playing on top of the step, and a parent would direct the child's attention to a toy from below the step. The child would look in the direction of the parent and toy, and would often approach the step's edge, but would not cross over it independently. This, despite persistent interest indicated by her fussy vocalizations, appeals to the parent for assistance (e.g., looking and vocalizing, reaching out with arms), or by creeping parallel to the step.

Given this general context, it became important to ascertain its meaning from the child's perspective. Several possibilities presented themselves, which may be organized as follows:

1. Interest in an object as a goal in itself: The child expressed her desire to obtain the toy/parent which she did not currently possess; enticing the child with a toy from the bottom of the step had the

effect of drawing the child's attention to the step, and her distress vocalizations, reaching, etc., expressed her fear of the step.

2. Conflict between the goal object and the means by which the goal could be obtained: The child wanted to reach a particular goal (e.g., the parent and/or toy), and this goal was blocked by the step. Thus, the child both wanted and wanted not to locomote over the step.

Option (1) was ruled out on the basis of the following developmental pattern observed over the 12-week period:

Phase I: Acquisition
   A: (25–28 weeks) child interested in step; would explore by patting floor on either side of step edge; no negative affect; no appeals for assistence in spite of sensorimotor limitations which precluded safe locomotion; parent either physically assisted or tried to direct child's attention away from step.
   B: (29 weeks) child could be enticed to climb up step with mild physical assistance; no negative affect associated with climbing up; refusal (turning away) or some distress vocalizations when enticed to climb down.

Phase II (30–32 weeks): Independent locomotion
Child would climb up and down step without assistance.

Phase III (33–37 weeks): Distress and refusal
Child would climb up step independently; distress vocalizations and refusals to climb down step unless provided with physical assistance.

Phase IV (after 37 weeks): Independent locomotion
Child would climb up and down step without assistance.

Because of the patterned fluctuations in negative affect associated with climbing *down* the step (but not *up* the step), it was reasoned that desire for the parent or object alone was not sufficient to produce distress and refusal. Similarly, it was unlikely that the step, as a feared object, produced her distress and refusal because she would climb up it without hesitation, would often approach the edge, and even reach over it to get a toy. Hence, her "problem" vis-a-vis the step was determined to represent a conflict within her goal structure: to climb and not to climb. Her distress vocalizations, refusals, and appeals for assistance were interpreted as manifestations of the disequilibration induced by the conflict.

Given that the nature of the conflict was to be examined in terms of the child's goal structures, it seemed advisable to assess her goal structures prior to the onset of the conflict. Knowledge of the evolution of her goal structures would provide insight to the disequilibration of those structures, and their re-equilibration. Because climbing up the step did not present a problem once the ability was initially acquired, the analyses below focus on the child's efforts to climb down the step.

Goal Structures During the Acquisition Phase

As mentioned previously, during the Acquisition Phase the child expressed interest in the step as an object in itself. Her activities with the step indicated that the step constituted a goal, and not a means to achieving other goals.

This is illustrated in the following narrative, in which the caregiver's attempts to block the child's goal (out of concern for her safety), resulted in fussy vocalizations which did not cease until she had once again gained proximity to the step:

> (Age=25 weeks)
> 8.02–8.15: Child crawls to step edge.
> 8.15–8.23: Mother lifts child, "Hold on you. Back you go," and moves her away from the step, close to some toys.
> 8.23–8.52: Child fusses when put down. Mother: "Uh-oh. What's the matter? Did I spoil it? Did I ruin your fun?"
> 8.52–9.20: Child stops fussing and crawls toward step, making excited, happy vocalizations.
> 9.20–9.44: Mother attempts to redirect child's attention to toys. Child continues toward step and reaches edge.
> 9.44–10.02: Mother: "Come back here," and lifts child, moving her away from the step. Child fusses when put down. Mother: "Are you mad again? You *are* mad again. You don't like it back here. What's the matter?"
> 10.02–10.42: Child climbs onto mother, fussing.
> 10.42–11.03: Child stops fussing and creeps to step edge. Mother follows.
> 11.03–11.49: Child puts hands over edge of step and pats floor below; chews on step edge. Mother: "There. You're right on the edge."

During the early period of the Acquisition Phase, and as indicated in the example above, the caregiver attempted to restrict the child's activities around the step. When the child expressed interest in the step as a goal, the caregiver would either attempt to redirect the child's attention, or would maintain physical contact with the child as she explored the step. Both of these strategies are present in the following example.

(Age=27 weeks)

3.23–3.30: Child and mother are above step. Child turns toward step, vocalizes, and pulls herself toward the step.

3.30–3.40: Child reaches the step edge. Mother grabs hold of child's pajamas, saying "Look. The kitty's over here," trying to direct the child's attention away from the step.

3.40–3.48: Mother continues to hold child's pajamas while child creeps along the edge of the step. Another verbal attempt to redirect the child's attention, "Come get your kitty."

3.48: The child turns away from the step and moves toward the cat. Mother releases her hold on the child's pajamas.

Thus, the parent's organization of the zone of free movement restricted the child's possibilities for locomoting over the step. Likewise, the zone of promoted action was organized to encourage the child's efforts in other endeavours (cat chasing).

The extent to which locomotions over the step were restricted by the ZFM was also apparent when the child expressed interest in a goal object which required her to traverse the step. The parent treated the step as an obstacle to the child's goal attainment and would simply lift the child over the step:

(Age=26 weeks)

11.00–11.43: In pursuing the cat, the child creeps to the edge of the step and places both hands over the edge and onto the floor below.

11.43–11.48: Mother lifts child and places her on the floor below the step. "There. You want to go chase the kitty? You can go chase the kitty now."

All of the observations cited above illustrate that the step constituted a goal object within the child's goal structure, and not yet a means to a goal. Likewise, the parent's organization of the ZFM/ZPA complex did not include locomotions over the step, although it allowed for the child's exploration of the step as an object of interest in and of itself. The important ontogenetic question concerns the way in which child and parent goal structures were organized as a totality so as to promote the development from step-as-goal to step-as-means-to-goal. Clues to this process are apparent in the following observation. Here, the parent restructured the child's interest in step-as-goal to step-as-means-to-goal:

(Age: 27 weeks)

4.47–4.59: Child sitting above step and mother sitting on step edge.

Mother attracts child's attention to a toy above the step and
then places the toy below the step.

4.59–5.12:   Child creeps to step edge. Mother grabs child's pajamas as
child lays down on belly, extends arms over edge and pats
the floor below the step, watching her own hands.

5.12–5.24:   Mother redirects child's attention to toy. Child alternates
hands on floor below step and knees above step, and in this
way slides over the edge while mother holds onto child's
pajamas. Child gets toy.

In this example, the mother initially organized the ZPA to promote
interest in an object on the other side of the step (4.47–4.59). Although
it appeared that the child's interest was engaged in the toy, leading her
to locomote towards it, upon reaching the step her interest became
focused on the step (4.59–5.12). However, the mother again drew the
child's attention to the toy, and assisted the child in locomoting over
the step and reaching the toy.

Throughout the Acquisition Phase, sensorimotor limitations precluded the child's safe, independent locomotion over step. The parent
always provided physical assistance. However, the first indication that
the child perceived the step as a physical obstacle, that is, *as a means
to a goal,* did not occur until she was 28 weeks of age:

(Age=28 weeks)
0.00–0.05:   Child is on top of the step, banging a toy on the step edge.
Father has both hands around child's waist.

0.05–0.57:   Child drops toy over step. Father: "Are you going to get your
rubber doughnut?" Child reaches over step and gets toy,
banging it on the floor below the step.

0.57–0.59:   Child turns body parallel to step, slapping the floor with her
hands.

0.59–1.45:   Mother calls to child and attracts child's attention to a toy
below the step but within child's reach. Child reaches and
gets toy, bangs and drops it below step. Again retrieves, bangs
and drops toy which then rolls beyond her reach.

1.45–1.59:   Mother: "Uh-oh." Child looks at mother. Mother: "Well,
what happened?"

1.59–2.05:   Child turns away from step towards father, pulls on father's
shirt.

2.05–2.26:   Mother tries to redirect child's attention to toy and puts it
on the edge of the step. Child turns, gets the toy and drops
it. Toy rolls off the step and out of reach.

2.26–2.43:   Mother: "There it is." Child fusses and turns away from step,
crawls onto father.

This observation illustrates that the child perceived locomotion over the step as an obstacle to goal attainment. She would reach over the step to attain objects that were within her reach (0.05–0.57 and 0.59–1.45), but refused to attempt locomotions over the step (1.59–2.05 and 2.26–2.43). This, indeed, is the first observation of a conflict within her goal structure.

In attempting to understand the nature of this first conflict, which immediately preceded the phase of Independent Locomotion, it is important to recognize that the assistance available to the child (parent physically holding on to her or her clothing) had not changed from the time she began to express an interest in the step at 25 weeks of age. Nonetheless, it was not until the observation above, at 28 weeks of age, that she evidenced reluctance to locomote over the step under these conditions of assistance. On the other hand, *when she had some degree of control over the conditions of assistance,* she would attempt to locomote over the step. This is illustrated in the following observation, also made at 28 weeks of age.

(Age=28 weeks)

5.08–5.21: Mother attracts child's attention to a toy from below the step, "Are you going to come down here? Huh?" Child creeps along the step edge to where the mother is sitting below the step.

5.21–5.42: Child reaches over the edge towards the toy. Mother: "Careful, sweetie," and grabs child's pajamas. "Will you come over? Will you come down?" Child alternately reaches hands over the step edge.

5.42–6.00: Child pulls on mother's sleeve, then reaches towards mother's leg. Mother moves leg toward child who then climbs onto mother using her as a "bridge" between the top and bottom of the step, and slides off step, over mother, and onto floor below step.

The observation above clearly illustrates that locomotion over the step figured in the child's goal structure as a means to goal attainment. This was initially expressed by pulling on the mother's sleeve and then reaching over the step edge for the mother's leg. The mother made available, and then promoted these efforts by moving her body into a position which made it possible for the child to use her as a "bridge."

In summary, observations made during the Acquisition Phase indicated that initially, the child's goal structure consisted of interest in the step as a goal in itself. Neither the child's goal structure nor the parent's organization of the ZFM/ZPA indicated that locomotion over the step constituted a means for goal attainment within the child's zone of proximal development. Later, however, the parent organized the ZFM/ZPA complex in ways that contributed to the child's differentiation between the step as an object of interest, and locomotion over the step as a means to a goal. As the beginning of this process of differentiation became apparent in the child's action, the parent promoted action within the child's zone of proximal development. Disequilibrations were observed in child–environment transactions and regulated by the caregiver such that successful locomotion over the step was achieved.

At 29 weeks of age, the child was independently locomoting over the step. This continued until she was 33 weeks of age, at which time she evidenced distress and refusals when encouraged to locomote over it.

Goal Structures During the Distress and Refusal Phase

This phase, like the Acquisition Phase, may be characterized in terms structural transformations of goal hierarchies. However, observations of the Acquisition Phase revealed a transformation from step-as-goal to step-as-means-to-goal. In contrast, it was argued previously that the Distress and Refusal Phase constituted a transformation from "to climb and not to climb," to step-as-means-to-goal. It will become clear in the analyses below that this difference has important implications for the process of disequilibration and structural transformation. For one, we will find that the zone of free movement is very loosely defined during this phase, probably due to the parent's knowledge that the child has already mastered the sensorimotor abilities required to traverse the step. This is indicated in the lack of "automatic" assistance provided (e.g., holding onto the child's pajamas). Furthermore, the parent's organization of the zone of promoted action vis-a-vis the child's goal structure is importantly different here, and constitutes a sort of reversal from that observed during the Acquisition Phase. Whereas the first phase was marked by parent actions which canalized the child's interest from the step to a toy, and thus promoted child activities resulting in the step becoming a means to a goal, during the latter phase, the parent capitalized on, and maintained, the child's *initial* interest in the toy, and restructured the setting so that the child's goal could be achieved. Again, the result was the child pursuing a goal which required the step to be used as a means to goal attainment. This is illustrated in the following observation.

> (Age=33 weeks)
> 6.59–7.18: Mother places a toy on top of the step where child is sitting. Mother: "Go get it. Go get your elephant." Child creeps forward and retrieves the elephant.

7.18–7.32:   Mother gets a different toy and entices the child over the step: "Want your keys?" Child creeps away from the step, taking the elephant with her.

7.32–7.42:   Mother takes the elephant from the child and uses it to entice her over the step. Child creeps away from the step and gets a different toy.

7.42–8.08:   Mother laughs: "She's going to get her Garfield." Mother takes Garfield, "Give me that. Come on. Are you going to come down here?" and uses it to entice child over the step.

8.08–8.20:   Child creeps toward step and sits, waving arms and vocalizing. Mother imitates child's vocalizations.

8.20–8.24:   Child creeps away. Mother: "Nope. She says 'no thank you.'"

8.24–8.39:   Mother moves closer to the step, "Come here baby. Come here you," enticing the child with a toy. Child creeps to mother's leg which is resting on the step. Mother: "Hello. Hello peanut. I'd be afraid of the step if I bonked my head, too."

8.39–8.41:   Child, sitting with one hand on mother's leg, reaches over the step towards the toys which are out of her reach.

8.41–8.46:   Child puts both hands on mother's leg.

8.46–8.50:   Child sits back and looks at toys. Mother entices.

8.50–9.19:   Child climbs down using mother as "bridge."

This example provides an interesting account of how parent and child jointly canalize each other's actions. The parent used the child's interest in a particular toy to promote locomotion over the step. At this point, however, the child would abandon interest in the particular object, and replace it with something else. The parent's action was thus canalized to the extent that she used the child's interest in the new object to again promote locomotion over the step. Successive abandonments ultimately lead to the parent's "recognition" that interest in a toy itself was not sufficient to produce locomotion. Thus, she restructured the task, explicitly treating the step as an obstacle to goal attainment (i.e., she moved closer to the step and put her leg on it to encourage the child to use it as a bridge, 8.24–8.39).

In the example cited above, disequilibration was manifested in the child's successive changes of object interest as a consequence of actions promoted by the parent. The parent then acted to regulate the disequilibration in a way that allowed successful locomotion over the step. In the observation below, a similar phenomenon occurs, although the disequilibration is manifested in distress vocalizations.

(Age=36 weeks)

12.00–12.56:   Mother entices child to climb down step. Child watches and vocalizes. Mother continues to entice. Child vocalizes and looks away. Child creeps to edge of step, sits, and fusses. Mother continues to entice.

12.56–13.03:   Mother places toy on top of step. Child reaches for it, pushes it over the step, sits back and fusses. Mother laughs: "You're being entirely silly."

13.03–13.10:   Child reaches towards the step edge and sits back. Mother moves to the bottom of the step and puts her leg on the step edge. Mother entices the child over the step with a toy.

13.10:   Child immediately climbs off the step and onto the mother, using her as a "bridge," and retrieves the toy.

In both of the observations above, the child used a strategy of locomotion which she originally used during the Acquisition Phase. That is, using the mother as a bridge between the top and bottom of the step. It was argued that the bridge strategy, as used during the first phase, represented a means, *under the child's control,* to goal attainment. This was taken as an indication that the child was actively differentiating between step-as-goal and step-as-means-to-goal. However, as used during the Distress and Refusal Phase, this same strategy seemed to have a different origin. The "assistance," as indicated in the following observation (also at 36 weeks of age), was symbolic.

(Age=36 weeks)

0.00–0.16:   Mother entices child with a toy from below step. Child leans forward and fusses. Mother continues to entice. Child continues to fuss.

0.16–0.25:   Mother extends her leg and touches the step with her foot. Child fusses while creeping to the edge of the step. Child touches the mother's foot with her hand, and then creeps over the step independently.

GENERAL CONCLUSIONS

In this essay, we explored different landscapes of the child–environment relationship, and the paths each provided to understanding the development of affect and intelligence. It was argued that Piaget neglected the developmental contributions of an active environment. Thus, his structure–energetic distinction failed to account for the role of affective expressions in organizing child–environment transactions. Observable sensorimotor and affective abilities were found to canalize parental organizations of the ZFM/ZPA complex, which, in turn, canalized subsequent child action and development.

On the other hand, Piaget's constructivistic notion of disequilibration was theoretically and empirically supported when buttressed with Valsiner's portrayal of an equally constructive environment. This was apparent from the analyses of goal structure transformations which took place within and between the parent and child. Development during the Acquisition Phase, from step-as-goal to step-as-means-to-goal, may be interpreted within Piaget's framework: The step took on value as a means in the context of satisfying a "need" (i.e., in leading to goal attainment). However, the step was initially a goal itself, and it was the parent who created the "need" by reorganizing the ZPA and canalizing the child's interest from step-as-goal to step-as-means-to-goal. Likewise, during the Distress and Refusal Phase, the parent organized the environment so as to produce opportunities for the step to be used as a means for acquiring particular goals. These results have important implications for understanding the relationship between affect and cognition. As it is typically stated, the goal of specifying *the relationship* between affect and cognition suggests that the two stand in static correspondence with one another. However, the results described above suggest that the relationship between them may follow a developmental course of its own. Specifically, it may become more visible during periods of disequilibration. Furthermore, the structural complimentarity of affect and cognition may be observed in the social regulation of conflict.

The empirical phenomena were found to support the argument that disequilibration is manifested in child–environment transactions. Affective and sensorimotor actions provided the parent with clues to the process of disequilibration, and thus, the state of overlap between the ZFM/ZPA and the zone of proximal development. Thus, disequilibration is not an activity of thought, but accomplished through the medium of social transaction.

The work presented here provides a glimpse of the child–environment relationship as a co-constructed totality. The ontogenetic consequences of this relationship were revealed in qualitative analyses of systems in transition. This convergence of theory and method provided an avenue for examining the intrinsic instability and contradictory nature of structural transformation. In this respect, it represents an attempt to move beyond that legacy of science which has produced, in the words of Engels,

> the habit of observing natural objects and natural processes in their isolation, detached from the whole vast interconnection of things; and therefore not in their motion, but in their repose; not as essentially

changing, but as fixed constants; not in their life, but in their death. (Engels, 1966, p. 27)

REFERENCES

Ainsworth, M., & Wittig, B. (1969). Attachment and exploratory behavior of one-year-olds in a strange situation. In B.M. Foss (Ed.), *Determinants of infant behavior* (Vol. 4, pp. 11–136). New York: Wiley.

Broughton, J. (1981). Piaget's structural developmental psychology III: Function and the problem of knowledge. *Human development, 24,* 257–285.

Bugental, D., Kaswan, J., & Love, L. (1970). Perception of contradictory meanings conveyed by verbal and nonverbal channels. *Journal of personality and social psychology, 16,* 647–655.

Campos, J., Hiatt, S., Ramsay, D., Henderson, C., & Svejda, M. (1978). The emergence of fear on the visual cliff. In M. Lewis and L. Rosenblum (Eds.), *The development of affect.* (pp. 149–182). New York: Plenum Press.

Engels, F. (1966). *Anti-Dühring.* New York: International Publishers.

Grossen, M., & Perret-Clermont, A. (1984). Some elements of a social psychology of operational development of the child. *Quarterly newsletter of the laboratory of comparative human cognition, 6,* 51–57.

Inhelder, B., Sinclair, H., & Bovet, M. (1974). *Learning and the development of cognition.* London: Routledge & Kegan Paul.

Janet, P. (1921). The fear of action. *Journal of abnormal psychology and social psychology, 16,* 150–160.

Kohlberg, L. (1969). Stage and sequence: The cognitive-developmental approach to socialization. In D.A. Goslin (Ed.), *Handbook of socialization theory and research.* Chicago, IL: Rand McNally.

Lewin, K. (1951). *Field theory in social science.* Chicago, IL: University of Chicago Press.

Perret-Clermont, A. & Schubauer-Leoni, M. (1981). Conflict and cooperation as opportunities for learning. In W. Robinson (Ed.), *Communication in development.* New York: Academic Press.

Piaget, J. (1962). *Play, dreams and imitation in childhood.* New York: W.W. Norton & Company.

Piaget, J. (1969). *The psychology of the child.* New York: Basic Books, Inc.

Piaget, J. (1971). *Biology and knowledge.* Chicago, IL: University of Chicago Press.

Piaget, J. (1973). *The child and reality: Problems of genetic psychology.* New York: Grossman.

Piaget, J. (1980). *Experiments in contradiction.* Chicago, IL: University of Chicago Press.

Piaget, J. (1981). Intelligence and affectivity: Their relationship during child development. *Annual Reviews Monograph.* Palo Alto, CA: Annual Reviews, Inc.

Prigogine, I. (1976). Order through fluctuation: Self organization and social system. In E. Jantsch & C. Waddington (Eds.), *Evolution and consciousness: Human systems in transition.* Reading, MA: Addison-Wesley.

Robinson, E., & Robinson, W. (1982). Knowing when you don't know enough: Children's judgements about ambiguous information. *Cognition, 12,* 267–280.

Super, C., Kagan, J., Morrison, F., Haith, M., & Weifenbach, J. (1972). Discrepancy and attention in the five-month infant. *Genetic Psychology Monographs, 85,* 305–331.

Valsiner, J. (1984a). Construction of the Zone of Proximal Development in adult–child joint action: The socialization of meals. *New Directions for Child Development, 23,* 65–76.

Valsiner, J. (1984b, August). *Children within their home settings: Canalization of child development through culturally organized physical environment.* Paper presented at the Inaugural European Conference on Developmental Psychology, Groningen.

Valsiner, J. (1985). Parental organization of children's cognitive development within home environment. *Psychologia, 28,* 131–143.

Valsiner, J. (1987). *Culture and the development of children's action.* Chichester, England: John Wiley and Sons.

Valsiner, J., & Mackie, C. (1985). Toddlers at home: Canalization of climbing skills through culturally organized physical environments. In T. Gärling & J. Valsiner (Eds.), *Children within environments; towards a psychology of accident prevention* (pp. 165–191). New York: Plenum.

Vuyk, R. (1981). *Overview and critique of Piaget's genetic epistemology 1965–1980* (Vols 1-2). London: Academic Press, Inc.

Vygotsky, L. (1962). *Thought and language.* Cambridge, MA: MIT Press.

Vygotsky, L. (1978). *Mind in society.* Cambridge, MA: Harvard University Press.

Walker, L. (1983). Sources of cognitive conflict for stage transition in moral development. *Developmental Psychology, 19,* 103–110.

CHAPTER 3

Developmental Tasks as Organizers of Children's Ecologies: Mothers' Contingencies as Children Learn to Walk, Eat, and Dress*

Thomas Kindermann   and   **Ellen A. Skinner**
Freie Universität,   Max Planck Institute for
Berlin (West)   Human Development and
Education,
Berlin (West)

For almost any caregiver behavior, it seems that one can identify both potentially facilitating and potentially detrimental consequences for the child. One set of caregiver behaviors that has been found in Western cultures to be associated almost exclusively with healthy child functioning is a constellation of behaviors referred to as contingent, sensitive, or responsive. In general, these constructs are used to characterize caregivers who respond consistently and appropriately to child bids (e.g., for help and attention) and who initiate interactions that are geared to the capabilities, intentions, goals, and moods of the child as well as to his or her current developmental level.

Research findings from naturalistic-correlational, experimental, and longitudinal studies indicate that parents who are more sensitive, con-

* The study described in this chapter was part of the project "Dependence and Independence in the Elderly: The Role of Social Interactions," directed by Margret M. Baltes at the Free University of Berlin and was completed while the first author was supported by the "Modellvorhaben zur Förderung des Wissenschaftlichen Nachwuchses in Entwicklungspsychologie," funded by the Volkswagen Foundation. We gratefully acknowledge the valuable discussions and support of Margret M. Baltes and Paul B. Baltes. We would also like to thank Jaan Valsiner for his insightful critique of some of the ideas contained in this chapter.

66

tingent, and/or responsive (relative to parents who are less so) have children who are more securely attached to them (Ainsworth, Blehar, Waters, & Wall, 1978; Belsky, Rovine, & Taylor, 1984), who perceive themselves as having more control over what happens to them (Skinner, 1986; Skinner & Connell, 1986), and who explore and examine their environments more (Easterbrooks & Goldberg, 1984; Jennings, Harmon, Morgan, Gaiter, & Yarrow, 1979; Riksen-Walraven, 1978). In addition, these children perform better on cognitive tasks (Beckwith & Cohen, 1983; Bradley, Caldwell, & Elardo, 1979; Donovan & Leavitt, 1978; Olson, Bates, & Bayles, 1984) and exhibit higher levels of social maturity in interactions with peers (Bakeman & Brown, 1980; Waters, Wippman, & Sroufe, 1979).

These aspects of child functioning are of such theoretical and practical importance that researchers have begun to ask themselves about the origins of individual differences in caregiver contingent and sensitive behavior. Because these questions are fairly recent, evidence pertaining to this issue can be described as sketchy at best.

After reviewing research aimed at identifying factors which contribute to responsive caregiver behavior, we will suggest an additional class of variables which may structure caregiver–child interactions, namely, *developmental tasks*. To illustrate several ways in which parent–child interactions are influenced by children's progression through developmental tasks, a study of mother–child interaction in everyday tasks is presented. Finally, we will argue that developmental tasks themselves are not fixed entities, but represent learning environments that are actively constructed jointly by the child and the caregiver in a given cultural and historical ecology.

RESEARCH ON THE FACTORS AFFECTING CONTINGENT AND SENSITIVE CAREGIVER BEHAVIOR

Two kinds of factors have been considered that may contribute to interindividual differences in caregiver behavior, namely, factors related to individuals (parents or children) and those related to the environment. Each will be reviewed briefly (for a more detailed review, see Belsky, 1984; Lamb & Easterbrooks, 1981; Skinner, 1985b).

Interindividual Difference Variables

Caregivers. On the side of the parent, researchers have hypothesized a stable personality characteristic, named, aptly enough, *sensitivity,* to account for individual differences in contingent and sensitive parent behavior. Ainsworth (1979), for example, includes sensitive–insensitive as one of four dimensions of parental personality (the others are accepting–rejecting, cooperative–interfering, and accessible–ignoring). Other researchers have attempted to specify the components of this personality characteristic (Brody, 1956; Brody & Axelrad, 1978; Lamb & Easterbrooks, 1981), identifying aspects such as intolerance, carelessness, self-centeredness, and persistence.

In addition, parent characteristics have been suggested which may facilitate (or hinder) the parent's ability to perceive, interpret, and respond to children's signals. Cognitive-developmental level (Sameroff, 1975), sex differences (Feldman & Nash, 1979; Lamb & Goldberg, 1980), differential physiological responsiveness (Leavitt & Donovan, 1979), and beliefs about the parental role in children's development (Kuczynski, 1984; Skinner, 1985b) have all been used to predict levels of contingent and responsive behavior.

Children. On the side of the child, typical studies have usually considered child personality to be an *outcome* of parental contingent responsiveness. However, recent work is beginning to explore aspects of children's temperament and behavior which may influence how sensitively their parents behave toward them. For example, although the findings are not conclusive, studies of children's temperament indicate that children who are characterized as being "difficult" (Bates, 1980) tend to have mothers who are less responsive to them (Milliones, 1978), or, over time, to produce such mothers (Campbell, 1979).

Other aspects of children's behavior also seem to influence how contingently parents respond to them. Child activity level and engagement seems to have an impact on parental sensitivity. For example, child passivity in problem-solving tasks has been shown to lead to less sensitive responding from mothers (Skinner, 1986).

Contextual Variables

The influences on parent sensitivity that are due to context have been studied at several levels of abstraction. At the most general level, research has shown differences in parental contingency as a function of socioeconomic status (Brown, Bakeman, Snyder, Frederikson, Morgan, & Hepler, 1975; Borduin & Henggeler, 1981). At a less general level, the effects of stress and social support have been documented, with more frequent and more sensitive interactions being observed for those parents and families who experience less stress and more social support (e.g., Crnic, Greenberg, Ragozin, Robinson, & Basham, 1983; Weinraub & Wolf, 1983; see Belsky, 1984 for a review). At the most specific level, research has shown that competing activities of the mother, such as caregiving for a second child (Kendrick & Dunn, 1980), result in less attentiveness and contingency on the part of the mother. Laboratory analogs in which mothers participated in competing cognitive tasks have also demonstrated that such demands reduce maternal interaction and responsiveness (Zussman, 1980).

As indicated in the introduction, the primary purpose of this chapter is to introduce an additional factor which we believe structures children's ecologies by influencing the amount of contingency that parents show toward their children, namely, developmental tasks. Before proceeding to this topic, however, we must make a brief detour to the constructs of contingency/sensitivity and developmental tasks.

Definitions of Constructs

Contingent and sensitive caregiver behavior. Although the terms *contingency* and *sensitivity* have been used interchangeably in the previous sections, more specific and differentiated definitions are needed for further discussion. Part of the confusion about definitions stems from the fact that these terms have been used in a wide variety of theoretical contexts, from learning theory to attachment theory to theories of learned helplessness.

For purposes of this chapter, contingency will be used in its statistical sense. That is, contingency refers to a probabilistic relation between two events. The extent to which parent behavior is contingent on child action can be described by comparing the likelihood that a certain parent behavior occurs following a specific action or behavior of the child, with the likelihood of that parent behavior in general (Seligman, 1975; Skinner & Connell, 1986; Suomi, 1980). According to this definition, contingent caregivers are ones who respond to their children's actions quickly, consistently, and discriminatively.

Equally important about this definition is what it *excludes*. No criteria are imposed about the *content* of contingent behaviors. This means that, for example, the parent who quickly, consistently, and discriminatively shakes her finger at the child when it cries is just as contingent as the parent who responds by picking the child up (Skinner & Connell, 1986).

In contrast, sensitive behavior is typically defined as behavior which is not only contingent but also appropriate. Although appropriateness has been defined in many different ways (Ainsworth, 1979; Bakeman & Brown, 1980; Clarke-Stewart, 1973; Elardo, Bradley, & Caldwell, 1975), the general emphasis is on behavior which shows responsiveness to the child's bids, signals, and intentions.

In sum, in the discussion which follows, contingency will be used to refer to response parameters and sensitivity will refer to behavior which is both contingent and responsive to the child's signals.

Developmental Tasks. It is difficult to provide a very straightforward definition of the concept of *developmental tasks.* For example, Havighurst defines a developmental task very generally as a "task which arises at or about a certain period in the life of the individual, successful achievement of which leads to happiness and success with later tasks, while failure leads to unhappiness in the individual, disapproval by the society, and difficulty with later tasks" (1972, p. 2). At the same time (p. 6), he notes that it is "largely arbitrary" which tasks are considered as developmental. Nevertheless, there are certain challenges in early childhood that most people would agree are developmental tasks, in that they are developmentally graded in their onset and are important and necessary steps in the developmental sequence of all children in a given culture.

Examples of very basic accomplishments that almost every child achieves during the first 2 years of life are the tasks of learning to walk, learning to eat, and learning to dress, go to the bathroom, and wash independently. In contrast to some later developmental tasks, these are usually accomplished in daily interactions with primary caregivers.

Although each is basic to human life, these three tasks are quite different from each other. In terms of how and when they are learned, walking appears to be a mostly biologically determined function, whereas eating and dressing are regarded as more culturally determined. To the extent that socialization can be described as teaching the "rules of the game" (Hetherington & Parke, 1979, p. 415), nobody has to be taught "how" to walk, but everyone has to learn how to eat and dress in a given culture and society.

However, this general view must be differentiated as soon as the material ecology is taken into consideration. Behavioral *competence* is only one side of the coin. *How to use competence* in a given setting is an issue of equal importance. For the tasks of learning to eat or dress, this is clearly the case. Children are able to swallow food right from birth. Learning what kind of food is eatable in a given environment and what is not, on the other hand, is a topic of further learning. At the same time, for appropriate eating in a given culture, specific kinds of tools have to be mastered and their competent use has to be accomplished beyond the basic capacity of swallowing.

Perhaps surprisingly, the same holds true for locomotive behavior. Mastery of walking per se need not necessarily be an issue of socialization. However, the *appropriate use* of mobile capacities almost always emerges as a socialization goal. For example, the need for accident prevention when children start to become mobile results in instruction, preventive reorganization in the family setting (child-proofing), and explicit training in interactions with the child (e.g., Valsiner & Gärling, 1985).

Thus, developmental tasks concern two issues. First there is the gain of a specific competence at a given point in development. Second, and often parallel to the first, there is the process of "canalization" of growing competencies into culturally and ecologically appropriate channels (Valsiner, 1984, 1986).

DEVELOPMENTAL TASKS AS ORGANIZERS OF CAREGIVER-CHILD INTERACTION PATTERNS

As described above, most research on the determinants of contingent and sensitive behavior has focused on individual difference factors, related to either parents or children, or on environmental factors. Although most people would agree that both factors make a contribution (e.g., Belsky, 1984), very little has been said about the conditions under which either or both of these sets of factors may contribute to contingent interactions.

The central argument of this chapter is that developmental tasks act as organizers of children's ecologies by influencing the patterns of caregiver–child interaction. More specifically, we argue that the process by which a child enters, learns, and accomplishes a developmental task structures the effort on the side of the child as well as the guidance on the side of the caregiver. In the discussion section, we will argue further that these developmental tasks are, in turn, a product of particular cultures which specify the appropriate age, sequence, and process of accomplishment.

At a general level, developmental tasks organize daily parent–child interactions in a given culture by reducing the influence of interindividual difference and environmental factors. For example, we would argue that, before the onset of the developmental task of learning to walk, the contingency between an infant's requests to be picked up and parents' picking up the infant will largely depend on a combination of interindividual difference factors (e.g., persistence of demands by child, caregiver's child-rearing style) and environmental demands (e.g., presence of material hazards). Hence, *before the onset* of a child's learning to walk, the amount of contingency in different parent–child dyads should vary and should be related to interindividual and environmental factors.

In contrast, *after the onset* of a developmental task, different parent–child dyads should come to resemble each other, in terms of contingencies in their interactions. During the process of learning to walk, for example, the contingency between child task-related behaviors and parent task-related behaviors should no longer be as easily predicted from interindividual and environmental factors.

Finally, *after* the developmental task has been *solved,* or, in our example, after the child is a competent walker, we would argue that dyads should no longer resemble each other as they did during the process of learning. Differences between dyads in terms of the contingencies for task-related behaviors should increase. Likewise, the relation between these contingencies and interindividual difference or environmental factors should increase.

How Parent–Child Interactions Can Be Structured by Developmental Tasks

At the most basic level, developmental tasks organize daily caregiver–child interactions by influencing the *kinds* of behaviors both caregivers and children show. On the side of the parents, new behaviors begin to appear that structure, guide, teach, and encourage developmental task-related behaviors. On the side of the child, attempts, demands to be allowed, and requests for help related to developmental task behavior should appear. These behavioral changes essentially signal the onset of a developmental task. After a developmental task begins, further changes in behavior should accompany the whole process of accomplishment. For example, mothers allow children to try to use a fork after they have achieved competence with a spoon.

In addition to qualitative changes in both parent and child behavior (i.e., the emergence of new behaviors), the *amount* or *frequency* of task-related behaviors should change with the onset of the developmental task. For example, before the child learns to dress himself or herself, dressing proceeds relative quickly—because it is done mainly by the caregiver. However, as soon as the child attempts and is encouraged to attempt to put on, for example, his or her own underpants, the amount of time spent dressing increases dramatically.

In terms of *contingencies,* during the accomplishment of developmental tasks, the relation between children's task-related behavior and parents' responses should change. For example, before a mother believes a child is ready to learn to eat with a spoon, she may keep the spoon under tight control (cf. Valsiner, 1984), no matter what the child requests. In contrast, after the onset of learning to eat with a spoon, the contingency between the child's bids for the spoon and the mother relinquishing the spoon should increase.

In addition to new contingencies that may emerge for the first time during a developmental task, the *level of contingencies* that existed previously may also change. For example, before a child can walk, the contingency between asking to be carried and being carried may be relatively high. However, while the child is learning to walk, this contingency may decrease. At the same time, the contingency between attempts to go down the stairs alone and mother permitting this behavior or only structuring it may increase.

We argue that these changes appear in a normative fashion, in that differences formerly existing between parent–child dyads will be overridden by the homogenizing process of change during the developmental task. As described earlier, these changes in contingencies have the cumulative effect of *reducing the interindividual differences between different parent–child dyads* during the time they are involved in solving the developmental task.

However, information about interindividual differences at various points in the process of accomplishing a developmental task, that is, information about how similar two dyads are in terms of their caregiver-contingencies, does not necessarily imply anything about the similarity between dyads in terms of their *patterns of change,* that is, information about whether contingencies change in the same direction or stay stable for both dyads.

Because this is a complicated point, an example will be used to illustrate it. Imagine two dyads which are not very similar to each other at one point in time: In one dyad, mother behavior is highly contingent on child behavior x but not on child behavior y, whereas, in the other dyad, the contingencies are exactly the opposite. From one time to the next, without increasing the similarity of the contingency patterns at either point in time, the *changes* that occur might nevertheless go in the very same direction for both dyads; for example, the contingencies in both dyads for both child behaviors might increase. And the reverse combination of high similarity between dyads at two points in time and different patterns of change is also possible.

We would argue that the similarity between dyads in terms of direction of change (or lack of change) in contingencies from one time to the next should also be heightened by the onset of developmental tasks. Before the developmental task, the amount and kinds of contingencies may be relatively situationally dependent, resulting in low similarity of changes in contingency measurements over time. During the task, *more consistency of change should be seen because the more homogenous process of passing through a developmental task dominates and clears out situational differences.* In other words, the process of proceeding through the developmental task itself leads to an increase in similarity between dyads in terms of changes in contingency patterns.

In sum, developmental tasks can organize caregiver–child interaction patterns by influencing the kind and frequencies of behaviors shown by both caregiver and child, by determining which contingencies will be significant and their level of significance, and by increasing the similarity between dyads in both the patterns of contingencies at one point in time and changes in contingencies across time.

Of course, some variability between dyads would probably still exist, even if children are compared who are in the same state of accomplishment of the same developmental task. Differences might exist, for example, in frequencies of particular behaviors and in the extent to which contingencies are elevated above their respective baselines. Of course, variability will also exist between different cultures. The point is that different dyads in a given culture will be relatively more *similar* (maybe even identical) with respect to which task-related contingencies are significant *during* the process of accomplishment of a developmental task. At these times, culture-specific guidelines of how and when children should be supported in learning developmental tasks will exert homogenizing influences on everyday interactions leading to high interdyad similarity relative to the times both before the onset of the developmental task and after the task is solved.

EMPIRICAL DEMONSTRATION OF HOW DEVELOPMENTAL TASKS CAN ORGANIZE MOTHER-CHILD INTERACTION PATTERNS

A study was conducted to examine the changes in mother–child interactions (and especially in mothers' contingent reactions to children's behavior) in three everyday tasks (walking, eating, and dressing) during the process when children become competent in these tasks. The question addressed was: In everyday mother–child interactions, is there evidence to be found that developmental tasks act as organizers of maternal contingencies?

Method

Sample. Six children, two each at the age of 9, 12, and 21 months, were observed in their homes interacting with their mothers. The dyads were selected out of a pool of mothers in a large West German city reacting to an announcement in a local magazine. Dyads with children of the same age were selected according to maximal comparability and *normative criteria* of development (see below for details).

Design. Interactions of each dyad were videotaped repeatedly 1 hour daily, eight times over a period of 100 days. During the study, the 9-month-old children grew to be about 13 months old, the 12-month-olds to be 16 months, and the 21-month-olds to be 25 months. The children will be referred to as the 9–13, the 12–16, and the 21–25 mon. groups.

Two days of videotaping were grouped together as one point of measurement. The first and second and the third and fourth points of measurement were separated by 2 weeks at maximum, while between the second and third there was a time gap of 2 months. Children were usually videotaped after getting up in the morning or after a nap in the middle of the day. As previous diaries of the mothers had shown, these were times when interactions typically were centered around shorter-lasting mealtime, dressing, washing, and toilet occasions. The selection of subjects and times of videotaping allowed for a design in which children of all age groups could be observed interacting in all three developmental tasks.

Mother's perception of child's learning in the developmental tasks. Independently of the videotaping, mothers were asked about their estimations of children's *current state of learning* in each of the three tasks. This was done at every measurement point. Additionally, the following questionnaires were used for the developmental description of the sample: (a) The KID-scale (Katoff, Reuter, & Dunn, 1978) for the age range of 9 to 16 months (using a German version currently under development by Hellgard Rauh and her colleagues at the Free University, Berlin), and (b) the Minnesota Child Development Inventory (Ireton & Thwing, 1979; German translation) for the age range of 12 to 25 months. Table 1 gives the developmental description of the children and the mothers' ratings of their children's status in the tasks.

According to normative criteria, the 9–13 mon. children were supposed to experience the developmental tasks of learning to walk and learning to eat as central tasks. Learning to dress was not supposed to represent a central issue in their interactions. Mothers' ratings of their learning confirmed these expectations (see Table 1).

For the 12–16 mon. children, however, the task of learning to walk was supposed to be largely solved, whereas learning to eat still was assumed to be a central task for them. Learning to dress, on the other hand, was not expected to be central yet. Again, these expectations generally were confirmed by mothers' ratings, with the exception that the mother of child 12a reported that her child was not completely competent in walking.

Table 1. Mothers' Reports of Children's Developmental Age (in Months) and Level, in General and in the Target Developmental Tasks

		Age groups in domains					
		9 Months		12 Months		21 Months	
		Child A	Child B	Child A	Child B	Child A	Child B
Overall Development							
Beginning of study	KID[a]	8.7	9.8	12.7	12.1		
	MCDI[b]					21.5	22.0
End of study	KID	13.2	13.4	14.0	13.3		
	MCDI					23.5	26.0
Developmental Task: Learning to walk							
Beginning of study:							
Mother rating[c]		2	3	3	4	4	4
KID Motor		9.8	10.1	11.5	12.1		
MCDI Gross Motor						39.0	30.0
End of study:							
Mother rating		4	4	4	4	4	4
KID Motor		14.0	13.0	14.0	14.0		
MCDI Gross Motor						48.0	39.0
Developmental Task: Learning to eat							
Beginning of study:							
Mother rating		0	0	2	2	4	4
KID Self-help		8.9	8.9	12.4	12.4		
MCDI Self-help						32.0	22.0
End of study:							
Mother rating		2	3	3	3	4	4
KID Self-help		12.4	13.2	13.0	13.2		
MCDI Self-help						42.0	36.0
Developmental Task: Learning to dress							
Beginning of study:							
Mother rating		0	0	0	0	1	2
KID Self-help		8.9	8.9	12.4	12.4		
MCDI Self-help						32.0	22.0
End of study:							
Mother rating		0	0	2	1	3	3
KID Self-help		12.4	13.0	13.0	13.2		
MCDI Self-help						42.0	36.0

[a] KID is the Kent Infant Development Scale (Katoff, Reuter, & Dunn, 1978); the total mean of the KID-scale includes the scores of all subscales; the maximum possible value of the KID-Motor scale is 14.0.

[b] MCDI is the Minnesota Child Development Inventory (Ireton & Thwing, 1979); the General score of the MCDI consists of items of several subscales.

[c] Mother's ratings of child's competence: 0 = Not yet learning; 1 = Starting to learn; 2 = Learning; 3 = Almost competent; 4 = Competent.

Finally, for the 21–25 mon. children, it was expected that both the tasks of learning to walk and learning to eat would be solved for the most part, whereas the task of learning to dress represented a central developmental task. Mothers' ratings indicated that this group's progress was consistent with normative expectations.

Behavior code. The videotaped interactions in developmental tasks were coded by trained observers in a way that the natural sequence of ongoing behavior was preserved. A coding system was used, based on the system employed by M. Baltes and colleagues (Baltes, Burgess, & Stewart, 1980; Baltes, Honn, Barton, Orzech, & Lago, 1983). (Although originally used to observe elderly people, the code has been successfully adapted for observations of children in institutions; see Baltes, Reisenzein, & Kindermann, 1985). The coding system was behaviorally oriented in that, for every behavior observed on the screen, one of 12 mutually exclusive and exhaustive categories were chosen. Of these categories, 6 referred to children's and 6 to mothers' behaviors.

The system was differentiated in such a way that, simultaneously with the classification of ongoing behavior, the behavior was also assigned to one of the three developmental tasks (behavior was coded as neutral if it was not related to walking, eating, or dressing/washing). In the following, for reasons of simplicity, the tasks of learning to dress, wash, and go to the bathroom alone will be referred to as the task of learning to dress.

Regarding mother behavior, four behavior categories are of special interest for our purposes.

(1) Coded as *dependence supportive behavior* were all mother behaviors that either involved direct help of the mother in one of the developmental tasks, or that involved offers of help without encouraging the child to engage in his or her own task-related activity. Thirdly, in cases where direct help was not involved, the dependence supportive category referred to mother behavior expressing appreciation and/or positive reactions towards child nonengagement once task-related activities had started.

(2) Coded as *independence supportive mother behaviors* were all behaviors that involved (a) either mothers' refusal to directly help the child when asked, or giving only minimal help; (b) mothers' encouragement of independent activity; or (c) mothers' positive reactions to the child's own activities in the tasks.

(3) Coded as *supportive of social engagement* were all mother behaviors that involved speaking or playing with the child, or behaviors to encourage, praise, or elicit (positive or negative) social activities from the child while he or she was engaged in walking, eating, or dressing. Note that speaking to the child about his or her performance in the tasks did not refer to this category but instead referred to independence or dependence supportive behavior.

(4) Coded as mother *other* behaviors were all remaining mother

behavior categories combined. These behaviors were not of special interest but were included in order to provide exhaustive categories for the contingency analyses.

Regarding children's behaviors in developmental task activities, the two categories of interest were *independent* or *dependent* behavior.

(5) *Dependent* behavior referred to waiting for help, asking for help, acceptance of help without showing engagement in the particular task, or refusal to behave independently when asked.

(6) *Independent behavior* referred to trying alone (irrespective of actual success), rejecting mothers' help, or using help as instrumental for the child's own activity in the task. The remaining categories of child behaviors consist of categories that are not relevant for the analyses, such as child positive and negative social behavior, sleeping and passive social behavior, and leaving the field of the camera. A detailed description of all categories can be found in Baltes and Reisenzein (1986). To give an impression of the coding procedure, three examples of transcripts and their coding are given in Table 2.

It is important to note that the definitions of independent and dependent child behavior, as well as those of independence and dependence supportive mother behavior, are *not* conceptually confounded with age or with competence: Every instance of the child attempting to behave independently or every instance of the mother giving even small opportunities to participate, was coded as *independent* (or *independence supportive* for mother behavior).

Coding procedure. Coding of videotapes proceeded randomly over tapes. In the coding procedure, every behavioral instance of child or mother behavior was registered in its natural sequence; children's ongoing behavior was re-recorded after 10 seconds if no new behaviors occurred. On the average, a new behavior was recorded about every 3 seconds.

Reliability checks were conducted for every coding session and showed neither indications of systematic changes in the observers' accuracy, nor interobserver differences. Mean reliability as computed with Cohen's kappa (Cohen, 1960) was .83 (SD=.11), ranging from one occurrence of a low .64 to several occurrences of 1.00 over time, and between .80 and .87 among the observers.

Results

Overview of data analyses. From a total of more than 24,000 behavioral events coded, the 17,132 that referred to developmental task interactions were considered. The analyses centered on the description of interaction patterns in the developmental tasks.

Table 2.   Coding of Interactions in the Three Developmental Tasks (Transcripts of Original Interactions)

Mother :	Comes out of the bathroom on the .... second floor and carries child with her	Dependence-supportive behavior
Child :	Gets carried	Dependent behavior
Mother :	Lets child down to crawl	Independence-supportive behavior
Child :	Crawls on the floor	Independent behavior
Mother :	Calls for attention and lets a package of paper towels fall down .... the stairs to interest child in climbing down	Independence-supportive behavior
Child :	Crawls near to look	Independent behavior
	turns around to climb down .... backwards	Independent behavior
Mother :	Praises child and adjusts child's .... position	Independence-supportive behavior
Child :	Climbs down backwards	Independent behavior
Mother :	Secures child's climbing with her hand	Independence-supportive behavior
Child :	Eats alone with a spoon sitting in the .... high-chair	Independent behavior
Mother :	Observes him and adjusts dishes	Independence-supportive behavior
Child :	Eats, but loses food from spoon	Independent behavior
Mother :	Tries to take over the spoon	Dependence-supportive behavior
Child :	Resists and does not give it	Independent behavior
Mother :	Takes second spoon and feeds with that	Dependence-supportive behavior
Child :	Eats what she feeds	Dependent behavior
Child :	Eats alone with other spoon	Independent behavior
Mother :	Tries to put on underpants	Dependence-supportive behavior
Child :	Resists and takes underpants himself	Independent behavior
Mother :	Encourages child to try alone	Independence-supportive behavior
Child :	Tries to put on underpants over head	Independent behavior
Mother :	Tries to help by taking pants off .... and tries to put them over feet	Dependence-supportive behavior
Child :	Takes pants away again and tries alone	Independent behavior
Mother :	Helps by holding hole open and letting .... child put his legs in	Independence-supportive behavior

To reconstruct sequential patterns in the interactions, the contingencies between mother and child behaviors were computed separately for each dyad, in each of the three developmental tasks, at each measurement point. Dependent and independent child behavior were used as the two possible antecedent events; the extent to which each of the four categories of mother behavior was contingent on each of these child behaviors was calculated. Sackett's (Sackett, 1977; Sackett, Holm, Crowley, & Henkins, 1979) LAG-sequential analysis was used to determine the extent to which the probability of a mother behavior, given that a specific child behavior preceded it, deviated from the expected baseline probability of that mother behavior.

For example, assume that a child showed independent behavior in the task of eating. Examples of possible mother responses are praising the child (independence supportive behavior), taking the spoon away and feeding the child (dependence supportive), starting a conversation or a play episode (social engagement supportive), or complaining that the child is messy (other behavior). The LAG program compares the unconditional probabilities (or expected probabilities or base rates) of each of these mother behaviors with its corresponding conditional probability, that is, the probability that the mother behavior occurs given a particular preceeding child behavior, using the binomial z - test. A significant elevation of the conditional probability over baseline indicates that that particular mother behavior is more probable, given that the child behavior preceded it. That is, the mother behavior is contingent upon that child behavior.

The analyses examined five ways in which developmental tasks might affect mother–child interactions: (a) by influencing the amount of task-relevant interactions that were shown by dyads, (b) by influencing the frequencies of behaviors shown by mothers and children, (c) by influencing the kinds and levels of significance of contingencies, (d) by influencing the similarity between dyads in the contingencies shown, and (e) by influencing the similarity between dyads in the patterns of change in contingencies.

Task-relevant interactions of mother and child. As a preliminary indication that the onset of a developmental task influences the extent to which mothers and children engage in behaviors centered around these tasks, one can examine the frequencies of task behaviors for each of the groups for which tasks are central, compared to the off-central groups. Table 3 presents the behavioral frequencies and percentages observed in each task.

Chi-square analyses revealed that the frequencies of mother–child interactions were significantly elevated above their expected frequencies in developmental tasks when the task was central for that age group when compared with the off-task groups (see Table 3). As can be seen in Table 3, for the dyads including 9–13 mon. children, 41% to 49% of all behaviors were observed in the task of learning to walk, and

Table 3. Frequencies and Percentages of Behaviors Observed in the Three Developmental Tasks

Developmental tasks:		Learning to walk		Learning to eat		Learning to dress		Totals per child	
Initial age	Child								
9 months	9 A	1196	(41%)	880	(30%)	862	(29%)	2938	(17%)
	9 B	1657	(49%)	1072	(32%)	648	(20%)	3377	(20%)
12 months	12 A	957	(34%)	998	(36%)	827	(30%)	2782	(16%)
	12 B	1513	(49%)	1134	(37%)	436	(14%)	3083	(18%)
21 months	21 A	545	(19%)	751	(26%)	1611	(55%)	2907	(17%)
	21 B	618	(30%)	281	(14%)	1146	(56%)	2054	(12%)
Totals per task		6486	(38%)	5116	(30%)	5530	(32%)	17,132	(100%)
Comparison of central vs. noncentral age groups									
X^2 (df=1) N=17,132		227.75 $p<.001$		270.70 $p<.001$		1744.10 $p<.001$			

Note. Boxes indicate developmental tasks that are central for the respective age group.

about 30% occurred in the task of learning to eat. Both tasks were supposedly central for this age group. For the 12–16 mon. children, about 35% of behaviors occurred in the task which was expected to be central for them, namely, learning to eat. In these same two youngest groups, behavior in the developmental task of dressing occurred infrequently; but for the 21–24 mon. children, more than 50% of behaviors were observed in this task, denoting it as central for this age group.

An examination of these percentages at the level of individual dyads showed that, for only one child, 12B, did the observed frequencies in a noncentral task (learning to walk) exceed the ones for the central task (learning to eat). This child was also slightly less developed in the task of learning to walk at the first points of observation (see Table 1 for developmental levels). Perhaps this indicates that, for child 12B, learning to walk was still a more central task than was expected. In general, it seems that the onset of a developmental task has the consequence that mothers and children show more behaviors relevant to this task.

Frequencies of behaviors. The raw data on which the remaining analyses were based, namely, the relative frequencies of each of the mother and child behaviors, and the contingencies for each combination of child-antecedent and mother-consequent behavior, appear in Table

4 (see Kindermann, 1986, for more detail). To account for differences in density of interactions in different developmental tasks, relative frequencies were computed separately for each mother and each child.

As discussed earlier, of interest was whether the *amount* of the behaviors shown by mothers and children changed as a function of the onset of a developmental task. As can be seen in Table 4, child dependent behavior was relatively high before the onset of a developmental task (e.g., 62% for one 12–16 mon. prior to learning to dress), decreased as the task progressed (e.g., 40% for one 21–25 mon., for whom learning to dress was central), and continued to decrease to a very low level after competence was reached (e.g., 17% for one 12–16 mon., who was competent in walking).

In contrast, for child independent behavior, the reverse pattern was seen. Before the onset of a developmental task, children showed almost no independent behavior (and remember, this category also included *attempts* to be independent); these percentages increased during the learning phase and accounted for almost 50% of child behaviors in a task after it was completed.

It should be noted that the trends for child dependent and independent behavior are not linearly dependent, because together they never accounted for more than 70% of child behavior, leaving a buffer zone of 30%. In addition, these cross-sectional patterns of age differences were paralleled by the results of age changes for each group over the 3 months of longitudinal observations (Kindermann, 1986).

Kinds and levels of contingencies. The third way in which developmental tasks may organize mother–child interaction patterns is by influencing (a) the kinds of behaviors mothers show as contingent to child behaviors and (b) the levels of significance contingencies reach at different points during the process of accomplishing developmental tasks. To examine this issue, analyses centered on child-dependent and -independent behavior, and on the two help-related mother behaviors, namely, independence supportive and dependence supportive behavior. Of interest was the extent to which each of the mother behaviors was contingent on each of the child behaviors at several points during the developmental tasks.

In Figure 1, the mother contingencies that were found significantly enhanced in dyads are presented as a function of mothers' estimates of children's progress through the developmental tasks. Levels of contingency, that is, deviations from baseline probabilities, were calculated at each of the four measurement points and then averaged. Therefore, mother behaviors not following as significant consequences of child independent or dependent behavior, or mother behaviors that are significantly inhibited consequences of child behaviors, were set to zero.

Table 4. Mother Contingencies Above Base Rates and Raw Percentages of Two Child and Four Mother Behaviors

Children		Antecedent Child behavior	Mother contingent behavior			
			Independence supportive	Dependence supportive	Social Engagement supportive	Other
Learning to walk						
9 mon. A	(56%)	Independent behavior	.09 (27%)	— (29%)	.04 (42%)	— (1%)
9 mon. B	(55%)		.09 (28%)	— (34%)	.04 (33%)	.03 (2%)
9 mon. A	(15%)	Dependent behavior	—	.44	—	—
9 mon. B	(17%)		.06	.27	—	—
12 mon. A	(47%)	Independent behavior	.06 (19%)	— (30%)	— (46%)	.04 (2%)
12 mon. B	(60%)		.01 (15%)	— (26%)	— (43%)	— (5%)
12 mon. A	(17%)	Dependent behavior	—	.40	—	.05
12 mon. B	(9%)		.02	.43	—	—
21 mon. A	(73%)	Independent behavior	.03 (51%)	— (20%)	— (21%)	.02 (4%)
21 mon. B	(54%)		.01 (27%)	— (19%)	— (49%)	.02 (4%)
21 mon. A	(7%)	Dependent behavior	—	.17	—	.18
21 mon. B	(8%)		.13	.31	—	.07
Learning to eat						
9 mon. A	(40%)	Independent behavior	.12 (21%)	— (53%)	.04 (19%)	— (2%)
9 mon. B	(55%)		.14 (38%)	.06 (40%)	— (14%)	— (3%)
9 mon. A	(39%)	Dependent behavior	—	.44	—	—
9 mon. B	(24%)		.25	.20	—	—
12 mon. A	(53%)	Independent behavior	.13 (35%)	.03 (25%)	— (32%)	— (3%)
12 mon. B	(51%)		.14 (34%)	— (36%)	— (25%)	— (2%)
12 mon. A	(16%)	Dependent behavior	.07	.32	—	—
12 mon. B	(23%)		—	.38	—	.06
21 mon. A	(70%)	Independent behavior	.05 (39%)	— (21%)	— (35%)	— (2%)
21 mon. B	(55%)		.06 (33%)	— (21%)	— (37%)	— (3%)
21 mon. A	(8%)	Dependent behavior	.05	.10	—	.27
21 mon. B	(16%)		—	.24	—	—

(continued)

Table 4 (Continued)

	Antecedent Child behavior	Mother contingent behavior			
Children		Independence supportive	Dependence supportive	Social Engagement supportive	Other
Learning to dress					
9 mon. A (9%)	Independent behavior	.18 (8%)	.20 (61%)	—	— (1%)
9 mon. B (11%)		.04 (8%)	.09 (65%)	—	.21 (3%)
9 mon. A (58%)	Dependent behavior	.02	.33	.01	.01
9 mon. B (58%)		—	.26	.06	.03
12 mon. A (13%)	Independent behavior	.20 (9%)	.11 (67%)	—	.04 (1%)
12 mon. B (14%)		.20 (14%)	.19 (67%)	—	— (1%)
12 mon. A (56%)	Dependent behavior	—	.33	—	—
12 mon. B (62%)		—	.31	—	—
21 mon. A (30%)	Independent behavior	.26 (29%)	.05 (47%)	—	.01 (2%)
21 mon. B (33%)		.33 (38%)	.02 (35%)	—	— (2%)
21 mon. A (40%)	Dependent behavior	.03	.34	—	.03
21 mon. B (29%)		—	.28	—	.03

Social Engagement supportive percentages: (37%), (17), (21%), (17%), (18%), (21%).

Note: Elevations of contingencies above baselines are given, averaged over four points of measurement. Dashes denote both nonsignificant and negatively significant contingencies. Percentages in the left most column, refer to child behaviors; percentages for mother behaviors appear in the other columns.

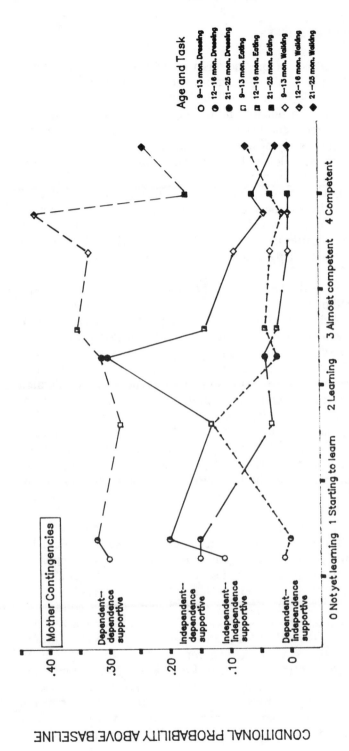

Figure 1. Mothers' help-related behavior contingencies for child task-related independent and dependent behaviors as a function of mothers' estimations of child learning in each of the three developmental tasks, calculated separately for the three age groups.

In the *pre-task phase,* before the onset of developmental tasks (children of the 9–13 and 12–16 mon. groups for whom learning to dress was not a central developmental task), high and significant contingencies prevailed. Mothers' dependence supportive behavior was highly contingent on child dependent behavior. At the same time, mother dependence supportive behavior was also contingent on child independent behavior, although at a lower level. In addition, independence supportive mother behavior in consequence of independent child behavior was contingent, but no more so than was dependent supportive behavior in consequence of independent behavior. This phase of developmental tasks seems to produce a *highly contingent* ecology and a highly *nurturant* contingency pattern: Regardless of what the child does or tries to do, mothers react highly contingently with dependence supportive behavior.

What happened with the onset of the *learning phase* of a developmental task? Although mothers continued to respond contingently to child dependent behavior with dependence supportive behavior, mothers no longer responded contingently to child *independent* behavior with dependence supportive behavior. Instead, mothers responded contingently to child independent attempts with only independence supportive behavior. What seemed to hold true in general for all children and all developmental tasks in the learning phase is that the independence supportive and the dependence supportive mother behaviors were contingent on the *complementary* child behaviors. This means, for example, that, when the child asked to be picked up, the mother was likely to pick him or her up (dependent–dependence supportive contingency), and when the child requested the spoon, the mother was likely to give it up contingently (independent–independence supportive contingency).

If any noncomplementary mother behavior showed elevated conditional probabilities, it was mother responses to child dependent behavior: Mothers responded contingently with independence supportive behavior. The pattern of contingencies in the learning phase of a developmental task can be described as *sensitive,* that is, mothers are highly contingent and at the same time are more likely to react contingently with complementary responses than they were in the pretask phase.

After *competence* is reached (as in the 12–16 and 21–25 mon. groups for the task of learning to walk, and for the 21–25 mon. group for learning to eat), the contingencies seemed to change again. A significant contingency of dependence-supportive mother behavior on dependent child behavior continued. However, as learning in the developmental tasks increased, this contingency dropped to a level lower than for any other phase in the developmental tasks. In addition, the independence-supportive contingency for independent (and for dependent) child behavior disappeared.

The ecology after a developmental task is completed might be described as *low contingent* and *dependent sensitive*. More specifically, mother behaviors are generally not contingent any more on child task-relevant behaviors. However, when children do show dependent behavior (and, as indicated in the previous section, after competence is reached this is a relatively rare occurrence), mothers still react contingently with dependence-supportive behavior when their engagement is necessary.

The role of developmental tasks in organizing contingency patterns thus can be clarified, at least in regard to mother help-related behavior. Before developmental tasks emerge as central topics of interactions, mothers behave nurturantly supportive: Dependence supportiveness is their main contingent response to both dependent and independent child behavior. This changes when developmental tasks are central. Dependence-supportive mother behaviors stay significant consequences of dependent behavior, but, increasingly, independence-supportive behaviors appear as consequences of child independent behavior. In general, during the time when tasks are central, mothers' predominant responses are sensitive (complementary) to child behaviors. This is different from the pattern of contingencies after competence is reached. At this point, the ecology can be described as ready to respond to (the rare instances of) dependent behavior, but no longer interested in (i.e., noncontingent to) independent behavior.

Similarity between dyads in patterns of contingency. If developmental tasks serve as organizers of contingency patterns, they should, as normative ecologies, heighten the similarity between different dyads at one point in development, especially when compared to the similarity between dyads during off-task periods.

To estimate the similarity between dyads in terms of the contingencies children experienced when interacting with their mothers, *rank order correlations* (Spearman-Rho) were computed between contingency scores of each pair of children in the same age group, separately for each of the three developmental tasks. In these computations, the deviations (positive or negative) in conditional probabilities of mothers' significant contingent behaviors from their expected baselines were employed; conditional probabilities not significantly differing from their baseline expectancy were taken as zero. Thus, "reliability coefficients" of eight maternal contingency scores (the four maternal behaviors in consequence of child independent and dependent task behavior) were examined. It was predicted that pairs of children of the same age would appear more similar to each other at times when a developmental task was central for them, compared to times before the onset or after the accomplishment of a developmental task.

Figure 2 presents the between-dyad similarity coefficients (rank order correlations), calculated separately per developmental task and age group, averaging across the four measurement points. Age groups and developmental tasks are lined up according to mothers' estimations of children's learning in each of the three tasks.

In the *pretask phase* (i.e., for the developmental task learning to dress for the 9–13 mon. and the 12–16 mon. groups), before the onset of a task, between-dyad similarity coefficients were not very high, averaging .38.

In contrast, for each age group in the *learning phases* of their respective developmental tasks (that is, for the 9–13 mon. age group, the tasks of learning to walk and to eat; for the 12–16 mon. age group, the task of eating; for the 21–25 mon. age group, the task of learning to dress) high interdyad correlations were found; for no task or age group were correlations less than .50. Indeed, the highest correlation, .85, was found during the central phase of a developmental task.

After developmental tasks were solved, that is, in the *competence phase* of all three tasks (the 12–16 month group for walking and the 21–24 mon. old children for walking and eating), the correlations dropped from a high of .65 to a low of .24, thus revealing greater differences between dyads, just as were found in the pretask phase.

To summarize these results: The more a developmental task becomes a central topic of interaction and the more children are learning that task, the more similar dyads become to each other in terms of contingencies children experience from their mothers (i.e., the *smaller* the interindividual differences). On the other hand, for children who are in the pretask or posttask phase, interindividual or interdyad differences seem to dominate the contingency patterns.

Similarity between dyads in patterns of change over time. To assess how similar dyads are in terms of the *changes* in their contingency patterns over the progression of developmental tasks—that is, the directions of changes in contingency scores—the same mother contingencies used before were evaluated. For purposes of this analysis, of interest was whether the conditional probabilities of mother behaviors as consequences of both child behaviors increased, decreased, or remained stable from each measurement point to the next. Note again that only significant deviations from baseline probabilities were used; thus, nonsignificant contingency scores were set to zero, and negatively significant contingency scores (which indicate inhibitions of mother behavior) were used as negative.

As an index of consistency of children's increases, decreases, and

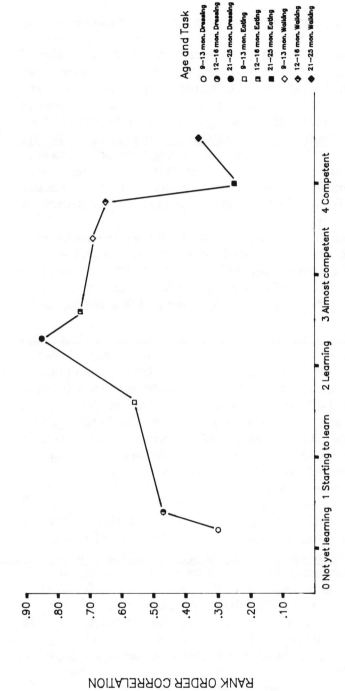

MOTHER RATING OF CHILD IN DEVELOPMENTAL TASK

Figure 2. Similarity between dyads in terms of mean rank order correlations of mothers' contingencies for child task-related behaviors, calculated separately for the three age groups in each of the three developmental tasks.

Age and Task

○ 9–13 mon. Dressing
◐ 12–16 mon. Dressing
● 21–25 mon. Dressing
□ 9–13 mon. Eating
◩ 12–16 mon. Eating
■ 21–25 mon. Eating
◇ 9–13 mon. Walking
◆ 12–16 mon. Walking
◆ 21–25 mon. Walking

RANK ORDER CORRELATION

.90
.80
.70
.60
.50
.40
.30
.20
.10

0 Not yet learning   1 Starting to learn   2 Learning   3 Almost competent   4 Competent

stabilities in contingency scores over time, Cohen's kappa (Cohen, 1960; Fleiss, 1975) was used. Kappa usually is employed as an index of interrater agreement after chance agreements based on the number of different categories are removed. In the present case, for every dyad and developmental task, it was ascertained whether, from each measurement point to the next, contingencies changed (a) in a positive direction (i.e., from a negative to a nonsignificant contingency, or from nonsignificant to positive); (b) in a negative direction (i.e., from positive to nonsignificant, or from nonsignificant to negative); or (c) remained stable. Kappa values, calculated for agreements in change scores between dyads of the same age and in the same developmental task, indicated the similarity of dyads in terms of the changes in their patterns of contingency over time.

Figure 3 gives the mean kappa scores (indicating the similarity of change) between the two dyads of the same age, averaged over all contiguous pairs of measurement points, separately for every age group and developmental task. In Figure 3, kappa values are lined up according to mothers' estimations of children's learning in the developmental tasks.

The results show that, before the onset of a developmental task (that is, learning to dress for the 9–13 and 12–16 mon. groups) the changes in mother contingencies were quite different for the dyads (mean kappa= .39 and .35). However, after the onset of a developmental task (learning to walk for the 9–13 mon. group, learning to eat for the 9–13 and 12–16 mon. groups, and learning to dress for the 21–25 mon. group), kappa coefficients indicated higher similarity between dyads in patterns of change (kappa ranging from .47 to .68). After competence was reached in the developmental tasks, the similarity in direction of change in contingencies from one point in time to the next continued to remain quite high (kappa ranging from .47 to .51).

Based on this information, the organizing mechanism of developmental tasks can be further specified: *Before* the onset of a task, both the comparability of dyads at a given level of development and the similarity of their change over time is quite low. With the *onset* of a developmental task, however, both the comparability across dyads at one point in time and the similarity of change over time increase. Furthermore, *after* children are competent in a developmental task, similarity between dyads at each point in time decreases again, but similarity in their patterns of change over time stays quite high (c.f., Kindermann, 1986, for analyses of these data which take into consideration the base rates of mother and child behavior).

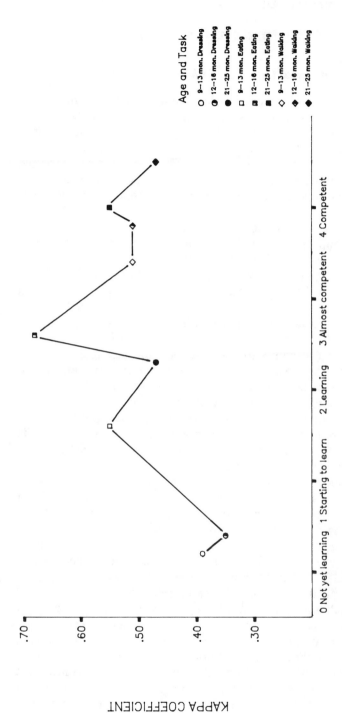

Figure 3. Similarity between dyads of the same age group in terms of changes over time in contingencies, calculated separately for the three age groups in each of the three developmental tasks.

MOTHER RATING OF CHILD IN DEVELOPMENTAL TASK

KAPPA COEFFICIENT

.70
.60
.50
.40
.30

0 Not yet learning   1 Starting to learn   2 Learning   3 Almost competent   4 Competent

Age and Task

○ 9–13 mon. Dressing
◑ 12–16 mon. Dressing
● 21–25 mon. Dressing
□ 9–13 mon. Eating
▣ 12–16 mon. Eating
■ 21–25 mon. Eating
◇ 9–13 mon. Walking
◆ 12–16 mon. Walking
◆ 21–25 mon. Walking

DISCUSSION

How Developmental Tasks Organize Children's Ecologies

The argument that developmental tasks organize caregiver–child inter-action patterns found empirical support in the results of a naturalistic observational study of mothers and young children as the children learned to walk, eat, dress, and wash themselves independently. Al-though conclusions must be qualified somewhat due to the small sample size, five ways were indicated in which the process of progressing through a developmental task organizes mother–child interaction pat-terns.

First, during the time when a developmental task is central for a particular age group, mothers and children engage in more interactions pertaining to that task, relative both to other tasks that are not central for that age group and to other age groups for whom that task is not central. Why this is the case is easy to imagine. Before the onset of a task (e.g., before a child is learning to eat), interactions in that task are usually accomplished quickly and efficiently by the mother (i.e., she feeds the child). When the child begins to learn in the task (e.g., when the child first attempts to use a spoon), the task-relevant inter-actions expand to allow extra time required for the incompetent (learn-ing) child to attempt and eventually to accomplish the task. And after the task is completed (e.g., after the child is able to eat with a spoon), the task-relevant interactions, just as in the pretask phase, take a relatively smaller amount of time to accomplish, although it is the child, and not the mother, who performs most of the task-relevant behavior (i.e., the child feeds himself or herself).

Second, developmental tasks appear to organize mother–child inter-actions by influencing the extent to which children show dependent and independent behavior. Prior to the onset of developmental tasks, children show high dependent and low independent behavior. As the task progresses, dependent behavior decreases and independent behavior increases, until, after the task is completed, independent behavior is high and dependent behavior is low.

It could be argued that such patterns of behavior are not the *result* of developmental tasks, but instead they are *alternative indicators* of the developmental task. Although, as indicated, it is not easy to for-mulate a clear or comprehensive definition of *developmental tasks,* in this study progress through a developmental task was measured by means of mothers' ratings of children's *competence* in performing the activities in the developmental tasks. In contrast, *child behaviors* referred to child dependent *behavior* (acceptance, request or waiting for help, and refusal to perform alone) and independent *behavior* (rejections of help, and bids to attempt or perform the task). Hence, progress through a developmental task is conceptually and operationally distinct from child independent and dependent behaviors. Even if a child cannot eat competently, the child can still ask for the spoon (independent behavior). And even when the child is able to walk, it can still ask to be carried (dependent behavior).

This means that the relation between a child's progress through a developmental task and the amount of independent and dependent behavior he or she shows is an empirical one. Of course, it is impossible to know the causal direction of the relations: It is possible that changes in child independent behavior and dependent behavior (and perhaps especially child bids to attempt task behavior) are one signal to mothers that the developmental task is starting.

The remaining three ways in which developmental tasks may organize mother–child interactions have to do with contingency patterns, that is, the extent to which mother behavior is predictable from or contingent on the child behavior which precedes it. Analyses examined how a child's progress through a developmental task (or as indicated above, the mother's rating of the child's progress) influences (a) the child behaviors to which mothers respond contingently, and the content of mothers' responses; (b) the similarity between dyads in the pattern of contingencies at each point in the developmental task; and (c) the similarity between dyads in the *changes* in contingency patterns over time.

Analyses revealed that, *before* the onset of a task, mothers show high levels of contingency for child behavior, and tend to respond to most child behaviors contingently with dependence supportive behavior. In addition, during the pretask phase, dyads do not ressemble each other either in their patterns of contingency nor in how these patterns change. In other words, then, individual differences may account for variability in how contingently and responsively (nurturant) mothers behave and how consistently they remain so over time. Whether these individual differences are related to other aspects of the dyad (or of the mothers or children individually) or of the situation cannot be determined in this study.

In contrast to the generally "nurturant" and heterogeneous ecologies of the pretask phase are the contingencies after the onset of a developmental task. During the *learning phase,* mothers no longer respond to independent child behavior with dependence-supportive behavior. Instead, both dependent and independent child behaviors are responded to *sensitively,* that is, with mother behavior that is complementary (i.e., dependence supportive mother behavior for dependent child behavior, and independence supportive behavior for independent behavior). It is also during the process of accomplishing the developmental task that dyads show the maximum resemblance to each other (and the minimum individual differences). Dyads are highly similar both in patterns of contingency at particular points and in patterns of change in contingencies over time.

The sensitive and homogeneous ecologies experienced by children during the on-task phase are replaced by a new pattern of contingencies *after* the developmental task is completed. During this time, the only significant contingency is between child dependent behavior and mother dependence supportive behavior. This contingency is lower than during the on-task phase, however, and the relatively low frequency with which children show dependent behavior after the task is completed means that children do not experience this contingency very often (Skinner, 1985a). Dyads do not resemble each other in terms of their patterns of contingency and, although they are similar in their patterns of change over time, these patterns are in general ones of stable and mostly low or nonsignificant contingencies.

In sum, children's progress through developmental tasks seems to organize children's ecologies by influencing the ways in which mothers interact with children, and especially the pattern and variability of maternal contingencies. The mechanism by which developmental tasks structure mother–child interactions remains to be determined. It may be that developmental tasks organize interactions only in the sense that they provide researchers with a frame for organizing assessment: They indicate the domain of interactions and the relevant behaviors that should be involved in systematic contingencies for children of certain developmental levels. In this case, a developmental task is simply a descriptive term, like age.

Alternatively, however, it is possible that the concept of *developmental task* may have some explanatory power. Developmental tasks may act as frames, not for the researcher, but for the caregiver. A developmental task may organize task-relevant interactions because it captures a set of cultural prescriptions about the timing and process of a child's developmental course. This possibility is addressed in the following two sections.

Why Do Developmental Tasks Organize Children's Ecologies?

In our view, developmental tasks organize parent–child interactions because developmental tasks are closely connected with both the goals of the children and the expectations of the parents. Especially important is the relation of developmental tasks (and their construction in certain cultures and historic eras) to the parents' perceptions of the appropriate sequence and timing of childrens' accomplishments.

In a given culture, parents' opinions about the "right" developmental trajectory in early childhood are presumably quite strong. Achievement of a developmental task is believed to be "necessary" in a certain time frame in order to guarantee further development. This idea is captured in concepts like "readiness to be socialized" (Maccoby & Martin, 1983), "sensitive period" (Ausubel & Sullivan, 1970), and "teachable moments" (Havighurst, 1972).

If this is the case, then the variability between different cultures in belief systems about early competencies of the child should result in actual differences in the onset, process, and achievement of these competencies, presumably mediated by differences in training practices stemming from these parental beliefs. That cultural differences in expectations about the appearance of certain behaviors are actually related to variation in children's performance has been documented by several researchers (Ainsworth, 1967; Harkness & Super, 1985; Konner, 1976; DeVries & DeVries, 1977). For example, the observation of Mead (1935, p. 57) that children of the Arapesh in New Guinea were able to stand alone by using their hands for stabilizing before they could sit alone, can be regarded as an example of a developmental sequence different from Western cultures and can be attributed to early training practices. Similarly, Super (1981) concludes in summarizing research on the precocity of African children in motor development that precocity is found only for those behaviors that are specifically taught and/or encouraged at early ages.

Cultural guidelines of when and how developmental tasks should proceed may influence actual caretaker behavior simply because developmental tasks of early childhood are tasks for the parents simultaneously. Kreppner (1983) refers to "socialization tasks," and Duvall (1971) discusses "family developmental tasks" as "those growth responsibilities that must be accomplished by a family at a given stage in development . . . if the family is to continue as a unit" (p. 51). Basic developmental tasks such as children's learning to walk, eat, and dress, in our view, become developmental responsibilities for the family as well. Hence, the onset of a developmental task for the child, that is, the point at which parents believe their child is ready to be socialized, should signal the onset of a developmental task for the caregiver as well and result in major shifts in caregiver behaviors.

Where Do Developmental Tasks Come From?

According to Havighurst (1972), developmental tasks emerge out of three sources: biological changes, sociocultural challenges, and individual expectations and values. It seems reasonable that, in the process of dealing with developmental tasks, all sources probably converge in their effects. In this chapter, we would like to highlight the role of cultural factors in defining developmental tasks. We hold that there exists some cultural relativity as to when and how developmental tasks emerge. In terms of timing, relativity exists across cultures with regard to when certain biological changes serve as indicators for the onset of tasks, when specific sociocultural challenges are recommended in order to demonstrate that parents are "good" at child-rearing, and when particular individual expectations for new achievements should appear. In terms of the process of completing developmental tasks, there probably exists relativity regarding the "necessity" of training, the particular supervision or guidance that is recommended, as well as the amount and duration of training or supervision that should be needed until some result is expected to be reached.

Considering only the developmental tasks of learning to walk, learning to eat, and learning basic body-care (dressing, washing, and toilet training), there seems to be vast variablility over cultures and historical epochs as to when these tasks are supposed to begin, how they are to be dealt with in terms of training, and when they are expected to be solved by the child (Mead, 1935; Konner, 1976; Valsiner, 1986). For learning to walk, for example, the practice of "swaddling" (Schenk-Danzinger, 1965; Solomons, 1978; Freedman, 1974) sets radically different conditions for learning than the recent use of "walkers" in the United States (Green, Gustafson, & West, 1980; Gustafson, 1984). Similarly, with regard to toilet training, the effects of early toilet training (DeVries & DeVries, 1977) in East-African Digo children seem to result in early advancements, compared to children of Western cultures. Evidence indicates that advancement can be attributed to differences in learning ecologies and training practices.

In addition, mothers' belief systems about early competencies and about the onset, process, and achievement of developmental tasks can be assumed to be affected by *material* ecological conditions. As Valsiner (1986) notes, cultural socialization goals are "already coded into the fixed-feature objects that surround the children" (p. 297). He points out that socialization goals for competent eating are defined in relation to culture-specific eating utensils, postures, and mealtime settings. Because the mastery of these aspects of tasks requires the achievement of certain levels of motor and cognitive skills, cultures which differ on these aspects would be expected to differ also in the pathways, timing, and training of these tasks.

In general, the identification of developmental tasks is not only a question of built-in affordances in utensils. The presence of hazards in the natural environment, as well as cultural rules about the inhibition of certain behaviors, may be an additional factor which plays a role in how and when developmental tasks are dealt with. For example, the presence of material hazards (e.g., stairs) may influence the extent to which parents allow certain competencies (e.g., walking) to be exercised. Or, if cultures have specific rules about the quality with which a certain act must be conducted before it is allowed (e.g., how messy a child is allowed to become in the process of eating), then the timing of accomplishment and the role of the caregiver in regulating child behavior should differ accordingly.

Cultural Relativity in the Study of Developmental Tasks as Organizers of Children's Ecologies

The previous sections highlight the dimensions along which cultures may differ in their construction of developmental tasks. What are the implications of these differences for our arguments about the way in which developmental tasks organize children's ecologies? Is it useless to apply the concept of developmental tasks when one attempts to understand the organization of caregiver–child interaction patterns in various cultures? Does it make sense even to try to compare cultures when they can differ so radically in their construction of developmental tasks? We recommend cautious optimism.

Why optimism? First, because we continue to hold that, across cultures, a child's status in a developmental task (e.g., the task's centrality for the child) structures caregiver–child interactions, including the amount of time spent in task-related interactions, the kind and level of behaviors shown, and especially the extent of contingency between caregiver and child behavior. Likewise, we hold that a dyad's progress through a developmental task affects its similarity to other dyads in terms of task-related interaction patterns at one point in time as well as change (or stability) of interaction patterns across time. Second, we recommend optimism because the concept of developmental tasks may provide a tool for making explicit the dimensions along which comparability between cultures can be achieved.

Third, if it is true, as we have argued, that developmental tasks derive their power to shape caregiver behavior through the caregiver's understanding about the nature, timing, sequence, and duration of children's developmental accomplishments, then several parameters helpful in comparing cultures have already been identified and these parameters can be empirically investigated. That is, we can discover the ways in which parents construct developmental tasks in different cultures (or other subgroups) and empirically determine if comparing cultures according to these dimensions brings us any farther in our understanding of structure and change in parent–child interaction patterns.

The notes of caution refer to the precise ways in which differential constructions of developmental tasks must be applied in order to shape empirical examination of the organizers of mother–child interaction patterns. Without underplaying the limitations of the present study, it may be helpful to focus on certain aspects of it which are analagous to the issues involved in cross-cultural comparison. The comparison in the present study of children of different ages in different developmental tasks may prove useful in this regard. What are the implications of some of the dimensions along which cultures may differ in their construction of developmental tasks?

At the most basic level, cultures may differ on *whether* a particular developmental accomplishment is regarded as a developmental task. In the case of learning to walk, eat, and dress independently, it is reasonable to assume that most cultures expect these competencies of their members, and so prescribe appropriate timing and methods of learning. However, cultural differences are apparent in the status given to later accomplishments. For example, in Western cultures, moving out of the house of the birth family is considered a developmental task, whereas, in many non-Western cultures, no similar expectation is present. Likewise, the developmental task in polygamous societies (Valsiner, 1985) of adjusting to the new spouse of one's current spouse may not be represented elsewhere.

Given that two cultures have indeed converged upon an activity as a developmental task, the cultures may still differ in expectations about the *timing* of developmental accomplishments. Hence, simply comparing dyads in which children are the same chronological age across cultures does not guarantee that the dyads are at the same point in a developmental task. Instead, an understanding of the normative expectations about the emergence of particular competencies is needed to ensure that the onset points in the two cultures can be compared. For example, in the present study, the age of onset differed for the three different developmental tasks under consideration. In this case, lining children up with respect to the onset of the tasks resulted in treating children who were different in age (9, 12, and 21 months old) as similar on the dimension of developmental task status.

Even if the dyads from different cultures are aligned according to task onset, if the *duration* of the accomplishment process of a particular developmental task differs across cultures, then the later points in the developmental task (e.g., learning phase, offset) cannot be lined up according to the same "real time" metric. One possible solution would be to use caregiver estimations of children's progress through the task as the "x-axis" instead of time. In the present study, this was done in order to allow the comparison of children in different developmental tasks which varied greatly in the length of time required to reach proficiency. For example, walking was "completed" as a task by all children by the end of the study, whereas dressing is a task that continues until about the age of five in the Western culture under consideration (when competence in tying shoelaces is reached). If children had been lined up according to real time since the onset of the tasks, information about changes in interaction patterns as a function of children's level of learning in the various tasks would have been lost.

What are the implications for cultural comparison if the *sequence* of steps in the task differs across cultures as well (e.g., as in the Arapesh described above)? In that case, the particular sequence of behavioral competencies used to define children's progress through a developmental task would have to be appropriate for the particular culture. Again, in the present monocultural study, the comparison across developmental tasks can serve as an analog: Mothers rated children's competencies on very different behavioral referents for the task of learning to walk than for that of learning to eat or dress. Nevertheless, when children were aligned according to mothers' estimations of their progress, meaningful patterns of change could be detected.

The matter becomes even more complicated when the notion is entertained that cultures may differ with respect to the *training practices* believed to be appropriate or necessary for children to achieve competence in various developmental tasks. In this case, although it would be expected that, across cultures, the onset of a developmental task would lead to increases in the amount or frequency of task-related caregiver–child interactions, the content or substance of behavior might differ from culture to culture. In the empirical illustration in this chapter, the particular categories of mother behavior chosen were independence and dependence supportive behaviors, precisely because in Western cultures parents tend to believe that their active "interference" facilitates children's progress through the developmental tasks of learning to walk, eat, and dress themselves. If, in other cultures, alternative belief systems exist in which the role of parent participation is otherwise defined (e.g., the strategy of choice is the modelling of desired behaviors), then the particular categories of behaviors that will be influenced by developmental tasks should be those which reflect parents' beliefs about their own role in children's learning.

It is interesting to speculate about the effects of developmental tasks in cultures in which parents believe that children are supposed to achieve competence in a particular task *without* interacting with caregivers. In this case, a *decrease* in parent–child task-related interactions would be expected to occur at the onset of the task, followed by an increase in interactions when the task is completed. Likewise, the patterns of contingency would be expected to show a general decrease in caregiver responsiveness during the learning phase of a developmental task.

Conclusion

This chapter began with a review of the factors which have been found to predict contingency in caregiver–child interactions. Based on the evidence provided here, it seems reasonable to add one more potential factor to that list, namely, developmental tasks. The precision gained by the use of the concept of developmental tasks (i.e., the specification of target behaviors, age groups, and domains of interaction which should be assessed) may also provide a mechanism for identifying some dimensions along which comparability across cultures may be achieved. Differences between cultures in expectations about the timing, duration, and sequence of developmental accomplishments may not prove to be an insurmountable barrier to studying the role of developmental tasks in organizing children's ecologies. As long as these elements are understood, dyads from different cultures may be aligned according to their progression through the culturally appropriate representation of the developmental task. Likewise, a fuller understanding of parental beliefs about their own role in children's developmental achievements (Sigel, 1985), as well as how these differ across cultures, should give us a handle on the precise categories of parent behaviors that will be structured by developmental tasks.

There seems to be evidence that the construction of developmental tasks for children does not proceed independently of context but is deeply rooted in historical and culture-specific expectations of caretakers for their children (DeVries & DeVries, 1977; Valsiner, 1984, 1986). The notion that the construction of developmental tasks may differ from culture to culture might simply indicate that the patterns of contingencies found may also differ across different cultures (or between any groups that are heterogeneous with respect to caregiver belief systems). At another level, however, it implies that the ecologies of development must be understood as scheduling and organizing forces in development. In early childhood, the caretaker exerts this organizing impact as he or she behaves in concert with the construction of developmental tasks according to prevailing cultural belief systems. The complexity of the relations among cultures, developmental tasks, developmental level, and patterns of caregiver–child interaction makes challenging the task of capturing the critical determinants of the dynamics in the developmental sequence.

REFERENCES

Ainsworth, M.D.S. (1967). *Infancy in Uganda*. Baltimore, MD: Johns Hopkins Press.
Ainsworth, M.D.S. (1979). Infant–mother attachment. *American Psychologist, 34,* 932–937.
Ainsworth, M.D.S., Blehar, M.C., Waters, E., & Wall, S. (1978). *Patterns of attachment*. Hillsdale, NJ: Erlbaum.
Ausubel, D.P., & Sullivan, E.V. (Eds.). (1970). *Theory and problems of child development*. New York: Grune & Stratton.
Bakeman, R., & Brown, J.V. (1980). Early interaction: Consequences for social and mental development at three years. *Child Development, 57,* 437–447.
Baltes, M.M., Burgess, R.L., & Stewart, R. (1980). Independence and dependence in self-care behaviors in nursing home residents: An operant observational study. *International Journal of Behavioural Development, 3,* 489–500.
Baltes, M.M., Honn, S., Barton, E.M., Orzech, M.J., & Lago, D. (1983). On the social etiology of dependence and independence in the elderly nursing home: A replication and extension. *Journal of Gerontology, 38,* 556–564.
Baltes, M.M., & Reisenzein, R. (1986). The social world in long-term care institutions: Psychosocial control toward dependency? In M.M. Baltes & P.B. Baltes (Eds.), *Aging and the psychology of control* (pp. 315–343). Hillsdale, NJ: Erlbaum.
Baltes, M.M., Reisenzein, R., & Kindermann, T. (1985, July). *Dependence in institutionalized children: An age-comparative analysis*. Poster presented at the 8th Biennial Meetings of the International Society for the Study of Behavioural Development, Tours, France.
Bates, J. (1980). The concept of difficult temperament. *Merrill-Palmer Quarterly, 26,* 299–319.
Beckwith, L., & Cohen, S. (1983, April). *Continuity of caregiving with preterm infants*. Paper presented at the Biennial Meeting of the Society for Research in Child Development, Detroit, MI.
Belsky, J. (1984). The determinants of parenting: A process model. *Child Development, 55,* 83–96.
Belsky, J., Rovine, M., & Taylor, D.G. (1984). The Pennsylvania Infant and Family Development Project, III: The origins of individual differences in infant-mother attachment: Maternal and infant contributions. *Child Development, 55,* 718–728.
Borduin, C.M., & Henggeler, S.W. (1981). Social class, experimental setting, and task characteristics as determinants of mother-child interaction. *Developmental Psychology, 17,* 209–214.
Bradley, R., Caldwell, B., & Elardo, R. (1979). Home environment and cognitive

development in the first two years: A cross-lag panel analysis. *Developmental Psychology, 15,* 246–250.

Brody, S. (1956). *Patterns of mothering.* New York: International Universities Press.

Brody, S., & Axelrad, S. (1978). *Mothers, fathers, and children.* New York: International Universities Press.

Brown, J., Bakeman, R., Snyder, P., Frederikson, W., Morgan, S., & Hepler, R. (1975). Interaction of black inner-city mothers with their newborn infants. *Child Development, 46,* 677–686.

Campbell, S. (1979). Mother-infant interaction as a function of maternal ratings of temperament. *Child Psychiatry and Human Development, 10,* 67–76.

Clarke-Stewart, K.A. (1973). Interactions between mothers and their young children: Characteristics and consequences. *Monographs of the Society for Research in Child Development, 38* (6–7, Serial No. 153).

Cohen, J. (1960). A coefficient of agreement for nominal scales. *Educational and Psychological Measurement, 20,* 37–46.

Crnic, K.A., Greenberg, M.T., Ragozin, A.S., Robinson, N.M., & Basham, R.B. (1983). Effects of stress and social support on mothers and premature and full-term infants. *Child Development, 54,* 209–217.

DeVries, M.W., & DeVries, M.R. (1977). Cultural relativity of toilet training readiness: A perspective from East Africa. *Pediatrics, 60,* 170–177.

Donovan, W.L., & Leavitt, L.A. (1978). Early cognitive development and its relation to maternal physiologic and behavioral responsiveness. *Child Development, 49,* 1251–1254.

Duvall, E.M. (1971). *Family development.* Philadelphia, PA: Lippincott.

Easterbrooks, M.A., & Goldberg, W.A. (1984). Toddler development in the family: Impact of father involvement and parenting characteristics. *Child Development, 55,* 740–752.

Elardo, R., Bradley, R., & Caldwell, B. (1975). The relation of infants' home environments to mental test performance from six to thirty-six months: A longitudinal analysis. *Child Development, 46,* 71–76.

Feldman, S.S., & Nash, S.C. (1979). Sex differences in responsiveness to babies among mature adults. *Developmental Psychology, 15,* 430–436.

Fleiss, J.L. (1975). Measuring agreement between two judges on the presence or absence of a trait. *Biometrics, 31,* 651–659.

Freedman, D.G. (1974). *Human infancy.* New York: Wiley.

Green, J.A., Gustafson, G.E., & West, M.J. (1980). Effects of infant development on mother-infant interactions. *Child Development, 51,* 199–207.

Gustafson, G.E. (1984). Effects of the ability to locomote on infants' social and exploratory behaviors: An experimental study. *Developmental Psychology, 20,* 397–405.

Harkness, S., & Super, C.M. (1985). The cultural construction of child development. *Ethos, 11*(4), 221–231.

Havighurst, R.J. (1972). *Developmental tasks and education.* New York: McKay.

Hetherington, E.M. & Parke, R.D. (1979). *Child psychology: A contemporary viewpoint.* New York: McGraw-Hill.

Ireton, H., & Thwing, E. (1979). *Minnesota Child Development Inventory,* Minneapolis, MN: Behavior Science Systems.

Jennings, K.D., Harmon, R.J., Morgan, G.A., Gaiter, J.L., & Yarrow, L.J. (1979). Exploratory play as an index of mastery motivation: Relationships to persistence, cognitive functioning, and environmental measures. *Developmental Psychology, 15,* 386–394.

Katoff, L., Reuter, J., & Dunn, V. (1978). *The Kent Infant Development Scale.* Kent State University, Kent, OH.

Kendrick, C., & Dunn, J. (1980). Caring for a second baby: Effects on interaction between mother and firstborn. *Developmental Psychology, 16,* 303–311.

Kindermann, T. (1986). *Entwicklungsbedingungen selbständigen und unselbständigen Verhaltens in der frühen Kindheit: Sozial-ökologische Analyse alltäglicher Mutter-Kind Interaktionen.* [Developmental conditions for independent and dependent behavior in early childhood: Social ecological analyses of everyday mother-child interactions] Unpublished dissertation, Free University of Berlin.

Konner, M.J. (1976). Maternal care, infant behavior, and development among the !Kung. In R.B. Bee & I. DeVore (Eds.), *Kalahari hunters-gatherers* (pp. 218–245). Cambridge, MA: Harvard University Press.

Kreppner, K. (1983, July). *Family and individual development: Socializing within the family.* Paper presented at the 7th Biennial Meetings of the International Society for the Study of Behavioural Development, Munich.

Kuczynski, L. (1984). Socialization goals and mother-child interaction: Strategies for long-term and short-term compliance. *Developmental Psychology, 20,* 1061–1073.

Lamb, M.E., & Easterbrooks, M.A. (1981). Individual differences in parental sensitivity: Some thoughts about origins, components, and consequences. In M.E. Lamb & L.R. Sherrod (Eds.), *Infant social cognition: Empirical and theoretical considerations.* Hillsdale, NJ: Erlbaum.

Lamb, M.E., & Goldberg, W.A. (1980). The father-child relationship: A synthesis of biological, evolutionary, and social perspectives. In R. Gandelman & L.W. Hoffman (Eds.), *Perspectives on parental behavior.* Hillsdale, NJ: Erlbaum.

Leavitt, L.A., & Donovan, W.L. (1979). Perceived infant temperament, locus of control, and maternal physiological response to infant gaze. *Journal of Research in Personality, 13,* 267–278.

Maccoby, E.E., & Martin, J.A. (1983). Socialization in the context of the family: Parent-child interaction. In E.M. Hetherington (Ed.), *Handbook of child psychology* (pp. 1–101). New York: Wiley.

Mead, M. (1935). *Sex and temperament in three primitive societies.* New York: Morrow.

Milliones, J. (1978). Relationship between perceived child temperament and maternal behavior. *Child Development, 49,* 1255–1257.

Olson, S.L., Bates, J.E., & Bayles, K. (1984). Mother-infant interaction and the development of individual differences in children's cognitive competence. *Developmental Psychology, 20,* 166–179.

Riksen-Walraven, J. (1978). Effects of caregiver behavior on habituation rate and self-efficacy in infants. *International Journal of Behavioural Development, 1,* 105–130.

Sackett, G.P. (1977). The lag-sequential analysis of contingency and cyclicity in behavioral interaction research. In J.D. Osofsky (Ed.), *Handbook of infant development* (pp. 623–649). New York: Wiley.

Sackett, G.P., Holm, R., Crowley, C., & Henkins, A. (1979). A Fortran program for lag sequential analysis of contingency and cyclicity in behavioral interaction data. *Behavior Research Methods and Instruments, 11,* 366–378.

Sameroff, A. (1975). Transaction models in early social relations. *Human Development, 18,* 65–79.

Schenk-Danzinger, L. (1965). Latente Reifung. Die kritische Zeitspanne bei mangelnder Funktionsübung. [Latent maturation: Critical periods when behavioral practice is lacking] In H. Heckhausen (Ed.), *Bericht über den 24. Kongress der Deutschen Gesellschaft für Psychologie,* (pp. 112–119). Göttingen: Hogrefe.

Seligman, M.E.P. (1975). *Helplessness: On depression, development, and death.* San Francisco, CA: Freeman.

Sigel, I. (Ed.). (1985). *Parental belief systems: The psychological consequences for children.* Hillsdale, NJ: Erlbaum.

Skinner, E.A. (1985a). Action, control judgments, and the structure of control experience. *Psychological Review, 92,* 39–58.

Skinner, E.A. (1985b). Determinants of mother sensitive and contingent-responsive behavior: The role of childrearing beliefs and socioeconomic status. In I.E. Sigel (Ed.), *Parental belief systems: The psychological consequences for children* (pp. 51–82). Hillsdale, NJ: Erlbaum.

Skinner, E.A. (1986). The origins of young children's perceived control: Mother contingent and sensitive behavior. *International Journal of Behavioural Development, 9,* 359–382.

Skinner, E.A., & Connell, J.P. (1986). Control understanding: Suggestions for a developmental framework. In M.M. Baltes & P.B. Baltes (Eds.), *The psychology of aging and control* (pp. 35–69). Hillsdale, NJ: Erlbaum.

Solomons, H. (1978). The malleability of infant motor development. *Clinical Pediatrics, 17,* 836–839.

Suomi, S.J. (1980). Contingency, perception, and social development. In L.R. Sherrod & M.E. Lamb (Eds.), *Infant social cognition: Empirical and theoretical considerations.* Hillsdale, NJ: Erlbaum.

Super, C.M. (1981). Behavioral development in infancy. In R.H. Munroe, R.L. Munroe, & B.B. Whiting (Eds.), *Handbook of cross-cultural human development.* New York: Garland STPM Press.

Valsiner, J. (1984). Construction of the zone of proximal development (ZPD) in adult-child joint action: The socialization of meals. In B. Rogoff & J.V. Wertsch (Eds.), *Children's learning in the "zone of proximal development": New directions for child development* (pp. 65–76). San Francisco, CA: Josey-Bass.

Valsiner, J. (1985, April). *Facilitation of children's social development in po-*

lygamic families. Paper presented at the Biennial Meeting of the Society for Research in Child Development, Toronto, Canada.

Valsiner, J. (1986). *Culture and the development of childrens' action: A cultural-historical theory of developmental psychology.* Unpublished manuscript, University of North Carolina at Chapel Hill, NC.

Valsiner, J., & Gärling, T. (Eds.) (1985). *Children within environments: Toward a psychology of accident prevention.* New York: Plenum.

Waters, E., Wippman, J., & Sroufe, L.A. (1979). Attachment, positive affect, and competence in the peer group. *Child Development, 50,* 821–829.

Weinraub, M., & Wolf, B.M. (1983). Effects of stress and social supports on mother-child interactions in single- and two-parent families. *Child Development, 54,* 1297–1311.

Zussman, J.U. (1980). Situational determinants of parental behavior: Effects of competing cognitive activity. *Child Development, 51,* 792–800.

PART TWO

Children's Construction of their Development under Cultural Guidance

INTRODUCTION

Co-constructivist theorizing about development involves ascription of the constructive role to the actions of the developing children. Contributions included in this part of the volume address cognitive, communicational, and personality implications of children's own construction of their development, and the use of socially available "resources" for such construction.

In Chapter 4, Frederick Verdonick extends the view on developmental tasks by way of conceptualizing those as *cognitive challenges* set up for the child in social interaction. These challenges are constructed by both the adult and the child in their joint action, and oftentimes it is not only the child but also the adult whose understanding of the interaction process is being challenged by some move on behalf of the other partner. In parallel with the dialectical perspective on parental reasoning (Holden & Ritchie, Chapter 2 in Volume 1), Verdonick outlines a viewpoint which is applicable to the social interaction which serves as the context for children's recall of familiar environmental settings. Verdonick's perspective, as well as his analysis of empirical research materials, is a good representative of the sociogenetic perspective on cognitive development that is exemplified in contemporary child psychology by the widening popularity of the work by Lev Vygotsky.

The emphasis on the active role of interaction partners, and on the empirical analysis of individual cases, is further developed by Julie Robinson (Chapter 5) on the material of phenomena of noncomprehension in the toddler–adult communication process. She develops an elaborate theory of human communication the core of which is *active negotiation of meanings* by the participants. Rather than construe meanings as fixed entities that "influence" partners who communicate, or "are used" by them (in some static form) in encoding and decoding of messages, Robinson accepts the dynamic nature of meanings which is a result of the continuous efforts of participants involved in communication to move *towards* a state of mutual understanding, reaching that state only under a restricted set of circumstances. Her approach is intellectually close to a similar perspective on "symbol formation" that is well known to those few who have been fascinated by Heinz Werner's work (Werner & Kaplan, 1963). However, Robinson's emphasis on the *cooperative* construction of meanings in the process of negotiations about "what the other side means" makes it possible for her to capture the adult's ways of feeding into child's speech development by virtue of limited understanding of what the child "wants to say." Both the child and the adult indicate at times noncomprehension of the other, and by that—challenge the other to try to make a communicative effort again. The adult's noncomprehension of the infant's or toddler's holophrastic messages may be the social context that guides the child's "persistent imitation" towards invention of new conduct.

However, all the negotiation of meanings between adults and children that can be observed in European, North-American, and Australian middle-class families may itself be afforded by the culturally structured understanding of what "makes sense" to expect while communicating with an infant and toddler. The cultural assumption—that the child under 2 years of age is an "equal" partner in interaction, who has something to "say to the adult," and intends to do so—constitutes the culturally structured background on which noncomprehension phenomena in adult–child interaction are made possible. If that assumption is not accepted by the adults, they will not provide noncomprehension feedback to infants' early gestures or vocalizations, and will not repeat or elaborate their own messages in the face of children's noncomprehending signals.

In the empirical part of her chapter, Robinson presents data on the process structure of negotiation of meaning between Australian mothers and infants/toddlers. The general model of the process of such negotiations has the strength of assimilating every possible sequence of interaction as a unique path structure within its limits. The particular empirical data about particular dyads illustrate the inferential usefulness of the general model, as every negotiation sequence is retained in the data, and can be retrieved in its uniqueness at any time. At the same time, Robinson's method allows for inductive generalizations about greater or smaller frequencies of different paths within the general model that are observed in empirical observations.

Finally, Eve Brotman Band (Chapter 6) analyzes the process of coping with varied frustrating events in middle childhood. Her clinical interviews with 6- to 12-year-old children reveal the readiness of use of different active ways in which children cope. Coping is an active process *par excellence*—children cope with problems that *they themselves* define as "problems," and in ways that challenge their cognition and action opportunities. The author's example demonstrate the intricate connection between children's thinking about their coping, and the structural organization of the environment within which the children have to cope. Situation specificity, as well as differential use of control strategies within situations, was found to be high in the children's self-reported coping. The coping means admitted by children include strategies that have been products of the internalization process, that is, have been used first by the children in interaction with others. In this respect, these coping means are examples of "fossilized behavior" in Vygotsky's sense—their roots are in the history of children's interaction with others, whereas their *current* form has already lost its connection with these roots.

REFERENCES

Werner, H., & Kaplan, B. (1963). *Symbol formation.* New York: Wiley.

CHAPTER 4

Co-Constructing Cognitive Challenges: Their Emergence in Social Exchanges*

Frederick Verdonik

Institute of Gerontology and
Department of Developmental Psychology
University of Michigan

INTRODUCTION

Several qualities of challenge that seem central to research on children's cognitive functioning and development are captured in the following set of observations. A group of five children meet on a regular basis outside a university library to use their skate boards. Jumping off the one step incline, which was learned at the beginning of the week, was now considered yesterday's news. The older kids showed them the trade secrets of making those board moves. Today their attention was riveted on the library steps and on how to make the two-foot jump off the side pillar of the steps. The failures were many and were often interspersed with conferences about the near-successes. The next day the children returned, rehashed their efforts of the previous day, and tried again. In all these actions it was apparent that *how* they conducted themselves on the skate board was a critical feature of their activity.

Germane to the concerns of the present paper on challenge in social exchanges, these children, through their interactions with one another, continuously constructed challenges for process and outcome in skate board performances. These challenges of how to skate board required

---

*I would like to thank the parents and children who participated in the study for their time, cooperation, and patience. Many thanks to Cynthia Adams, Denise C. Person, and Jennifer Smith for their editorial comments. Finally, a special thanks to Jaan Valsiner and Irving Sigel for their comments, encouragements, and challenges.

them to represent, reconstruct, incorporate, and elaborate upon past actions in their present performances. Indeed, they frequently shared descriptions, comments, explanations, and evaluations of previous skate board performances. Through these communicative processes, there existed a system for maintenance and transmission of standards, values, status, and content on how to skate board—a collective challenge between group members. Guided by these shared representations and reconstructions of past conduct, these children routinely transformed the library environment into an exciting and personalized place to develop, practice, and perfect their board skills.

Cognitive challenges occur frequently in social settings, and are promoted by various social institutions (e.g., family and schools). For example, educators repeatedly discuss the need to construct challenging perspectives and curricula for children to facilitate their cognitive growth (Gagne & Briggs, 1974; Kozol, 1972; Holt, 1969; Bruner, 1963, 1971; Goodman, 1960; Conant, 1961). Many parents are also invested in their children being challenged in school and play. While valued by the adult community of our culture, there is little known about the social processes of constructing cognitive challenges. Indeed, there are fundamental differences between educational theories based on beliefs that adults should construct challenges for or with children. Given these considerations, the dynamic(s) of constructing cognitive challenges between adults and children is an important issue, which is addressed in this chapter.

The social activities that we choose or are forced to participate in with others are often experienced by adults and children as either challenging or boring. Challenging activities are typically referred to as interesting, memorable, engaging, and fun, while boring activities are often regarded as tedious and dull. There are important behavioral consequences of these perceptions of activities. For instance, when faced with a boring activity, we either distance ourselves and disengage from it at the first opportunity, or reorganize, supplement, and/or redefine the activity in such a way that it is more challenging. Yet only some activities are experienced as challenging, and these experiences often wane. Nevertheless, social activities that are experienced as challenging (e.g., a discussion or a game) may have significant impact upon cognitive functioning and development and, thereby, merit the attention of researchers.

With few exceptions (Ratner, 1980, 1984), cognitive challenge in social interactions has been ignored as a category of social experience which affects children's cognitive processes and their development. It may be through participation in challenging activities with peers and adults that children's cognitive functioning is initially developed, and then subsequently practiced and refined. However, from observations of everyday activities such as skate boarding, it is evident that cognitive challenges frequently emerge and unfold in social interactions that are embedded in routine activities.

A basic thesis of this paper is that cognitive challenges constitute important realms of social experience for the operation and development of children's cognition. The objective of the present chapter is to discuss and provide illustrations of how cognitive challenges are constructed in joint activities by adults and children. Towards these ends, I will begin with a comparison of two broad conceptual frameworks for understanding cognitive challenges in social interactions. In the section that follows, some case studies will be presented as descriptions of the social challenges that contribute to children's cognitive functioning and development. In the last section, some tentative conclusions about cognitive challenges will be given.

CONCEPTUALIZATIONS OF COGNITIVE CHALLENGES IN SOCIAL SETTINGS

Surprisingly, cognitive challenge has received little attention as a scientific construct, even amongst those theories that emphasize goal-directed behaviours. Instead, the main focus of research on goals has been devoted to means–ends relation. However, there are several constructs currently used in the general research literature of information processing (I.P.) that implicate challenge as an important social experience of goal-directed behaviour. The general contributions of the I.P. framework to the perspective of social challenge given in the present paper will be outlined.

Information Processing Perspective

There are several constructs that implicate a need to consider challenge; namely, the terms *problems, task demands,* and *problems space.* In general, activities requiring cognitive processes that are not routine or well practiced as a primary goal or subgoal would be considered a *problem* to be solved (Simon & Hayes, 1979; Hayes, 1966; Forehand, 1966; see Gagne, 1966, for a theoretical discussion). In a research context, a problem is typically embodied in the form of a standardized goal which is made explicit to all subjects, and must be attained by information processing. The problem is usually inferred to exist for any subject by virtue of the instructions presented to subjects which impose *task demands.* A task analysis is sometimes used to describe objectively the demands of a specific task by defining cognitive strategies and processes that are needed to solve a given problem.

Complementary to the objective properties of a task, *problem space* reflects the internal dimensions of task demands (Newell & Simon, 1972; Klahr & Wallace, 1972). It is "a collection of symbolic representations and operations that are determined by the task environment and the problem space in turn determines the program that can be actually used" (Klahr & Wallace, 1972, p. 154). As a transformation of the external task environment into an internal representation, it is typically assumed that the problem experienced by subjects in their problem space is equivalent to the objective qualities of the task environment.

Cognitive challenge would be a discrepancy in the problem state between the internalized goal(s) or subgoal(s) of a task and the existing limits on the information processing system to complete the task goal(s) (Simon, 1972). Content of cognitive challenges would be determined by a subject's internalized representation of a goal or subgoal presented in the instructions. In both cases the form of the challenge would be determined (predominantly) by the externally defined demands to carry out the stated goals of a task. Furthermore, developments of the processor to meet challenges would include differentiation and integration of knowledge states (i.e., goals and knowledge elements) in relation to internal transformations on the knowledge states (Klahr & Wallace, 1972). With respect to cognition in social exchanges, most I.P. positions would *not* make qualitative distinctions between individual and social cognitive processes (e.g., Pask, 1975; Clippinger, 1977; Lewicki, 1986). Cognitive processes in social exchanges are frequently analyzed as distinct information processing units. While descriptions of feedback loops and interdependencies are given, there are no unique social qualities in these analyses. Hence, challenge in a social exchange is reduced to *rational* properties of distinct individuals.

Having drafted what is one of several possible versions of cognitive challenge from an I.P. perspective, its main contributions to the present concept of social challenge are distilled in the form of the following postulates.

1. Cognitive challenge is a *constructive* process that involves transformations of the external task environment into internal representations.
2. Cognitive challenge involves a *discrepancy* between goal or subgoal of a task and existing constraints on information processing to complete the goal or subgoal.

While these postulates are based on a generic I.P. perspective, the computer metaphor itself is rejected as an adequate description of social challenge for two reasons. First, the research paradigm has almost exclusively focused on challenge processes within individuals. This bias towards the individual as the unit of analysis reflects mechanistic and reductionistic assumptions about cognition and are inherent in the computer metaphor (Bursen, 1978; Reese, 1976; Neisser, 1963). Descriptions of cognitive challenge in social exchanges indicate that a level of analysis which attends to the social qualities of cognition may be warranted (Halbwachs, 1980 [original work published in 1952]; Perlmutter, 1952; Yukes, 1954; Kvale, 1977; Meacham, 1977; Olson, 1979; Ratner, 1980, 1984; Verdonik, 1980, 1984, 1986a; Rogoff & Gardner, 1984). Insofar as a computer metaphor of cognition precludes or obscures a social level of analysis, an I.P. framework is not descriptively adequate of conjoint information processing in social exchanges.

A second limitation of an I.P. perspective is related to its overemphasis on objective demands imposed by tasks. The lack of concern for intersubjective experiences of a problem suggests that these experiences are equivalent to external demands on cognition for all subjects, or are epiphenomena produced by information processing and therefore external to cognitive processes. Intersubjective experiences refer to shared or partially shared interpretations of the "world" between members of the same group, which may be temporary or lasting in effect upon individual group members (cf. Rommetveit, 1980; Schutz, 1945). In either case, intersubjective variables, such as *interpretive* transformations of task goals and subgoals in the construction of a problem space, are rarely discussed. Yet these intersubjective interpretations do impact information processing through constituting the definition of a goal (Wertsch, 1984) and, in part, by creating a task which is experienced as a challenging problem to be solved (Verdonik, 1986b; Feigenbaum, 1986).

Contrary to the arguments by some I.P. researchers (e.g., Simon, 1972), failure to attend to intersubjective transformations of task demands may reflect more than an oversight in the I.P. research program (Neisser, 1963). Indeed, it may point to the limitations of I.P. approaches to model human cognitive processes. Specifically, computers do not have intersubjective experiences of a problem or task demands (e.g., felt discrepancies in abilities to achieve, and felt progress towards meeting a task demand or solving a problem). One can program some information *about* these intersubjective experiences as information units, but the social experience itself is beyond computer simulation or use of the computer as a metaphor for human cognition.

It is claimed in this paper that the *experience* of information processing derived from intersubjectification contributes more than new information to the process of problem solving. This experience of information processing is regarded as a critical quality of social challenge. Within a group context, intersubjective experiences are part of a shared world of interpretations based on "a stock of previously given experiences of it, our own experiences of it, and those [experiences] handed down by teachers and parents" (Schutz, 1945, p. 533). Intersubjectifications of external information are social experiences that contribute to the relation of "information processors" to an activity and to one another as intentional actors in an activity (cf. Leon'tev, 1979). The remaining part of this paper will be devoted to the conception of challenge as a dialectical process of intersubjective and externally defined information.

A Dialectical Perspective of Social Challenge

Let me begin with a working definition of social challenge. *Social challenge* is a *shared experience of discrepancy* between available collective resources and collective resources necessary to attain a desired goal. With a felt discrepancy, group members also share a high motivation, value, and interest in attaining the goal in the face of the discrepancy. These intersubjective experiences of discrepancy and their components occur on several levels of social interactions that are not always articulated in social exchanges.

Types of intersubjective experiences. Two types of social experience have been differentiated, based on Schutz's work (1945), that have relevancy to intersubjective experiences of cognitive challenge: social reflection and active social experiences.[1] *Social reflections* are experiences that can be differentiated, recollected, and reflected upon in detail by group members. A social experience of conduct is yielded by the reflective attitude adopted by group members. In contrast, *actual social experiences* are undifferentiated and fleeting. They exist in the actuality of being shared between group members. Actual social experiences are perceived, yet they are neither delineated as circumscribed social experiences nor accessible for group reflection (cf. Werner & Kaplan,

---

[1] Both types of social experiences were initially applied to individuals as the unit of analysis. However, they contents and form of intersubjective experiences may differ qualitatively from their counterparts on the individual level. Intersubjective meanings of cognitive challenge, as social experiences of discrepancy in collective resources available to attain a shared goal, can also be described in terms of these experiences. In the description below they are modified to have parallel meanings within a social level of analysis—a collective experience of cognitive challenge.

1963). Social reflections and actual social experiences are not mutually exclusive modes of social experience. In a single social exchange there may be multiple dimensions of intersubjective challenge, some that are embedded in the sharing of an actual experience and others that are subject to a reflective attitude by group members.

By comparison, it is conduct as a reflective experience which has received the most recognition in the anthropological literature (e.g., Garfinkel, 1964; Geertz, 1983). Insofar as actual social experiences elude or preclude a reflective attitude, researchers have mitigated the contributions of active experiences to the meaning of activities (Schutz, 1945). Yet it is on this level that we experience the immediacy of a group's excitement, interests, expectations, motivations, values, and engagements as a cognitive challenge which emerges between group members. Moreover, actual social experiences may contribute to processes of unfolding and maintenance of cognitive challenges through forging an affective relationship between group members, and between group members to the goal (cf., Sigel, 1986; Werner & Kaplan, 1963). Ultimately, these immediate and shared experiences in relation to concurrent reflective experiences may determine the initial and continued engagement of group members in cognitive processes (e.g., depth of processing), motivate elaborations upon old challenges, and inspire the advent of new challenges.

Contents and forms of social experiences. Two aspects of cognitive challenge that are socially experienced are content and form. The *content* of social challenge refers to the shared goal or subgoal to be attained by group members. Importantly, empirical research strongly suggests that participants in an activity often negotiate and redefine goals throughout the activity (Wertsch, 1984; Wertsch, McNamee, McLane, & Budwig, 1980). Thus, the contents of shared goals are not necessarily fixed or stable, and are subject to change in a single activity.

The *form* of a social challenge, which is the emphasis of the present chapter, refers to the co-constructed and given constraints on how a goal or subgoal can be attained. These intersubjective and objective constraints define the range of appropriate behaviors for reaching a shared goal (i.e., the "legal" rules). Adherence to these rules implicitly and explicitly regulates how group members process information and, thereby, affects cognitive outcomes. Group members typically try to complete activities within some acceptable interpretation of the "legal" rules. However, under some conditions, the act of violating old rules and constructing new rules can be perceived as creativity. In both cases, the social value system of how to meet a challenge dictates and organizes the degrees of freedom for information processing.

Content and form of a cognitive challenge are always interrelated, for the waxing and waning of a social experience in one affects the other. For instance, after repeated trials of skate boarding off a ramp and children's mastery of this activity, the actions that constituted a path to their goal became boring. The increased boredom in the content of the activity seemed to inspire a collaboration or competition amongst children to develop a new set of behavioral forms that challenge their skate boarding skills. Specifically, one skater changed the angle of the incline so that it was more difficult for everyone to complete the jump. The steeper incline led to a change in how they made the jump, because their feet would leave the surface of their boards when they were in mid-air. Consequently, they would not land on the ground with their feet on the board. After several unsuccessful trials, one child suggested a technique for insuring that the board would remain underneath his feet. Assuming a crouched position as he approached the incline, he held onto the board when in mid-air and then let go of the board upon hitting the ground. When a successful jump was (eventually) completed using this procedure, this form became the valued action for making the steep jump. Thus, there were indications that shifts in the saliency of challenge components (e.g., forms and contents) occur after some degree of mastery was experienced over repeated trials.

In the prior examples of skate boarding, there was no formal ordering of challenges by groups members. A flexibility and fluidity in the emergence of challenges seemed to exist. However, in contrast to these instances of relatively open-ended challenges, there are many instances in which learning and development occur in formal systems, such as school. These formal systems of learning tend to regulate the order of cognitive challenges for children. It is apparent that when children enter into these institutional activities, a fixed set of social rules about how to master an activity or skill is often imposed upon them. For example, in typical American schools cognitive challenges are organized by teachers who implement a school curriculum or establish their own class syllabus. These fixed or semifixed rules constitute social orderings of cognitive challenges that are valued ways of completing an activity. For children, the ordering of challenges may be initially enforced by adults who have power within institutions (e.g., teachers or administrators). Gradually, children are socialized to accept and internalize the ordering of the cognitive challenges as positive values and "natural" sequences for learning and development. Thus, it is important to recognize that cognitive challenges differ in the degree to which they are ordered, formalized, and enforced in social exchanges.

So far the focus of attention has been on describing social challenge in general. The making of cognitive challenges has remained in the background of the discussion. For the remaining sections of the chapter, emphasis will be the emergence and unfolding of the formal features of cognitive challenges in social exchanges, and the experiential components underlying these developments.

Emergence and unfolding of cognitive challenges in social exchanges. A social relationship between participants is a dynamic medium through which the form of cognitive challenges is co-constructed. The term *co-constructed* is used as an interpersonal construct in which people engage one another as an *effort after shared meaning* (Bartlett, 1964). Group members represent and interpret each other's actions, motives and perspectives in a sequence of exchanges. These social exchanges often yield intersubjective agreement about the goals and means–ends relations of a task (e.g., Wertsch, 1984; Rogoff & Gardner, 1984), and an affective bond between group members (Sigel, 1986). During this process, each group member serves as an external object to the subjective interpretations of the other participants. Through being situated in the development of group processes (e.g., differentiation of power, social roles, physical and cognitive labor), cognitive challenges are woven into the fabric of an activity as shared goals toward which participants aspire. Importantly, these co-constructive processes yield a shared relation to a goal which is different from external meanings of the task, as defined in the instructions and the subjective meaning of the goal.

Social exchanges as constitutive processes of cognitive challenges. The types of social exchanges that potentially contribute to the formation of cognitive challenges are implicit in research on adult–child interactions conducted by Sigel and his associates. Sigel emphasizes that social behaviors create discrepancies between internal and external representations of events, between two internal representations of events, and between two external representations of events (Sigel & Cocking, 1977). These discrepancies are viewed as social processes that distance group members from the ongoing present. Moreover, social behaviors minimize or maximize "distancing" in situ, which, in turn, enables the development of children's representational capacities.

Distancing behaviors typically take the form of inquiries. High-distancing inquiries require a respondent to transform representations beyond the information given to or immediately experienced by a respondent. For example, questioning processes that request explanation, synthesis, and analysis of information require representations of this information that are beyond the here and now. In contrast, *low* distancing behaviors require transformations of experience that are tied to the immediate context of experience. For example, questions that request a respondent to label objects that are present may minimize opportunities to distance from the present situation (i.e., decrease cognitive discrepancies). The results of Sigel's research showed that high-distancing behaviors by adults in social exchanges with their children are positively correlated with children's development of representational competencies (Sigel & Cocking, 1977; McGillicuddy-DeLisa, Sigel, & Johnson, 1979; McGillicuddy-DeLisa & Sigel, 1982).

Some orchestrations of high- and low-distancing behaviors in social interactions may constitute *co-constructive* processes that yield collective representations of goals as shared challenges (I. Sigel, 1986, personal communication, June, 1986). For instance, adults and children may first tacitly negotiate the meaning of a goal and the range of paths to reach the goal (Wertsch et al., 1980). Questions and answers may be calibrated between adults and children so that a shared discrepancy is experienced and understood (cf. Brown, 1979). The co-constructions, if successful, result in a mutual investment toward attaining a goal and a shared value for a range of means–ends relations. Once experienced, the subsequent actions by adults and children may be directed at attaining the goal as a shared challenge.

Interestingly, the positive effects of high-distancing behaviors on cognitive processes *in* these interactions may be particularly salient for challenge situations. Cognitive functioning between the group members may be heightened because of the intensity of engagement (actual social experience) in situ. Also, the positive effects of high-distancing behaviors on subsequent individual development may result from practicing representational skills when retelling and reflecting upon triumphs and failures with group and nongroup members. However, if participants fail to co-construct a shared commitment to a goal, they may risk a reduction in the group potential to benefit from distancing behaviors and/or a total disruption in the activity.

Thus far, descriptions of co-constructive processes underlying the emergence and unfolding of cognitive challenges have been outlined. The term *co-construction* has been reserved for social dynamics that yield intersubjective experiences of cognitive challenges. However, co-construction is only half the story, for intersubjective interpretations are wedded to objective qualities of an activity. Attention is now directed to the relation between objective and intersubjective qualities that constitute the whole formation process of cognitive challenge in a group interaction.

Dialectical nature of co-constructions. From the present perspective, cognitive challenge is a *dialectical synthesis* of co-constructive processes and external definitions of a task. The objective features enter into the co-construction as constraints on behaviors to be interpreted, because these co-constructive processes necessitate an object of interpretation. These external constraints are *re*-presented by participants as objectives of the task to be interpreted and solved when creating means to carry out an activity. Whether participants view external task demands as objects to avoid, manipulate, and/or incorporate, the objective qualities of the task are ever present. It is on this basis that cognitive challenges in groups are said to always develop within a dialectic relation between objective and intersubjective meanings of the task.

By dialectic synthesis, it is meant that from an initial set of external demands in an activity (e.g., instructions) emerges a set of opposite yet complementary intersubjective experiences of the activity. A felt need to synthesize the definitions may arise from tension between the two poles of the activity. In these cases, the dialectical synthesis reflects a continuous process of intersubjectification of the object, and the objectification of intersubjective interpretations (cf. Leon'tev, 1979; Piaget, 1980, 1985). However, group members may also acquiesce to one pole over the other, the intersubjective or the objective.

In sum, general principals of cognitive challenges in social exchanges were outlined. The primary purposes of these discussions were to promote an interest in the topic of shared cognitive challenges, and to provide some framework for understanding the developmental issues related to shared cognitive challenges. With these objectives in mind, in the section that follows, a case-study approach is used to glean insights from the social dynamics underlying the emergence and unfolding of cognitive challenges.

CASE STUDY DESCRIPTIONS OF CHALLENGES IN SOCIAL EXCHANGES

Case studies will be presented as windows to view the dialectics of objectification and co-construction within dyads. In particular, reconstructive processes between mothers and their children are used to explore how cognitive challenges are formulated. It is an ideal domain to examine shared challenges because adults and children frequently make memory demands upon each other when guiding, supporting, and structuring information about the past (Verdonik, 1980, in press; Ratner, 1980, 1984). These demands undergo social transformations and seem to emerge as shared challenges to remember.

The data to be reported were generated from a study of joint efforts to reconstruct the past (i.e., joint reconstructive episodes). One aspect of the study was to investigate how remembering processes between mothers and children are initiated. Challenge was employed as a heuristic to guide descriptions of how mothers and children constructed goals to remember.

The research method was as follows. Four- or seven-year-olds and their mothers were asked to construct jointly a model of their local environment with building blocks.[2] Participants were asked to build a minimum of eight places on a 6' × 6' plastic sheet positioned on the floor. The activity implicitly required each mother–child dyad to remember information in the service of the modeling activity, but they were not told that it was a memory-related study. The sessions were videotaped in the homes of subjects. (See instructions in Appendix A.)

In the present study, there were many levels at which participants formulated and expressed challenges of remembering. However, the challenges to be discussed are restricted to the building of places that contribute to the completion of the activity. Furthermore, in the examples to be presented, all cases were viewed as formulations of shared challenges because they met one (or more) of the following criteria: participants were aspiring to complete an established, shared goal for which they have expressed some experience of discrepancy; and participants were creating shared constraints on how a goal could be attained. Both criteria require explicit statements between participants that suggest some shared experience of cognitive discrepancy. As such, the unit of analysis is the dyad and not the individuals, because the emerging or existing discrepancy is expressed (and therefore assumed to be experienced) as demands upon cognitive resources of the dyad.

The case studies will be focused on three general areas of social memory challenge: dialectics of social challenge, creating constraints on reconstructions, and politics of initiating shared challenge. Illustrations of social dynamics of shared memory challenge will be discussed within each of these areas.

Dialectics of challenge. It was suggested in a previous section that the synthesis of objective and intersubjective dimensions of the task is a critical feature in formulating a shared challenge. The dynamics of the dialectic were observed in the following dialogue between a 4-year-old and his mother that followed immediately after the experimenter presented the task instructions.

C: Let's make a house. [Pause]
M: Okay. Whose house?
C: We're making it together. (Child picks up some blocks)
M: I know. But who's house is it? [Pause]
C: (Child plays with the blocks in his hand) A house.
M: Our house. Okay.

---

[2] The method outlined in this chapter was part of a more comprehensive study of the development of social reconstructive processes between mothers and their children.

C: Yeah. Ah . . . Any house (Child places two blocks on the plastic sheet to make a house)

M: No, but we gotta make a house we know sweetie. [Pause]

C: (Child stops building) Just one thing. I don't know how to make a door.

M: Don't worry about the door. I think we can pretend we know that the door is there. [Pause] Now whose house are we doing?

C: (Child looks for a block) Ours.

M: Okay.

The task instructions presented to both participants a set of goals to make real places in their neighborhood. However, upon beginning the activity, the child reformulated the task demands that were stated in the instructions by suggesting that they make "a house." From the mother's inquiry about "whose house" emerged an explicit conflict about their interpretations of the place to be modeled.

In response to the implicit conflict between the objective and constructed goals, a compromise solution (synthesis) of building their house was proposed by the mother. The mother's suggestion was a synthesis because it embodied the child's interests in making a building, her interpretation of the task, and also observed the objective rules. In the remaining segments of their dialogue, the mother's reformulation of the challenge was discussed by the participants, and it was gradually integrated into the activity as an accepted goal.

It was evident that the social exchanges that led to the accepted challenge were also ridden with conflict. For instance, in response to his mother's suggestion, the child confirmed his mother's suggestion to make their house, and then explicitly negated the meaning of her suggestion by stating that they could make "any house." In doing so, the place called "our house" was transformed into a special case of "any house." At this point the mother re-presented the concept of an of an official rule in her use of the word "gotta." However, she also adds an interpretation of the objective rule: the places modeled must be places that "we know." The notion of "real" place was embodied in "we know," yet it also differed from the objective rules of making places that exist in their neighborhood. The mother's interpretation of the objective rules implied a shared experiential knowledge of places as a criterion for including places in their model. The rule created a more restricted range of acceptable places to be modeled, and, as such, it generated a new framework to formulate challenges.

Sharing challenges and integrating them into the activity can be view as a gradual process of socialization in which resisted interpretations are reformulated and cast into shared framework of meaning. For instance, the child phrased the problem of constructing the door in a manner that preserved his interpretation of the overall task (any house) and immediate meaning of a house. He used the indefinite article once again (a door) rather than a personal form (e.g., our door) to make his point. In response to the child's concern (challenge) about the construction of the door, the mother added another interpretation to the objective rules which essentially eliminated the child's challenge to build a door. This rule can be summarized as follows: buildings do not have to represent all aspects of places, and they can pretend that nonrepresented things are included in the model. In addition, the mother checked her child's meaning of the place they were building. This inquiry by the mother may have been prompted by the child's use of the indefinite article and/or a feeling that they never reached an explicit consensus. As illustrated in this example, the child and mother eventually share the memory for the place through social exchanges that formulated and then reformulated their interpretations.

The child's agreement to make a place called "our house" seemed to yield a shared challenge on two levels. First, after discussing the place to be made, both participants actively contributed to building a representation of their house, continued to refer to the place as "our house," and used this representation as a device to generate new places to be modeled. Second, and perhaps more importantly, the explicit rule of making places that "we know" was honored by both participants as a criterion of inclusion for the duration of the activity. The formulation of their subsequent challenges of places to model assumed the operation of this rule.

With the right blend of re-presentation of the objective rules and shared interpretation, participants who were bored sometimes renewed their shared aspirations to make places. For instance, participants often collaborated to bracket objective rules, and, in doing so, they recalibrated the task demands to a manageable discrepancy based on their active experience of demands and felt potential to realize them. Bracketing refers to a *communicative device* which acts to suspend the technical meaning of the objective task while *simultaneously* recognizing that the objective rules exist.

Bracketing objective rules seems to allocate participants with more degrees of freedom to co-construct goals that are experienced as challenges. It also seemed to yield higher levels of shared incentives to make places in the model. The following dialogue between a 4-year-old and his mother exemplifies how bracketing is enacted.

C: I don't know what else.
M: Well how about [Pause] What's you're favorite . . . What do we like to do tomorrow when we wake up? Where would you like to

go? [Pause] Where is there a nice place to go so that we could build it? [Pause] When you wake up tomorrow what d'ya want to do?

C: To the aquarium. Go to the aquarium.

M: You want to go to the aquarium? Hmm. That we have to take a car to. [Pause] Do you want to build the aquarium?

C: Yeah. [Pause]

M: Well may be we could pretend that its in our neighborhood. [Pause] Alright, so where should we build it?

The mother stated in an interview after the first session that pretending served several functions. First, and foremost, it allowed her and the child to finish the activity with a shared commitment to its completion. Indeed, the child's resistance to making more places was reduced, and both participants seemed reinvested in the task. Second, the bracketing of the neighborhood rule neither denied the meaning of this rule as a constraint on their actions, nor suspended the rule of making real places. Bracketing the neighborhood rule was, in her opinion, the best way to be engaged in the activity in a meaningful way while completing the objective goals of the activity.

As suggested in the previous examples, the dialectics of challenge are instantiated in various forms of social exchange. A form of particular interest is illustrated in the following dialogue between a 7-year-old and his mother. Specifically, a shared criterion in remembering places was experienced at a later point in the activity, when the social dynamics changed, as an unrealistic challenge. The transcript below begins with both the mother and child naming and building all the adjacent stores along a main avenue.

M: And then Mario's.

C: No. No. Pino's. (Mother places a block to mean Pino's)

M: The broker. (Mother places a block) And then the Chinese restaurant. (Mother places a block)

[The mother and child continue to add stores. After completing that street, the child returns to the places he was building.]

M: Do I have to do all of it logically?

C: What's logically?

M: You mean down Seventh avenue where every store is? or can I space these (refers to locations where building blocks will be placed to represent another street along the avenue).

C: What? Uh, end it at Fifteen Street.

M: Excuse me! [Pause] We're going all the . . . I don't know all the stores.

C: Then go to Ninth street.

In the beginning of this episode the mother and child built upon each other's contributions. They established a rhythm which both of them seemed to enjoy and which met their aspired level of descriptive adequacy (i.e., criterion of memory performance). However, after the child disengaged from the joint effort, there was a shared expectation that the mother would continue to represent all the places on the rest of the avenue. This expectation was evident in her question about whether she should continue their previous efforts, and it was also evident in his casual comment that she should continue building all the places for another 14 streets. The mother perceived these demands as unreasonable and stated that she could not meet the previous level of performance. Once the expectations were questioned by the mother, a recalibration of demands was proposed by the child. Interestingly, the challenge to build places to Fifteenth Street changed, yet they did not reassess the expectation about remembering all the places on each street.

Two additional observations about the previous example are worth mentioning. First, the mother initially framed her response to the expectation that she would go to Fifteen Street as a shared endeavor ("*We're* going all the . . ."). Second, she immediately assumed personal responsibility for not being able to meet these expectations ("*I* don't know . . ."). These exchanges suggest that the division of labor created a paradox between co-constructing challenges and meeting these challenges. The primary paradox was that they developed performance expectations based on their collaborative efforts (giving her a "we" experience) but she was then left with the reality of facing the two-person challenge by herself (giving her an "I" experience). Indeed, the mother's petitioning to change their expectations suggests that, in the differentiated form of labor, she *felt* accountable to her son. Yet, despite the "we-ness" of the process and product, her comments indicate that the shared challenge had developed a strong individual component.

Creating shared constraints on reconstructions. The modification of rules, standards and values for how the model-making activity should be performed was a central part of the intersubjective construction of cognitive challenges. These co-constructive processes were important because they constituted shifts in the task from standardized to optional constraints on information processing that varied within and across dyads. The following example highlights the significance of added constraints for the emergence of memory challenges in this activity. The transcript begins with the mother suggesting another place to build.

M: Wanna do Christopher's house?
C: Oh, okay. [pause] I'm not gonna make everything.
M: Well . . . [pause; mother and child build]

M: Is anybody else's house on second street? [pause; child looks at second street in model] On this side? (mother gestures to one side of second street in the model, but she does not point to a specific location)

C: No. But I know Rachel.

M: No. She's just way, way down here (mother gestures to a location off the plastic sheet) [pause] Who lives over here? (Mother points to a specific location on Second Street in the model). [pause; child looks off into the distance and then looks at mother] Christopher's house is over here (mother points to exact location). So who's right over there? (mother points to location). Somebody who lives underneath? A friend of mine? [pause] He goes to Berkeley-Carroll? [pause; mother reaches for blocks to build with] You know who I mean.

C: Meach?

M: Noo. A little boy your age [pause] lives underneath Vivian's house?

C: Yes. Justin.

M: I thought you knew him.

The use of a restricted geographic area, namely Second Street, to guide and organize their memories for other places is a "proximity strategy". The role of this practice as an acquired standard for adequacy and a shared device for generating challenges was clarified when the child violated the implicit rule of descriptive adequacy. First, he said that he was not going to make everything and then he suggested places that were not in the designated geographic location. In response to these violations, the mother repaired and re-presented their commitment to a certain level of descriptive adequacy by asking questions, pointing to particular locations, and providing shared information to orient the child.

If not intended, a by-product of the proximity strategy was that an entire area was described to the best of their efforts before starting another location, and their use of previously made places as a framework enabled new memory challenges to emerge. In addition, the use of the proximity strategy afforded the mother and child with a method to meet new memory challenges. Specifically, the systematic use of the proximity strategy gradually generated a physical organization of places in a geographic area, which could be used in subsequent reconstructions to model other places. For instance, when the mother suggested that they build another house on Second Street, she already shared with the child an established reference system of familiar streets and houses. Together with the mother's verbal descriptions of places, the physical organization provided an accurate reference for the child to infer "Justin's house" from its relative location. Thus, regulative power of some reconstructive strategies to create new challenges and methods to meet these challenges may change over the course of an activity.

In some dyads criterion of adequate description sometimes took extreme forms that reflected the upper limits of intersubjective modifications of the task. The following dialogue (between a 7-year-old and his mother) is an example of strong commitment to high standards of adequate description and the enactment of these standards as shared challenges. The example begins with the child questioning the mother about the meaning of a place that she just completed.

C: So what is over there? (Child points to a set of houses that the mother just made).
M: That's three stories. Three stories. (Mother points to each of the blocks representing a floor of the building).
C: What . . .
M: Those aren't as tall as . . . (Mother gestures to another set of buildings that she made).
C: Yes they are. (Child makes a comparison between the sizes of the building being made by the mother and the other set of buildings).
M: They are? [Pause]
C: Four . . . Ever think of Adam's house? He lives on the third floor. And they have one floor above. Ever think of that?
M: Okay. Got to use lots of orange blocks.

[There is a break in the dialogue. The mother takes away the large red blocks that she used to make the buildings, and she uses smaller orange blocks so that all of the buildings are the same size.]

M: This is really to scale, isn't it?
C: Yeah.
M: Everything is exact.

By comparison, the level of memory demands maintained by the dyad in the present example exceeded the memory demands generated by other dyads in the study. Indeed, intentions of the these participants to create a scale model were best described by the child at the beginning of the activity: ". . . think of what it (the size of the buildings) would look like if you were in a helicopter." However, while the mother collaborated with the child to maintain the scale of the model, it was the child who initiated and enforced these rules. For instance, in the example above, the mother violated the scaling rule. In response the child tried to reconfirm their commitment to scaling the model by immediately re-presenting the rule as a criterion of descriptive adequacy.

In ways such as this cognitive challenges were maintained by his dyad as shared goals.

Politics of initiating challenges. It appears that the processes of setting challenges are embedded in the politics of social exchanges (e.g., roles, status, and power of group members). Feelings of efficacy in the development of shared challenges may come from the responses by others to a participant's initial efforts to formulate a shared goal—a goal that both participants aspire to complete. These politics of experience warrant investigation because they may affect the pathways constructed by participants to reach a shared goal, and aspirations of dyads to continue toward a goal.

In assuming a tutorial role, adult guidance, support, and structuring of children in activities may be experienced by children (on occasion) as insincere, annoying, boring, and/or oppressive. It was evident in the present study that questioning children sometimes undermined their power to initiate and maintain a shared challenge. The following dialogue exemplifies the power struggle between a 7-year-old child and his mother when he tried to formulate a shared commitment and aspiration to remembering. The episode begins with the child inquiring about the name of a place that they had previously made in their model.

C: What's this? (Child points to a previously made place)
M: What's across from the drug store? (Mother refers to the place that they were making, which is across from the place of interest to the child).
C: Across from the drug store? I don't know.
M: You told me the first time. I'm not gonna tell you unless you remember.
C: What did I say?
M: Don't know? You can't ask me that.
C: Let's see. What is that darn thing? Well . . .
M: You told me in the beginning. That's why we put it there.
C: Well, I forget.
M: Across the street from the drug store, what do you get? What's over there? [Mother points to a location in the model]
C: The little market. [Child says it boldly]
M: Okay. [Pause] Don't talk like that [Mother refers to the child's tone of voice]

The child's initial request for help was sincere. It reflected a functional need to remember information that he had forgotten. In asking the question, he suggested a goal of remembering which he expected to share with his mother as a challenge. However, the mother immediately reframed the child's inquiry by responding with a question that undermined his intention to construct a shared challenge with symmetrical roles. Thus, there was a collaboration between the mother and child to reach a shared memory, but the mother regulated the information needed to reconstruct the name of the place and, thereby, controlled the child's participation in the reconstructive episode.

The asymmetry of the mother–child roles in the example above was two-fold. First, it was evident to the child that his mother knew the answer to his question. Second, there was no doubt that his mother would help him to remember the name of the place, but it was also evident to the child that she would not give him the answer. Indeed, the mother did support and guide the child's remembrances of the name to a successful conclusion. Yet, despite their success in reconstructing the name of the place, the child may wonder why she refused to answer his question when it was evident that she knew the answer, why he must answer her questions, and what happened to his initiation of a partnership in remembering.

Within our culture we assume that an asymmetry in adult–child interactions reflects a natural order of power relationships (Erikson, 1950). Children are suppose to be universal novices and, therefore, require teachers. Adults have more experience which then justifies their roles as teachers of children. In the light of these cultural expectations, consider what would happen if the power relationship between mothers and their children roles was reversed. How would a mother experience the inquiries of her child if the sincerity of a child's questions was suspect? An example of such a reversal occurred in the following dialogue between a 4-year-old and his mother. The child's inquiries seemed to shift the mother's authority and power in the activity.

M: So what else should we make?
C: Mom, what were . . . What was this? I forgot. (Child points to a place which they previously made)
M: This was the whale place? Right? (Mother points to the target place)
C: Ah . . . What was this? (Child points to another place that they made) I forgot (Child giggles).
M: You remember! What is it? You're checking me.
C: No. I'm not checking you.
M: Uhmm.
C: Seals. [Pause] And what was this? (Child points to another place) And this? I forgot (Child points to another place).
M: What do you do when you . . . when you're eating in here (mother points to the place that they were originally making before the child began to question her)
C: And . . . What is . . .

M: You remember Heather went to the Aquarium, Michael? . . . For her first time?

C: Uh Huh.

M: Did she like it?

C: That was her last time.

M: So, is there anything else you want to build?

C: No.

In this dialogue the motivation for the child's initial inquiry about the identity of the whale house is unclear. He may have forgotten its meaning, or he could have initiated the question–answer sequence as a game to divert his mother's attention from the task. Regardless of the child's original motives, his motivation in asking the subsequent questions about places were not related to a failure to remember. The fact that the child gave the answer to his second inquiry indicates that his question was not motivated by a need to remember.

As a challenge to remember, the mother treated her child's original inquiry as a sincere question. The child's inquiry resembled her own questioning procedures during other parts of the activity. In the questions that followed, the mother sensed his playful attitude and questioned her child's motivations for initiating these inquiries. The mother failed to see the resemblance between her own questioning style during other parts of the activity and the child's form of questioning in the present episode. Rather, the mother seemed to interpret the child's questions as an evaluation of her competency. Moreover, given that the child knew the answer to his own questions, she may have regarded these question–answer sequences as irrelevant to the completion of the activity. The mother's interruptions of the child's questions and her attempts to redirect their attention to the building of the aquarium supports this interpretation. Similar to the mother's perceptions of the child's actions in this episode, the child may experience his mother's constant inquiries about information that she knows as evaluations of his competency and as off-task behaviors.

The previous example raises an important dilemma for the question–answer sequences that occur between adults and children. If adults assume that their "tutorial" roles are also genuine because children need challenges for their development of cognitive competencies, then giving them the answer would be viewed as detracting from children's "educational experience" in deriving the answer. This belief seems to hold true even when cognitive challenges are met by a child through an adult's constant support and guidance. However, adults must also reflect upon what else a child is learning in social experiences when his or her genuine inquiries are rejected or mitigated in importance.

Perhaps adults are also challenging children's status and efficacy as initiators of shared challenges. Are these children learning to suspend their communicative needs to know and tell? Are they acquiring coping skills to deal with the frustration generated by the tutorial dialogues that adults impose upon them? Are children also acquiring cultural forms that help them to formulate cognitive challenges with others, or are they learning to undermine the cognitive challenges initiated by others who have less power, knowledge, or ability?

CONCLUSIONS

In the present chapter it was argued that goals differ with respect to people's commitment and aspirations to achieve them. As such, the construct of shared challenge was discussed as an important realm of social experience for the functioning and development of children's cognitive processes. However, the present chapter is intended only as a prolegomena on the topic of dialectics of shared cognitive challenge. The theoretical framework and case studies were set forth to encourage further consideration of the relation of people to goals, the emergence and unfolding of commitment and aspiration to goals within adult–child interactions, and the impact of shared challenges upon children's cognitive development.

Shared challenge as a unit of social participation holds promise as an important developmental construct, because it embodies the notions of aspiration, commitment, and discrepancy between being and becoming in a social context. Shared challenge goes beyond current day notions of discrepancy, insofar as it does not regard all discrepancies as having the same meaning for participants. Rather, challenge constitutes a particular class of discrepancy. Moreover, shared challenge is different from the traditional concepts of motivation as a drive or state of arousal. As a social experience of a goal, shared challenge was presented as a co-construction between group members to each other in relation to the objective goals of the task. Hence, the construct of shared challenge provides a relatively different framework for thinking about children's cognitive development.

The power of shared challenge as a developmental construct is tied to the intersubjective component of communication. The social meaning of a goal and the transformation of social meaning by participants are emphasized, and direct attention to people as creators of their own development (cf. Lerner & Busch-Rossnagel, 1981). In the co-construction of cognitive challenges, children and mothers set the trajectory, content, and tempo of their development. In this way the dialectic of external and intersubjective demands builds into the developmental process a space for participants to create the cutting edge of their growth. Therefore, a central concern which derives from this perspective is: What degree of political freedom does a child possess to truly share in the co-construction of his or her own cognitive challenges?

REFERENCES

Bartlett, F. (1964). *Remembering: A study in experimental and social psychology* (rev. ed.) London: White Friars Press (Original work published 1932).

Brown, A.L. (1979). Theories of memory and the problem of development: activity, growth and knowledge. In L.S. Cermak & F.I. Craik (Eds.), *Levels of processing in human memory.* Hillsdale, NJ: LEA.

Bruner, J. (1963). *The process of education.* New York: Vintage Books.

Bruner, J. (1971). *The relevance of education.* New York: W.W. Norton & Co., Inc.

Bursen, H.A. (1978). *Dismantling the memory machine.* Boston, MA: D. Reidel Publishing Company.

Clippinger, J.H. (1977). *Meaning and discourse: A computer model of psychoanalytic speech and cognition.* Baltimore, MD: The John Hopkins University Press.

Conant, J.B. (1961). *Slums and suburbs.* New York: Signet Books.

Erikson, E. (1950). *Childhood and society.* New York: W.W. Norton & Co., Inc.

Feigenbaum, P. (1986). The development of questioning as a means of framing problems and posing challenges. In R. Cocking (Chair), *Challenge as a dimension of development.* Symposium conducted at the Sixteenth Annual Symposium of the Jean Piaget Society, Philadelphia, PA.

Forehand, G.A. (1966). Epilogue: Constructs and strategies for problem-solving research. In B. Kleinmuntz (Ed.), *Problem solving: Research, method, and theory* (pp. 355–383). New York: John Wiley and Sons, Inc..

Gagne, R.M. (1966). Human problem solving: Internal and external events. In B. Kleinmuntz (Ed.), *Problem solving: Research, method, and theory* (pp. 128–148). New York: John Wiley and Sons, Inc.

Gagne, R.M., & Briggs, L.J. (1974). *Principles of instructional design.* New York: Holt, Rinehart and Winston, Inc.

Garfinkel, H. (1964). Studies of the routine grounds of everyday activities. *Social Problems, 2,* 225–250.

Geertz, C. (1983). *Local knowledge.* New York: Basic Books, Inc.

Goodman, P. (1960). *Growing up absurd.* New York: Vintage Books.

Halbwachs, M. (1980). *Collective memory.* (F. Ditter & V. Ditter Trans.). New York: Harper & Row. (Original work published 1952.)

Hayes, J.R. (1966). Memory, goals, and problem solving. In B. Kleinmuntz (Ed.), *Problem solving: Research, method, and theory* (pp. 149–170). New York: John Wiley and Sons, Inc.

Holt, J. (1969). *The under-achieving school.* New York: Dell Publishing Co., Inc.

Klahr, D., & Wallace, J.G. (1972). Class inclusion processes. In S. Farnham-Diggory (Ed.), *Information processing in children* (pp. 143–172). New York: Academic Press.

Kozol, J. (1972). *Free schools.* New York: Bantam Books.

Kvale, S. (1977). Dialectics and research on remembering. In N. Datan & H. Reese (Eds.), *Life-span developmental psychology: Dialectical perspectives on experimental research* (pp. 165–190). New York: Academic Press.

Leon'tev, A.N. (1979). The problem of activity in psychology. In J. Wertsch (Ed.), *The concept of activity in Soviet psychology* (pp. 37–71). New York: M.E. Sharpe Inc.

Lerner, R.M., & Busch-Rossnagel, N.A. (1981). Individuals as producers of their own development: Conceptual and empirical bases. In R.M. Lerner & N.A. Busch-Rossnagel (Eds.), *Individuals as producers of their own development: A life-span perspective.* New York: Academic Press.

Lewicki, P. (1986). *Nonconscious social information processing.* New York: Academic Press.

McGillicuddy-DeLisa, A., & Sigel, I. (1982). The relationship between parents' beliefs about development and family constellation, socioeconomic status, and parents' teaching strategies. In L. Loasa & I. Sigel (Eds.), *Families as learning environments for children* (pp. 261–299). New York: New York: Plenum.

McGillicuddy-DeLisa, A., Sigel, I., & Johnson, J. (1979). *Parental distancing, beliefs and children's representational competence within the family context* (ETS RR 80–21). Princeton, NJ: Educational Testing Service.

Meacham, J. (1977). A transactional model of remembering. In N. Datan & H. Reese (Eds.), *Life-span developmental psychology: Dialectical perspectives on experimental research* (pp. 261–284). New York: Academic Press.

Neisser, U. (1963). The imitation of man by machine. *Science, 139* (3549), 193–197.

Newell, A., & Simon, H.A. (1972). *Human problem solving.* Englewood Cliffs, NJ: Prentice-Hall.

Olson, R. (1979). *The constitutive processes of memory in organizational communication.* Unpublished doctoral dissertation, Ohio State University.

Pask, G. (1975). *Conversation, cognition, and learning.* New York: American Elsevier Publishing Co., Inc.

Perlmutter, H. (1952). *A study of group and individual memory-products.* Unpublished doctoral dissertation, University of Kansas.

Piaget, J. (1980). *Experiments in contradiction.* (D. Coltman, trans.). Chicago, IL: The University of Chicago Press.

Piaget, J. (1985). *The equilibration of cognitive structures: The central problem of intellectual development* (T. Brown & K. Thampy, trans.). Chicago, IL: University of Chicago Press. (Original work published 1974.)

Ratner, H. (1980). The role of social context in memory development. In M.

Perlmutter (Ed.), *Children's memory: New directions for child development* (pp. 49–68), No. 10. San Francisco, CA: Jossey-Boss.

Ratner, H. (1984). Memory demands and the development of young children's memory. *Child Development, 55,* 2173–2191.

Reese, H.W. (1976). Models of memory. *Human Development, 19,* 291–303.

Rogoff, B., & Gardner, W. (1984). Adult guidance of cognitive development. In B. Rogoff & J. Lave (Eds.), *Everyday cognition: Its development in a social context* (pp. 95–116). Cambridge, MA: Harvard University Press.

Rommetveit, R. (1980). On 'meanings' of acts and what is meant and made known by what is said in a pluralistic social world. In M. Brenner (Ed.), *The structure of action* (pp. 108–149). Oxford, England: Basil Blackwell.

Schutz, A. (1945). On multiple realities. *Philosophy and Phenomenological Research, 5,* 533–551.

Sigel, I. (1982). The relationship between parental strategies and the child's cognitive behavior. In L. Laosa & I. Sigel (Eds.), *Families as learning environments for children* (pp. 47–86). New York: Plenum.

Sigel, I. (1986). Cognition-affect: A psychological riddle. In D. Bearison & H. Zimiles (Eds.), *Thinking and emotion* (pp. 211–229). Hillsdale, NJ: LEA.

Sigel, I., & Cocking, R. (1977). Cognition and communication: A dialectic paradigm for development. In M. Lewis & L. Rosenblum (Eds.), *The origins of behavior. Volume 5. Interactions, conversation, and the development of language* (pp. 207–226). New York: Wiley.

Simon, H.A., & Hayes, J.R. (1979). Understanding written instructions. In H.A. Simon (Ed.), *Models of thought* (pp. 451–476). New Haven, CT: Yale University Press. (Original work published 1974.)

Verdonik, F. (1984, June). *Memory development in the context of social interactions.* Paper presented at a Max Planck Institute Conference on "Memory development: Universal changes and individual differences," Bavaria, F.R.G.

Verdonik, F. (1980). *Memory development through social processes.* Unpublished manuscript, City University of New York, Graduate and University Center, New York.

Verdonik, F. (1986a). *Memory functioning and development through individual and social processes.* Dissertation, City University of New York, Graduate and University Center, New York.

Verdonik, F. (1986b, May). Unfolding and emergence of challenges for remembering. In R. Cocking (Chair), *Challenge as a dimension of development.* Symposium conducted at the Sixteenth Annual Symposium of the Jean Piaget Society, Philadelphia, PA.

Verdonik, F. (in press). Reconsidering the context of remembering: The need for a social analysis of memory processes and their development. In F. Weinert & M. Perlmutter (Eds.), *Memory development: Universal changes and individual differences.* New York: Erlbaum.

Werner, H., & Kaplan, B. (1963). *Symbol formation: An organismic-developmental approach to language and the expression of thought.* New York: John Wiley and Sons, Inc..

Wertsch, J. (1984). The zone of proximal development: Some conceptual issues. In B. Rogoff & J. Wertsch (Eds.), *Children's learning in the "zone of proximal development": New directions for child development* (pp. 7–18), No. 23. San Francisco, CA: Jossey-Boss.

Wertsch, J., McNamee, G., McLane, J., & Budwig, N. (1980). The adult–child dyad as a problem-solving system. *Child Development, 51*(4), 1215–1221.

Yukes, H. (1954). *Some effects of group properties upon recall.* Unpublished doctoral dissertation, New York University.

APPENDIX A

Instructions to the Model-Making Activity

I want you (addressing the child) and your mother to make on the plastic sheet places that you know in (name of locale is given), the neighborhood you live in. There are blocks of different shapes and sizes over here (point to location). I put these things over here, but you can move them if you want.

You can make any place in (name of locale is given) that you want. But there are two important rules. First, the places must be real places—places that I could go to and see if I wanted to. Second, the places must be in (name of locale is given).

You can work on these places separately or together, and you can help each other in any way you want. I want you to make a total of eight places, and if you want to make more that's okay. So I'll move out of your way so that you can begin.

CHAPTER 5

"What We've Got Here Is a Failure to Communicate": The Cultural Context of Meaning

Julie Ann Robinson

Department of Psychology
La Trobe University
Bundoora, Victoria 3083
Australia

Misunderstandings don't exist; only the failure to communicate exists.
—Senegalese proverb

"Why do you not understand what I say? It is because you cannot bear to hear my word . . . you are not of God."
—Gospel of John

Communication is a process through which the lack of understanding that initially exists between individuals may be overcome. Humans differ in a multitude of ways. Each individual is a unique and changing combination of dispositions, interests, beliefs, knowledge, and abilities. As a consequence of this diversity, and the lack of a well-developed telepathic sense, people do not automatically understand one another's intentions or desires. Through communication, the thoughts, feelings and information held by one can be made known to others. It should be noted, however, that the process of communication is abandoned short of complete understanding. In a spirit of economy, speaker and listener are usually content to establish shared knowledge at the level perceived as being minimally sufficient for current purposes.

Communication, by facilitating the sharing of information, serves several important functions. It contributes to the ability of groups of interdependent persons to live together efficiently and in relative harmony. It allows information necessary for survival to be held in common. It is a means by which technology and culture can be transmitted between groups and from one generation to another.

This chapter explores the ways in which cultural information is transmitted in the course of casual conversation. It also explores the ways in which the cultural context influences the form and content of conversations. These two are mutually embedded: conversation in culture, culture in conversation. In exploring the ways in which this mutual influence is expressed, conversations involving infants or young children will be a particular focus.

Whatever the age of the participants, communication is a process through which understanding can be achieved. However, not all attempts to communicate increase understanding. On some occassions this is deliberate. Speakers may use communication to mask their thoughts, feelings and knowledge: They may deceive. At other times the speaker may wish to share information, but the listener may be unreceptive. By not attending to the message, by selective attention, and by distorting the speaker's meaning, listeners can cause attempts to communicate to fail. In yet other instances, the attempt to share knowledge may be sincere but unsuccessful. That is, the listener may fail to receive or fail to understand the message. Regardless of these failures, however, communication can be viewed as a process in which meaning is negotiated.

THE NEGOTIATION OF MEANING

Whatever the society, there is initially some lack of understanding between individuals. This is a necessary consequence of the changing nature of human emotions and knowledge, and the situation-specific nature of speech. The study of conversation allows one to trace the development of understanding on a microscopic scale. Conversation can be seen as a problem solving task in which meaning is discovered by "negotiation"[1] (Golinkoff, 1983) or "collaboration" (Clark, 1985; Clark & Wilkes-Gibbs, 1986). In conversation, both speaker and listener accommodate their knowledge of the other and their future conduct in the light of the unfolding revelations provided by their partner's behavior. For example, the speaker makes inferences about the proficiency with which the listener can use the signal system, his or her

---

[1] The term is used here in a broader sense than it has been in previous discussions (e.g., Golinkoff, 1983)

level of interest in the topic, and the extent of prior relevant knowledge. This information is used by the speaker when choosing an appropriate signal. Under ideal conditions, competent speakers diligently monitor listener responses to their messages. The information they glean allows them to revise their assessments of their listeners, and subsequently to refine their choice of messages. Meanwhile, under similarly ideal conditions, competent listeners decode their speakers' messages and interpret them in the context of earlier messages and their world knowledge. Newly received messages allow listeners to verify or reject their interpretation of earlier ones. By generating and testing hypotheses in this way, understanding develops between listener and speaker.

Of course, ideal conditions rarely present themselves. The behavior of the speaker and listener are influenced, not only by the demands of the conversation in which they are engaged, but also by factors external to it. Consequently, there are many cases in which neither the speaker nor the listener are optimally efficient in their problem solving during conversations. Such factors as emotional stress, fatigue, level of interest in the topic, and the presence of competing demands on attention influence their behavior. When the efficiency of speaker or listener is lowered, the negotiation process may be prolonged. In some cases these factors may even cause the negotiation to be abandoned. However, the negotiation process is generally robust to deviations from optimal communication conditions.

The process of negotiation between speaker and listener occurs in the most mundane and the most learned conversations. However, the negotiation of meaning is often not directly observable in either case, as the example below shows.

Example 1

> host: Would you like something to drink?
> guest: Coffee, please.
> host: Okay. I have expresso or cappucino.
> guest: Cappucino.

The process only becomes observable in some special, though not rare, communicative contexts. For instance, negotiation of meaning can be seen when listeners signal that they have received a message that cannot be reconciled with prior messages from the same speaker.

Example 2

> guest: Coffee is the worst. I just can't go near the stuff. Uggh.
> host: Sorry to interrupt, but would you like something to drink?

> guest: Coffee, please.
> host: Coff—I'm sorry. What did you say?
> guest: Coffee.
> host: Coffee? I don't . . . I thought you said you didn't like coffee.
> guest: No. I only meant that I don't like it at night. It keeps me awake.

In this case, "Coff—I'm sorry. What did you say?", and the utterances that follow it, are noncomprehension signals (i.e., signals that indicate that the speaker's attempt to communicate has failed). In this instance, they indicate that the listener cannot grasp the speaker's communicative intent given the conversational context of the message. On other occasions, the initial lack of understanding between speaker and listener may not be bridged because the speaker's vocabulary is more sophisticated than the listener's, or because the listener lacks necessary background information. There are also many occasions on which the speaker's signal is not received intact by the listener. Clearly, incomplete reception of the signal hinders, and often prohibits, its correct interpretation. In each of these circumstances, the listener is likely to provide a noncomprehension signal. When this is done, the negotiation of meaning becomes observable.

The importance of negotiations following failed attempts to communicate can be easily and vividly illustrated. Many of us are familiar with a game (sometimes referred to as the "broken telephone game") in which a message is transmitted from one person to another through a series of intermediaries. The intermediaries are expressly forbidden to make requests for repetition or clarification. The result is a message that is unrecognizable by the time it reaches the final player. Were the information being conveyed necessary for survival, the degradation of the message would have serious consequences. Noncomprehension signals are therefore central rather than peripheral components of the process of communication. Clearly, the outcome of the game would be quite different if the listener were allowed unlimited repetitions and clarifications of the prior speaker's signal.

The negotiation of meaning is also observable during language learning, whether the student is an adult or a child. Most language is learned through listening and speaking, rather than through formal instruction. In this context, the meaning of any word or phrase is derived by a process of successive approximations. Even when language is learned in an academic setting, the appropriate use of words and expressions, and subtle discriminations between synonyms are learned gradually, often through an implicit negotiation with an absent author.

There are thus two major opportunities to gain access to the process of negotiation that underlies all communication, but which often remains hidden. The first of these occurs when attempts to communicate fail, and the speaker and listener actively negotiate the meaning or function of prior speech. The second occurs during language learning as the basis for shared understanding is laid through negotiation.

Motivation and Cultural Organization

It was noted earlier that communication is a tool for the transmission of culture. What was not noted was that the communication system is itself part of the culture that it transmits. Cultures exert direct influence over patterns of communication. They specify what may be said, in what way, to what audience, at what time. They also produce more subtle effects on organization. Particular topics are more salient in some cultures than in others, appropriate patterns of gaze between speaker and listener vary, and so on. Communicative interactions can not be separated from the cultural context in which they are embedded. Communication is a tool by which culture is transmitted, but it is a tool that is shaped by the culture it transmits.

Given the functions that communication may serve, it is not surprising that both speaker and listener are often highly motivated to resolve misunderstandings when they occur. However, the level of motivation the speaker and listener exhibit largely depends upon the meaning encoded in the message, and its salience to each of the individuals. These, in turn, are influenced by the cultural context. Thus, as a listener, I am more likely to signal that the message has not been understood if the speaker is providing directions to the nearest hospital, than if he is engaged in greeting behavior. Similarly, I am more likely, as a speaker, to repeat the message when the listener does not understand, if I have made a request, than if I have made a comment on a minor feature of the environment. Teachers are likely to find their students more receptive to instruction about some signals than others, and the willingness of a teacher to provide instruction also varies (as children who have asked their mothers the meaning of a word, and been told simply that it is "a bad word," can attest). It can be seen that speakers and listeners are likely to differ in their motivation to negotiate with one another whenever they evaluate the salience of the message differently.

It was noted earlier that, in addition to the subtle role cultural factors play (above), cultural conventions also exert a more direct influence on conversation. For example, the culture regulates when and how meaning is negotiated after an attempt to communicate has failed. It also assigns the roles of teacher and student, the content and method of instruction about communication, and its developmental timing.

Cultural rules tend to be context-specific, and thus, ways of conversing that are appropriate in one context may not be in others. The speech style known as "baby-talk" may be appropriate in Western cultures when one addresses an infant, lover, pet, or invalid (Snow & Ferguson, 1977) but may not be appropriate when addressing someone of higher status than oneself. Noncomprehension signals, being a form of social speech, are also subject to cultural organization. Thus, for example, some forms of noncomprehension signals are more appropriate in some settings than others. In English-speaking countries, the noncomprehension signal "Huh?" is appropriate only among children and with listeners with whom one is intimate, and then only in the context of informal conversation. It would not, for example, be heard very frequently in the course of legal proceedings. Such cultural preferences for some signals over others are often explicitly taught to children. For example, Australian mothers expend much effort training their preschool-aged children to say "I beg your pardon" rather than the less polite "What?" when they fail to hear or fail to understand. Thus, the culture specifies which of several forms serving the same function is appropriate in a particular context.

In other cases, the cultural organization of communication may influence, not only the way a person speaks, but also whether he or she speaks. For example, under some circumstances the listener may not signal that the speaker's attempt to communicate has failed, even though such is the case and the topic had high salience. This is likely to occur when the failure of an attempt to communicate may reflect unfavorably on the speaker's competence to encode the message, or on the listener's attentiveness, knowledge, or intellectual abilities. In some communicative contexts, the achievement of mutual understanding may be of secondary importance. For example, the creation of an impression of attentiveness and shared attitudes and knowledge may be valued more highly than the actual achievement of these ends through negotiation. Thus, on a first date or during a job interview, the listener may not mark failed attempts to communicate.

Other cultural constraints apply in ritualized communication. During a wedding ceremony or a formal debate, the allocation of speaking turns is prescribed, as, to some extent, is the content. Consequently, even when the message is a highly salient one to the listeners, it is usually culturally inappropriate, for example, for them to interrupt with a noncomprehension signal. Thus, it is normally assumed that the groom has inquired into the meaning of the words "forsaking all others" prior to his arrival at the church, and that any desired modifications in the vow will have been made before, rather than during, the ceremony. It would, at the very least, be considered undiplomatic were he to interrupt the proceedings in order to have the priest enumerate the specific types of relationships that are and are not prohibited by the vow.

The use of noncomprehension signals is also regulated in formal debates. In this context noncomprehension signals are neither completely forbidden nor necessarily insincere. It is appropriate for a participant to declare that he or she is unable to follow the reasoning of one of the opposition speakers.

Example 3

> debater: I confess that my learned opponent has far more wit than I. His reasoning is so far superior to my own that I was completely unable to grasp the relevance of the connection he made between the literary works of "The Great Bard" and our current topic in this debate: the deployment of "Star Wars" technology by the United States. Perhaps future speakers for our opposition will be able to shed more light on this fascinating and vital connection.

It is also appropriate for debaters to highlight a mishearing or misunderstanding of their own position by their opposition.

Example 4

> debater: It is clear that our opposition did not clearly hear what was said by our last speaker. This could be the only possible explanation for the line their argument has taken, since it is inconceivable that they should have deliberately misrepresented our position. For their elucidation, and to save them from further embarrassment, I would like to reiterate our position.

However, because the sequence of speakers and the duration of each turn are prescribed by the rules governing debates, the timing of these noncomprehension signals differs from that found during casual conversation. All team members usually pass their noncomprehension signals to the speaker who will next represent the team. He or she determines the priority of each of these, given the constraints set by the duration of the speaking turns, then awaits the opportunity to present them. The speaker must also frame noncomprehension signals so that they comply with the rules of politeness established for debating. Thus, in example 4 (above), the speaker may believe that the misrepresentation made by the opposition was indeed intentional, but feel that an explicit accusation to this effect would be inappropriate.

Of course, one cannot always ascribe the listener's failure to provide an appropriate noncomprehension signal to the influence of motivation and cultural organization. In many instances, listeners are unaware that a message has been addressed to them. Negotiation need not be abandoned in such cases. Speakers may themselves signal that the listener has not received the message (e.g., "You haven't listened to a word I've said") or has not understood it (e.g., "It was a joke Bill. I don't really want you to do it"). It should be noted, however, that cultural rules also regulate the contexts in which speaker-produced noncomprehension signals are appropriate. Example 4 shows the way in which the timing of speakers' noncomprehension signals can also be influenced by cultural rules.

Shared Knowledge

From the description of communication that has been outlined above, it is clear that establishing an understanding will be more difficult for some speaker–listener pairs than others. Motivational factors and cultural organization are two factors that influence the degree of difficulty. Familiarity is another. It has previously been noted that some knowledge must be shared by speaker and listener if communication is to take place. Two types of knowledge play roles in shaping patterns of communication. The first, and more general of these is shared cultural knowledge.[2] Similar world views and similar cultural conventions will aid the process of communication even when these views and conventions do not directly concern communication.[3] Of course, when the rules do pertain to the communication process, the problems are even greater. The difficulties an absence of this shared cultural knowledge raises for the task of communication can be seen in examples 5 and 6 below.

Example 5

[As an American tourist leaves a guesthouse, he greets a villager who is seated near the entrance]

---

[2] For a broader discussion of the role of shared knowledge, including physical copresence and linguistic copresence, the reader is directed to Clark and Carlson (1981). In the scheme provided by these authors, what have been listed here as personal familiarity, cultural conventions, and world views belong to the category of shared knowledge provided by "community membership."

[3] This was brought home by a communication failure of my own. I attended a religious service with a fellow student who had been raised without the concept of a god or gods (in the People's Republic of China). She found, not only the service, but also my attempts to explain it, to be quite unintelligible.

American: Hi, how are you?
Nepali: [to himself: How rude! Prying into my intimate thoughts and
            emotions! But I will not be discourteous. I will speak with
            him.] Where are you going?
American: [to himself: Why didn't he answer me? I don't know him.
            Why is he interested in where I'm going? What is he after?
            Perhaps he wants to know how long I will be away so that
            he can rob my room.]

Here the two individuals interpret each others communications in the light of their differing cultural expectations. Each unwittingly raises the suspicions of his listener by violating these expectations. The intention of both speakers to convey a friendly greeting is lost and the attempt to establish a shared understanding fails.

We expect things to be said in the way in which we are accustomed to talk ourselves: things that are said in any other way do not seem the same at all but seem rather incomprehensible.

Aristotle, *Metaphysics*, Book 2

Example 6

[Fieldworkers are conducting a nutrition survey in the barrio of Malitbog, The Philippines]

After breakfast, the researchers stayed for a while and asked a number of questions: "How many times do you eat in a day?" "What constitutes your breakfast, lunch and supper?" . . . She hedged questions and gave generalized answer. Then she would look at the people around who, perhaps, taking the hint would contribute an answer they thought the researchers wanted. . . . (She) borrowed money from Sambi so that they could purchase in town the things they told the researchers they serve at each meal. "They are coming back tomorrow and it would be shameful if they found that we do not actually eat the things we told them we do" . . . for a stranger to ask about what people eat, how many times they eat, and so forth, is a breach of proper conduct.

(Jocano, 1969b, p. 268–9)

The dialogue in example 5 is a hypothetical one designed to illustrate the way cultural differences in the appropriateness of conversational topics may influence the perceived meaning of communications. In the context of this example, the cultural differences coincide with differences in nationality. However, such differences also exist within national boundaries, as can be seen in example 6. Jocano (1969b) reports that the people of the barrio are ashamed of having insufficient food for their families. A villager may share such problems with friends, but it is impolite for strangers to make direct inquiries about so personal a topic. In consequence, the villagers draw on their knowledge of the values of "outsiders" and attempt to construct a satisfactory reply, thereby completely subverting the researchers' intentions.

In contrast to the abandonment, distortion, or protraction of negotiation processes that occurs when cultural knowledge is not shared by speaker and listener, are cases in which conversational partners have experienced very similar processes of enculturation. In this latter case, they come to the communication process having already negotiated the significance and meaning of some experiences, the nature of the physical world, and so on, with parents, peers, and teachers. The knowledge and beliefs that emerged from these earlier negotiations do not need to be negotiated in each new conversation, since they are assumed to be shared within the cultural group. (Many of these issues will, nevertheless, be negotiated more than once in a lifetime.)

A particularly dramatic illustration of the role of shared knowledge in shaping patterns of conversation is provided by Tolstoy.

Example 7

"I have long wished to ask you something."

"Please do."

"This," he said, and wrote the initial letters: W y a: i c n b, d y m t o n. These letters meant: "When you answered: it cannot be, did you mean then or never?" It seemed impossible that she would be able to understand the complicated sentence.

"I understand," she said, blushing.

"What word is that?" he asked, pointing to the n which stood for "never".

"The word is 'never'," she said, "but that is not true." He quickly erased what he had written, handed her the chalk, and rose. She wrote: I c n a o t.

His face brightened suddenly: he had understood it. It meant: "I could not answer otherwise then."

She wrote the initial letters: s t y m f a f w h. This meant: "So that you might forget and forgive what had happened."

He seized the chalk with tense, trembling fingers, broke it, and wrote the initial letters of the following: "I have nothing to forget and forgive. I never ceased loving you."

"I understand," she whispered.

Anna Karenina, Part 4, Chapter 13

A new understanding developed between these two conversational partners, even though they had not previously negotiated the meaning of these particular signals. The illustration can not be dismissed as the product of poetic license, since it was modelled after an event that occurred in Tolstoy's own life. Vygotsky (1986, pp. 237–238) used this example to show that the role of speech is minimized whenever people live in "close psychological contact." In contrast, even elaborated and redundant speech may be insufficient to achieve shared understanding when participants hold divergent world views. It is clear that, in this illustration, the estranged lovers share more than a cultural heritage. They also share the history of their own relationship. This personal familiarity is the second type of shared knowledge that shapes the pattern of communication. In this case too, many negotiations relevant to the communication at hand have been completed prior to its commencement.

Thus, members of an established family share an accumulation of knowledge gained from observation and earlier communications. This familiarity often simplifies the listener's problem-solving task. Previous knowledge of the speaker's behavior patterns, disposition, and likes allows the listener to reject some possible interpretations of the speaker's message and favour others. As any family member will attest, however, familiarity with the speaker does not guarantee error-free transmission and interpretation of signals. It does, however, allow many "short-cuts" in the process of negotiation.

Although the way in which the conversation was simplified in the extract from *Anna Karenina* may appear unusual, the extent of the abbreviation was not. Consider the following interchange between two co-workers as they pass in the hall.

Example 8

co-worker 1:   Tonight?
co-worker 2:   Six-thirty?
co-worker 1:   Fine.

The two co-workers know that they meet on a regular but flexible basis to have a drink and discuss marketing strategy after work. Each knows that she has received a memo announcing an upcoming marketing meeting, and that the other will have received the same. They know that they always meet in the same place, but that the time of the meeting varies with their responsibilities. Although more familiar and less dramatic than Tolstoy's example, the extent of condensation in this example is at least as great. Compare the conversation as it appears in example 8 with the still brief, but "minimally" complete rephrasing found in example 9 below.

Example 9

co-worker 1:   Do you have time to meet me at Rosie's Bar to talk about marketing strategy after work tonight?

co-worker 2: Yes. But not until 6:30pm. Is that convenient?
co-worker 1: Fine.

Among conversational partners who are highly familiar with one another, and who share common goals, one would expect abbreviated communications to be the rule rather than the exception, with the extent of the abbreviation being roughly proportional to the degree of familiarity, and the form of the abbreviation being tied to their past history of negotiating meaning.

Just as familiarity with the speaker often simplifies the listener's problem-solving task in interpreting the signal, so the speaker's familiarity with the listener may aid him in isolating the source of listener difficulty and in choosing an appropriate repair response when an attempt to communicate has failed. For example, if the speaker is certain that the listener had necessary topical knowledge and a vocabulary that included all the words used in the signal, he may deduce that the listener's difficulty lay in receiving the message, and choose to repeat his message at a louder volume.

It can be seen that the most accessible negotiations of meaning are likely to occur when the listener and speaker share little cultural and personal information, yet are highly motivated to achieve successful communication. Misunderstandings are likely when the listener has limited knowledge of the speaker's disposition, beliefs, and preferences, or when reception of the signal is inhibited. The listener (or speaker) is likely to signal that such a misunderstanding has occurred when the message is a salient one, for example, when the partners are interdependent. The process of negotiation will be extended if the speaker and listener do not share the same signal system. Many of these circumstances co-occur whenever members of different cultures meet and when one tries to communicate with an infant.

Due to the limited range of communicative responses available to preverbal infants, the negotiations in which they take part have several distinctive features. Of necessity infants' signals are often simple in structure and non-specific with regard to the intention they encode. Thus, it may not be possible to determine from the signal itself whether an infant's communicative intention in offering an object is "Hold this for me, I'm finished with it," "Show me how this works, I'd like to play with it" or "This is the first turn in a give-and-take game." The signal can only be understood if the recipient of the object has attended to contextual information and been led to a "rich interpretation." Because infants' turns are usually brief, negotiations involving adults and infants are characterized by the relatively quick exchange of conversational turns. In addition, the feedback adults provide following infants' attempts to communicate are almost invariably as long or longer than the original signal.

A FRAMEWORK FOR STUDYING THE STRUCTURE OF NEGOTIATIONS

In order to describe the process of negotiation, it is useful to have a well-developed taxonomy of the types of conversational turns available to speaker and listener, and a plan of the sequences in which these turns may be used. A general model of the process of negotiation in conversation is presented here (see Figure 1). The model is necessarily overly simple. For example, it allocates turns to only two participants. Clearly, many conversations involve more than one speaker and one listener. However, for the current purpose of denoting the possible sequences of action in the negotiation of meaning between a mother and her preverbal infant the model is adequate without further elaboration. The form of the model presented here is one designed to be generally applicable to conversations involving two persons. For that reason it includes two "moves" that are unlikely to be made by infant communicators in response to feedback from their adult partners. These are the prompt for acknowledgement and the noncomprehension signal. It is possible to make both these moves using nonverbal signals. However, they require more extensive understanding of the norms and subtleties of dyadic conversation than would usually be attributed to infants under 18 months of age.

Any model of the negotiation process must reflect the fact that communication can sometimes be accomplished in a small number of conversational turns, while, at other times, it is achieved only after a very prolonged interchange. Regardless of their length, however, all negotiations are composed of combinations of four types of turns: attempt to communicate, listener feedback, speaker response, and termination. Possible combinations of these turns are summarized in Figure 1.

The First Turn: The Attempt to Communicate

The first turn in any negotiation sequence is the initial attempt to communicate. This attempt may take either vocal or nonvocal forms, or may combine signals in both channels. Not all vocal behavior is communicative. Such vocalizations as grunts made due to exertion, babble, and self-directed talk are signs rather than signals (Clark, 1985). On the other hand, many nonvocal behaviors, such as pointing, spon-

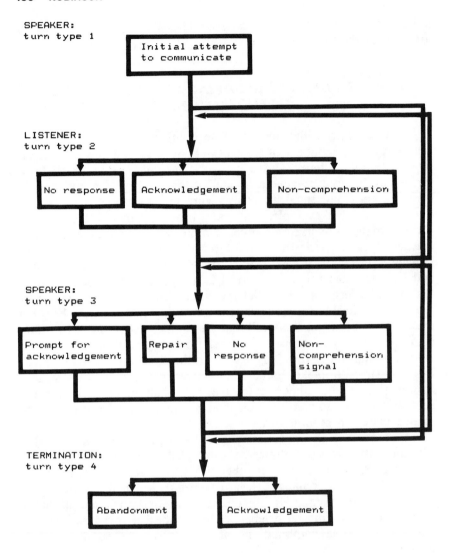

SPEAKER:
turn type 1

Initial attempt
to communicate

LISTENER:
turn type 2

No response   Acknowledgement   Non-comprehension

SPEAKER:
turn type 3

Prompt for acknowledgement   Repair   No response   Non-comprehension signal

TERMINATION:
turn type 4

Abandonment   Acknowledgement

Figure 1. Flow chart of possible turns in the negotiation of meaning

taneous offering of objects, and gestures that model a functional behaviour while not themselves being functional (e.g., when a child
stretches an arm towards a toy without attempting to complete the
reaching act), serve as signals.

The termination of one attempt to communicate and the initiation
of another is usually marked by a pause, but can also be marked by
a change in the phonological character of the vocalization, or change

in the target of a gesture. These changes are often accompanied by movement in the direction of the speaker's gaze.

The Second Turn: Listener Feedback

The second turn in a negotiation sequence consists of listeners' responses to the speaker's attempt to communicate. These responses can be sorted into three broad categories. Firstly, a listener's behavior could signal that the speaker's attempt to communicate had not been received or had not been comprehended, a noncomprehension signal. Secondly, it could signal that the child's attempt to communicate had been received and comprehended, an acknowledgement. Thirdly, the listener may fail to provide feedback regarding the success or failure of the speaker's attempt to communicate, a "no relevant response."

It is sometimes the case that listeners fail to comprehend the speaker's signal. If the listener is aware that this is the case, he or she may provide a signal of noncomprehension. A diverse array of terms has been used to refer to feedback signalling that an attempt to communicate has failed (Cherry, 1979). Many of the terms used in previous studies refer to only a subset of all noncomprehension signals. The complete set of such signals includes considerable variety. As has been noted earlier, they may be made either by the speaker or the listener. In addition, they vary along three other dimensions: syntactic form, type of response requested from the speaker, and source of listener difficulty (see Table 1).

Alternatively, the feedback provided by the listener may indicate that the speaker's attempt to communicate was successful. Listener acknowledgements may be verbal or nonverbal, and can assume several forms. They may for example, be minimal filler responses (e.g., "Mm," "Oh," nodding of the head). They could also provide an appropriate answer to the communication (e.g., by returning a greeting, handing a child the desired object, or providing requested information). Alternatively, the listener may signal that he or she had received the message by correcting it with regard to its truthfulness or its acceptability.

Example 10

      mother: Where's the pussy cat?
      infant: [points to a picture of a dog]
      mother: That's not a pussy. That's a puppy.

Example 11

      infant: [whimper]
      mother: You're a big girl now. Big girls don't cry.

Table 1. A Classification System for Noncomprehension Signals

Source of difficulty	Form	Type of repair requested
Reception	Declarative	Nonspecific repetition e.g., "I can't hear you." "You'll need to say that again." Specific repetition e.g., "Sorry. I missed the start of that."
	Imperative	Nonspecific repetition e.g., "Speak up." Specific repetition e.g., "Say the first part of that for me again."
	Interrogative	Nonspecific repetition e.g., "What did you say?" Nonspecific confirmation e.g., "Are you talking to me?" Specific repetition e.g., "What was the last word?" Specific confirmation e.g., "Did you say, 'He's never been there'?"
	Nonverbal	Repetition e.g., cupping hand to ear, beckoning movements
Interpretation	Declarative	Nonspecific repetition e.g., "I don't follow you" Specific repetition e.g., "I didn't understand anything after X." Elaboration e.g., "I don't know what 'plucked' means."
	Imperative	Nonspecific repetition e.g., "Say that for me again." Specific repetition e.g., "Say that last bit again." Elaboration e.g., "Tell me what 'plucked' means again."

Table 1.   A Classification System for Noncomprehension Signals (Continued)

Source of difficulty	Form	Type of repair requested
	Interrogative	Nonspecific repetition e.g., "What do you mean?" Specific repetition e.g., "You want what?" Nonspecific confirmation e.g., "Are you rousing (fussing) at me?" Specific confirmation e.g., "That wasn't the right one?" Specification e.g., "Which block are you talking about?"
	Nonverbal	Repetition e.g., tilting or turning head while narrowing eyes, shrugging shoulders Confirmation e.g., holding up object

The listener might also correct the pronunciation or completeness of the speaker's communication.

Example 12

    infant: Dere.
    mother: Over there. Yes. The puppy's over there.

An imitation or repetition of the speaker's vocalization may also signal acknowledgement.

Example 13

    infant: Ook.
    mother: Ook-ook. That's what the owl says.

An additional two forms of acknowledgement merit separate consideration. In the first of these the listener signals understanding in the course of refusing the speaker's request.

Example 14

    infant: Bot-bot.
    mother: No. You've had enough. You can wait until we get home.

The second anomalous form of acknowledgement is largely restricted to conversations involving infants or young children. Games such as peek-a-boo and pat-a-cake, as well as extended rounds of imitation, involve sound and gestural play.

Although refusals and a continuation of sound or gestural play are forms of acknowledgement, their conversational function differs from that of other acknowledgements. In particular, refusals and sound or gestural play invite the speaker to repeat or recast his or her previous signal. This is not true of the category of acknowledgements in general. In the context of developmental research, the anomolous property of these two acknowledgements is especially troublesome. Any study that seeks to examine the selectivity with which infants provide repetitions and reformulations of their message following failed attempts to communicate would be contaminated by the inclusion of refusals and sound play in the general category of acknowledgements.

The third type of listener response provides the speaker with no feedback regarding the success or failure of the attempt to communicate. Included in this category are attempts by the listener to distract the speaker from his or her topic, silence, and tangential or unrelated responses.

On many occasions, the listener's response to the speaker's attempt to communicate involves several utterances. In such cases, it is possible for more than one type of feedback to be represented within the listener's conversational turn. If all utterances within a turn are of the same type (i.e., all acknowledgements, noncomprehension signals or "no responses"), only one classification need be made. However, when more than one type of feedback is found within a turn, it is advisable to assign the turn to the multiple categories that appear relevant. Thus, while the categories outlined in Table 2 are mutually exclusive and exhaustive for any single utterance, a multi-utterance turn may be assigned to all three categories. In example 15, the listener provides both a noncomprehension signal and an acknowledgement within a single turn.

Example 15

> infant: Yuh. [Leans towards a table containing several objects. A ball
> is under the table.]
> mother: Which one? Oh. I see it. [Hands the ball to the infant.]

The Third Type of Turn: Speaker Response

The third type of turn in the negotiation of meaning marks the speaker's response to listener feedback (or the absence of it). When a noncom-

Table 2. A Classification System for Listener Responses to the Speaker's Attempt to Communicate.

1) Acknowledgements
   - a) filler
   - b) explicit feedback
   - c) appropriate answer
   - d) corrections
   - e) imitation
2) Anomalous acknowledgements
   - a) refusals
   - b) continuation of sound or gestural play
3) Noncomprehension signals
   - a) clarification questions
     * requests for repetition/recast
     * requests for confirmation
     * requests for specification
   - b) declarative noncomprehension signal
     * request for repetition/recast
     * request for specification
   - c) imperative noncomprehension signal
     * request for repetition/recast
     * request for specification
4) No relevant response
   - a) silence
   - b) attempts to distract the speaker
   - c) tangential or unrelated speech

prehension signal has been sent, or when the listener fails to provide feedback, the speaker may elect to make a conversational repair. Repairs serve as correction responses to aid the noncomprehending listener (Jefferson, 1972). They may assume any syntactic form. Consequently, repairs are generally categorized, not by their meaning or form, but by their relationship to the original signal. The one exception to this rule is the form-based "Yes/No" category of repairs, which may follow a request for confirmation.

There are three broad categories of repair responses. The first is a response that serves to confirm or disconfirm the listener's interpretation of the initial signal. This is the "Yes/No" response referred to above. Secondly, the speaker may repeat part or all of the initial signal. Thirdly, the speaker may reformulate the initial signal while maintaining the same communicative intent.

Repairs may also be made using the gestural channel of communication. Confirmation and disconfirmation responses may be made by nodding and shaking the head, respectively. If the initial signal was in gestural form, a repetition repair would necessarily also be gestural.

Similarly, a verbal signal can be augmented or substituted for by a gesture, such as pointing.

A schematic summary of this taxonomy of repair responses can be found in Table 3. As in the case of the taxonomy of noncomprehension signals provided in Table 1, the distinctions between types of repairs are possible theoretically, but are often not so in practice. For example, it may be very difficult to determine whether a communicative signal is a repetition or reformulation of a previous signal when the "speaker" is a preverbal infant.

Alternatively, the speaker may not receive or not respond to listener feedback. For example, he or she could continue the conversation with a new (though related) message, could fall silent, or could be distracted to pursue a new communicative intention. Each of these responses can be classified as "no relevant response" because they do not continue the negotiation of meaning.

Although it is unlikely to be made by an infant, a third speaker response to listener feedback is possible. It involves the speaker requesting a signal of acknowledgement from the listener. Many negotiation episodes continue until a strong display of understanding is provided by the listener.

Example 16

    speaker: It's my turn next.

Table 3. A Classification System for Repair Responses

Category	Subcategory	May be appropriate for these noncomprehension signals
Confirmation/ Disconfirmation	Confirmation	Request for confirmation
	Disconfirmation	Request for confirmation
Repetition	Partial	Request for confirmation Request for repetition
	Complete	Request for confirmation Request for repetition
Reformulation	Elaboration	Request for confirmation Request for repetition Request for specification
	Substitution	Request for confirmation Request for repetition Request for specification

              In addition reformulations may be
                * partial or complete
                * phonetic, lexical and/or syntactic

listener: [Silence]
speaker: Okay?

Example 17

    speaker: Put that comic book away and start working on the mathematics problem on the board.
    listener: [Silent. Continues previous activity.]
    speaker: Did you hear me?

Finally, the speaker himself may signal that an attempt to communicate has failed. Two distinct types of noncomprehension signals can be produced by the speaker. The first signals that the listener has not received, or not understood, his message.

Example 18

    listener: So you want me to be there at eight.
    speaker: No. You weren't listening to me. I can't be there until eight. You have to get there at least an hour earlier if we're going to get tickets.

A second type of speaker-initiated noncomprehension signal indicates that the speaker himself has failed to receive, or failed to understand, the listener's feedback.

Example 19

    listener: So you want me to be there at eight.
    speaker: Huh?
    listener: At eight.
    speaker: Oh. Yeah. . . . Did you see what that guy was wearing?!

When the speaker signals that he has failed to receive or failed to understand the listener's feedback, one negotiation of meaning (the listener's) becomes embedded in another (the original speaker's).

Bringing Negotiations to a Close

The fourth and final type of turn in a negotiation sequence marks its termination, either because it was abandoned by both parties or because communication has been accomplished. The conversational functions of final turns in negotiations are not unique. Most are acknowledgements or "no relevant responses." They are noteworthy only because they mark the end of one event in the event sampling procedure.

Table 4.   A Classification System for Speaker Responses to Listener Feedback

1) No relevant response
    * silence
    * a new message on the same topic
    * change of topic
2) Repair
    * Confirmation/disconfirmation
    * Repetition
    * Reformulation/augmentation
3) Prompt for a signal of acknowledgment from the listener
4) Noncomprehension signal
    * signalling listener noncomprehension
    * signalling own noncomprehension

It is clear that the negotiation of meaning may extend over more than four turns. It is also clear that some negotiation episodes can be described accurately by using only some of the four types of turns discussed above. Regardless of the length of the sequence, however, each participant's turns can be described using the four-level framework that was summarized in Figure 1.

The current discussion relates to all negotiations of meaning that occur during the course of casual conversation. However, it has earlier been noted that the process of negotiation is most accessible to study when an attempt to communicate is initially unsuccessful. Thus, negotiation sequences in which a noncomprehension signal occurs are of special interest. In particular, the focal conversational sequences in the current chapter are those in which meaning is negotiated between infants and their conversational partners following a failed attempt to communicate.

THE INFLUENCE OF CULTURE ON THE NEGOTIATION OF MEANING BETWEEN PARENTS AND YOUNG CHILDREN

It was noted in the first section of this chapter that cultural factors influence the course of the negotiation of meaning. Because of this, the negotiation of meaning conveys more than the speaker's immediate message. It also reveals information about the culture that gave it birth. The negotiation of meaning can thus be studied on two very different levels of analysis: the overt structural level and the often implicit cultural level.

The immediate and overt function of the exchange between speaker and listener can be studied using the model outlined above. In this way one might, for example, study cross-cultural differences in the structure of negotiations that occur between adults and young children. However, the implicit transmission of cultural information cannot be studied using this framework. Other tools are required to effect its study. The current section of this chapter explores the ways in which cultural information is reflected in negotiations of meaning. The focus of discussion remains conversations between adults and very young children.

Different Assumptions; Different Negotiations

Clearly, the negotiation of meaning is a process through which infants may receive information about the organization of communication and about the wider philosophical background of the culture. The infant is a novice to both. Information about the rules governing the organization of communication is transmitted indirectly in, for example, the form and timing of negotiations. For the infant, then, there is a sense in which "the medium is the message."

An example may help to illustrate the ways in which cultural information may be implicitly transmitted by the form the conversation takes. Australian adults spend much time engaging infants in games in which they can play an active role despite their limited repertoire of responses (e.g., catch and throw, pat-a-cake, peek-a-boo). Infants are also treated as partners in the speech mothers direct to them. Thus the pattern of communication too fosters reciprocity. In both cases the infant is assigned not only the role of audience but also that of participant.

Example 20

mother:	Are you ready?
child:	[holds his arms out towards mother]
mother:	Here it comes!
	Here it comes!
	Oh! Did you get it?
child:	[child holds the ball in the air triumphantly]
mother:	What a clever boy!

An even more subtle form of cultural transmission also occurs in casual conversation. Just as communication is shaped by the cultural content it transmits, so the cultural content that is transmitted to infants of different sexes at different ages is structured by the wider culture. It is obvious that cultures differ in their beliefs about the nature of infants, and that these differences are reflected the types of interactions infants experience. The fact that adults speak to infants at all transmits information to them about their social station.

Observations of adult–infant conversations in industrialized countries reveal that adults wish to treat infants as conversational partners. Much of the speech between adults and infants is dominated by adults' attempts to establish a shared system of signals. Two means to this end are often adopted. Firstly, the adult provides the meaning of the standard signals and expressions of the culture, tests the child's knowledge of these signals, and clarifies ambiguities and misinterpretations when they arise (as in examples 21, 22, and 23, respectively).

Example 21

[An Australian mother's speech to her 14-month-old daughter as they look at a picture book]

> mother: There's a puppy dog.
> 'N' a pussy cat.
> What ' the puppy dog say?
> Rrow, doesn't he?
> Rrow, row-row-row.
> And what's the pussy cat say?
> Meow.
> There's the fish.
> The fishy.
> 'N' an egg.
> And a goat.

Example 22

[Interaction between an Australian mother and her 13-month-old son as they look at a picture book]

> mother: Where's the rooster?
> What does the rooster say?
> infant: Oooh.
> mother: Oooh?
> He does not.
> Does not.

Example 23

[An Australian mother's speech to her 9-month-old daughter]

> mother: Look at those little yellow beads.
> You go and get them for mummy.
> No.
> Not the red ones.
> Those ones over there.[Points]

Secondly, adults attempt to negotiate and fix the meaning of the infant's idiosyncratic signals (as in examples 24 and 25). These too can form the basis of a shared signal system, albeit one that is relatively short lived and has only a small number of initiates.

Example 24

[Interaction between a U.S. mother and her 14-month-old son]
    mother: People.
    infant: Pee-pee.
    mother: Is that what "Pee-pee" means?
               People?
    infant: Pee-pee [points towards door of the playroom].
    mother: What does "Pee-pee" mean?

Example 25

[Interaction between an Australian mother and her 11-month-old son]
    infant: Ah-du.
    mother: Ah-du?
               That's not dad.

It is clear from these examples that, despite the current emphasis on the implicit transmission of cultural norms, transmission also takes place explicitly. On some occasions the content of conversational turns may provide direct instruction about a culture's rules for communication. In the examples above, the failure of attempts to communicate and the process of language learning are mutually embedded. Such embedding can be expected whether the infant is learning standard signals from the mother, or whether the mother is learning idiosyncratic signals from the infant.

The signal system of the culture is, however, but one of the pieces of cultural information being explicitly transmitted in adults' speech to infants. For example, adults also specify the types of behaviours valued in the society (example 26), normative sex-appropriate preferences within the culture (example 27), and the nature and purpose of objects in the child's environment (example 28).

Example 26

[Australian mother's speech to her 12-month-old son, who is playing with a baby doll]
    mother: Give him a cuddle.
               Give him a cuddle.

Yes.
That's right.

Example 27

[As in example 26]
    mother: Doll's is girls' stuff, isn't they?

Example 28

[Australian mother's speech to her 16-month-old son]
    mother: Put the lid on the box.
              Look.
              It goes on here.
              See?
              On the box.

However, whether subtle or explicit, we know little about the influences of culture on language development. What knowledge we have is largely derived from studies of syntax. Very few emphasize the process of interaction.

Our ignorance of the types of communication children are exposed to across cultures may have important consequences for our understanding of language development. The types of parent–child interactions that have dominated the child development literature—those drawn from white, middle-class families in industrialized nations—may not be good reflections of the way the majority of the world's children learn language. This is likely to be the case because many cultures assign primary caregiving duties to siblings rather than parents, and because the cultural goals and assumptions held by white, middle-class parents are not shared in many other cultures. Indeed, they are often not shared by other subcultures in the same country. This does not discount the value of studies of white, middle-class parents and their children. It emphasizes, however, that these studies tell *a* story, not *the* story, and that no adequate understanding of the fulfillment of the human potential for language can be achieved solely based upon them.

The focus on white, middle-class values is, of course, not solely the product of the populations on which research has been conducted. Language researchers, being in the main white and middle-class themselves, have been induced with the same assumptions about the nature of infants and the type of skills one must learn in order to be a competent communicator. Both the questions researchers frame and the way they interpret the information they gather are necessarily influenced by such cultural factors. This does not, in itself, make the data or the interpretations less valuable. It does, however, highlight the importance of explicit statements about the culturally based assumptions of the research population and of the persons conducting the research. To date such statements have not been provided in language development research. Of course, cultural assumptions are difficult to identify when they are shared by researchers, their peers, and the population under study. However, they can be made visible by juxtaposing them with the assumptions made by members of other cultures. Therefore, a brief survey of adult-infant communication in four non-Western cultures follows. This suggests the wide variety of ways in which the negotiation of meaning can be constructed.

The Kaluli of Papua New Guinea

Many cultures hold assumptions about the nature of infants, the function of language, and the course of language development that differ from those reflected in most current analyses. One of these is the culture of the Kaluli in the southern highlands of Papua New Guinea. It is a culture that is distinguished by the absence of a babytalk register (Schieffelin & Ochs, 1983), or at least of a babytalk register that is similar to those found in other language systems (Snow & Ferguson, 1977). This alone would cause the communicative interactions in which Kaluli infants participate to take a distinctive form. However, the absence of a babytalk register appears to stem from distinctive Kaluli beliefs about infants and language, and these beliefs have a wider influence on speech directed to children.

The Kaluli report that infants have no understanding *(asugo andoma)*. The meaning of this expression is somewhat ambiguous, since Kaluli mothers often appear to behave as though their infants had considerable ability. For example, they attempt to shape their infants' unsocialized behaviors by "shaming" *(sasidiabo)*. If an infant reaches for something he is not supposed to touch, a mother may ask "It is yours?!" Kaluli mothers clearly expect this disciplining technique to be effective. Therefore they must, at minimum, assume that the infant can correctly interpret their communicative intent. (It is possible that they also expect the infant to understand the social prohibition against interfering with another's property.) Nevertheless, in accord with the belief that infants "have no understanding," Kaluli mothers rarely treat their infants as conversational partners. Imperatives and rhetorical questions are directed to them, but no verbal response is requested or expected from an infant. One would therefore not expect that noncomprehension signals would be directed to infants. They would be inappropriate on two counts. Firstly, they are redundant unless the infant is perceived to have made an attempt to communicate. Secondly, they are of limited use when infants are not expected to be able to do anything more than begin or cease activity in response to the spoken word (Schieffelin & Ochs, 1983).

Kaluli infants are not deprived of exposure to language. Indeed, they hear a rich variety of speech: they are greeted, expressive vocalizations are directed to them, and they hear speech directed to others as they are carried by their mothers in the fields and in the longhouse. However, the "protoconversations" (e.g., Trevarthen, 1977) in which adults and infants often engage in other cultures, and which have been thought to be an important precursor of language development (Trevarthen, 1979), are absent. Mothers and infants rarely gaze into each others' eyes, a pattern consistent with the Kaluli practice of not looking at the person to whom one is speaking. Neither do mothers interpret, and give vocal expression to, gurgles, cooing, or apparent infant preferences.

Nevertheless, mothers often take the speaking role of the infant. In Kaluli society, speaking ability is a primary indicator of social competence and a primary medium of social contact. As a result, learning how to talk is a major goal of socialization. While this may appear to be very "Western," its consequences are very "un-Western." Since one of the goals of communicative interactions is to display one's competence and independence, mothers often sit their babies facing away from themselves and towards the larger social group in the longhouse. On seeing this, older children will often greet the infant and address speech to him or her. The mother, in turn, will begin to move the infant, and speak on his or her behalf, in a high-pitched, nazalized voice. Thus, for Kaluli infants, most communicative interactions involve at least three participants, and, of these participants, it is their role that is the least important. When the mother "speaks" for her infant, she does not attempt to speak the thoughts and desires of her infant (since these are not believed to exist). Indeed, within the Kaluli culture it is inappropriate for anyone to talk about the feelings or thoughts of another. Instead, mothers appear to enact a social role, engaging in behaviors that are more characteristic of an older child than an infant. For example, when speaking for a baby, mothers take an assertive stand and use well-formed utterances. Thus, they present an image of a competent and self-controlled individual on the infant's behalf. Mothers do not use behavioral cues from their infants in framing these "dialogues."

Example 29

[Conversation in which a Kaluli mother speaks to Abi on behalf of her 3-

month-old son, Bage. Abi, the infant's brother, is holding a stick on his shoulder in a manner similar to that in which heavy patrol boxes are carried. A patrol box is usually carried on a pole between two men]

Abi:	Bage!
	Do you see my box here?
	Do you see it?
	Do you see it?
Mother:	(in high-pitched voice) My brother. I'll take half, my brother.
Abi:	(holding stick out) Mother, give him half.
	Give him half.
	Mother, my brother—here, here take half X
Mother:	(in her usual voice) Put it on the shoulder.
Abi:	(rests stick on infant's shoulder)

(Schieffelin & Ochs, 1983, p. 123)

The Kaluli note the onset of infant babbling *(dabedan)* but believe that these sounds do not serve a communicative function. Nor do they believe that babbling is related to later language development. For the Kaluli, language emerges when the child is first able to use two particular words, the words referring to *mother* and *breast*. However, the Kaluli manner of speaking to children does not become more "Western" once the child is perceived to be using language. When the child is judged to have begun speaking, the Kaluli embark upon a program of instruction through modeling. An adult or older child will provide an appropriate utterance followed by the command "say like that." Even at this stage, however, the content of the modeled utterance is not derived from the child's thoughts or emotions, but is based on what the other person considers to be culturally appropriate.

Once the child is acknowledged to be making attempts to communicate, noncomprehension signals emerge in speech to children. For the Kaluli, the responsibility for failed communications lies with the speaker. Mothers and other listeners make no effort to interpret unclear signals from the child. Instead, they attempt to elicit clearer signals by providing feedback meaning "Huh?" and "What?" Thus, young children are often provided with noncomprehension signals. Once children are able to speak, they are also taught to provide noncomprehension signals when they have not understood the speech of others. At an early age, children receive direct instruction, through modeling, of the ways in which this may be done. Thus, in the negotiation of meaning, very young children have similar communicative status as other members of the longhouse: They are expected to provide competent communication, and expected to require competent communication from others.

In summary, the patterns of communication found in this culture are very different from those reported in studies of white, middle-class families in industrialized countries. It can be seen that Kaluli culture influences the organization of communication. In consequence, patterns of communication convey cultural information. That is, the form and content of speech, as well as its developmental timing, are derived from, and therefore reveal, Kaluli beliefs concerning infants and communication. This content and form convey cultural information that may not be taught to children explicitly. Kaluli patterns of negotiation of meaning reveal beliefs about the responsibilities of speaker and listener, the lack of understanding of infants, beliefs about the way children learn language, and so on.

Few other anthropological studies of language development provide information specifically relevant to the negotiation of meaning. Many of those studies that are available are, nevertheless, useful in highlighting the assumptions white, middle-class parents and researchers bring to the context of communication. They also suggest different ways in which meaning might be negotiated with infants (or reasons why such negotiations might not take place).

One of these studies was conducted among the inhabitants of the island of Panay in the Philippines (Jocano, 1969a,b). Here, the cultural assumptions about language and infants are different from both those among the Kaluli and those of the white middle-class, and it would appear that negotiations are similarly different.

The People of Malitbog, The Philippines

In the barrio of Malitbog, language is not only a medium of communication but also has supernatural properties. For this reason, language skills have direct consequences for one's physical well-being. Infants are therefore very vulnerable until they are able to speak.

> Should the pulse of two individuals beat at the same time their eyes meet, the one who utters the first word casts a ?usug power over the other. The ?usug causes severe stomache ache. . . . Because infants cannot talk, they are liable to die from ?usug.
>
> (Jacano, 1969a, p. 29)

Not surprisingly then, adults consider changes in infants' communication patterns to be important developmental milestones. From the youngest ages, infants are exposed to a rich linguistic environment. They are sung to, and addressed both in an "everyday" speech style and in babytalk. Their status in conversation is, however, rather complex. In some aspects they are treated as equal partners. Thus, Jocano (1969a) reports that, even before children can fully respond to the speech of others, adults speak to them as though they are competent. In other respects however, children are assigned a subordinate role in conversation, especially once they are weaned. This status is likely to have a direct impact on the negotiation of meaning.

In the barrios, politeness is necessary to sustain social interaction. Villagers display great sensitivity to the shame of having their errors noted by others.

Example 30

Bado was somewhat drunk when he entered the house of Mal?am Itkit to join a group of young people who came to visit the old man. Because he did not call out, "Panagbalay" before entering, Mal?am Itak was mad. He spoke to him in a loud voice: "No character, no shame. You do not even bother to call out before entering." Bado unsheathed his bolo and lunged at the old man. Cooler heads and quicker hands prevented him from inflicting harm. When subdued, Bado kept saying: "Why did he shame me, why did he shame me?"

(Jocano, 1969b, p. 275)

Thus it is usual for rebuttals and criticism to be given diplomatically. Members of the barrio are sensitive to the shame felt when one is disagreed with or when one's language or behavior are noted as being inappropriate. The influence these considerations exert on casual conversation can be seen in an example from in another barrio.

Example 31

"Isn't it better to beautify the character *(Kalooban)* of the individual rather than the house?" . . . "Maybe so," he said. "But my father taught me a proverb which may answer your question. . . . If one beautifies the house, the character of the person becomes beautiful, too." . . . "Then why is it that my character is ugly when my home is beautiful?" I asked. His eyes twinkled as he answered: . . . "Because you are always out of your beautiful house and here in the muddy villages most of the time."

We both laughed. His answer is a classic in combining repartee with compliment—an act of rebuttal coupled with praise.

(Flavier, 1978, p. 133–134)

However, the pronounced attempts to avoid affront to one's conversational partner that can be expected in adult–adult speech appear to be abandoned when adults address children.

Example 32

[An old Philippino man to a young boy who is crying]

Huh—stop crying or I will cut off your testicles. Do you like to be a
kapun (i.e., castrated)?

(Jocano, 1969a, p. 42)

Example 33

[A Philippino grandmother shouting at a young girl who is crying]
Stop your crying and be a good girl or I will pull your clitoris and wind
it around your neck.

(Jocano, 1969a, p. 42)

Much of this change in tone can be accounted for by the role
seniority plays in organizing all social relationships in Malitbog. Whether
as children or adults, interactions between members of different gen-
erations are prescribed by cultural rules. Thus, except in extreme
circumstances, individuals do not verbally express disagreement with
older members of the barrio.

In addition to these general prescriptions are special rules governing
children's speech to adults. For example, whenever children address
their parents they are expected to lower their voices as a sign of respect.
Failure to do so brings swift reprisal. In addition, children are not
permitted to mention the names of their parents, either in referring to
them or in speaking directly to them.

Of particular relevance to the negotiation of meaning, however, is
the prohibition against children disputing with older persons, and the
general social rule that "a Malitbog child is better seen than heard"
(Jocano, 1969a, p. 77). Given the accumulated direction of available
evidence, it would appear unlikely that children in Malitbog often signal
that their speech has been misunderstood by an adult. Indicating that
an adult had made an error would need to be done carefully. Indeed,
given the subordinate status of children as conversational partners, all
negotiations of meaning between adults and children may occur relatively infrequently. Adults in Malitbog seem unlikely to find the speech
of children as salient as white, middle-class parents do.

Yet for the children of Malitbog, there are long and frequent releases
from the restrictions adults impose on their vocal behavior. From the
time an infant is able to walk, he or she spends most of the daylight
hours outdoors, in the company of other children. While the parents
work, siblings and other older children assume responsibility for the
supervision of young children. Thus, the language-learning child may
have greater exposure to the speech of other children than that of
adults. Many of the games that occupy these daylight hours appear to
involve considerable quarreling and negotiation (Jocano, 1969a). Thus,
it seems likely that most negotiations occur in the context of peer

interaction. For this reason the negotiations of meaning experienced by children in Malitbog are likely to have quite a different structure to those reported in studies of interactions between middle-class parents and their infants.

The Qalandar, Pakistan

Another anthropological study makes clear the connection between cultural beliefs and language directed to children among the nomadic entertainers of Pakistan, the Qalandar (Berland, 1982). As in the barrio, so here, language skills have survival value. In this case, however, the focus is on economic survival. It is not surprising, then, that the verbal abilities of infants and young children are explicitly fostered. Several aspects of the Qalandar world-view suggest that the negotiation of meaning between adults and infants and young children is likely to occur regularly.

Qalandar society is an egalitarian one in which there are few status distinctions between children and adults. Young children are actively involved, not only in the tent's economic activity and its rewards, but also in some decision making. Communicative interactions involving infants and very young children also reflect the egalitarian nature of Qalandar society. For example, the Qalandar pride themselves in their facility for creative abuse. Very young children are both the originators and targets of this abuse.

Example 34

[Young Qalandar daughter to her father who has been scolding her]
Stop barking. . . . go put your head in your mother's vagina.
(Berland, 1982, p. 112)

Example 35

[Qalandar mother expressing her displeasure to her daughter]
You are made of feces!
(Berland, 1982, p. 112)

The novelty this egalitarianism holds for the sedentary communities is turned to economic advantage in an entertainment routine called the "joking child" *(bacha jhamura)* that is a standard in the Qalandar repertoire. The routine is normally performed by an adult male and a child, and by the age of four all Qalandar children have already learned half-a-dozen roles by rote.

Example 36

[A typical *bacha jhamura* routine between a father and his son]

father:	Bacha jamuray!
child:	Waa Waa!
father:	Is a sheep bigger or a lamb?
child:	Lamb!
father:	Is a father bigger or a son?
child:	Son!
father:	Is a teacher bigger or a student?
child:	Student!
father:	I am your father.
child:	And I am your grandfather!
father:	Is mother bigger or daughter?
child:	Daughter!
father:	How many wives do you have?
child:	Two!
father:	Where do they sleep?
child:	On *charpoy!*
father:	Where do you sleep?
child:	In the fireplace!
father:	Why did you perform this?
child:	For my stomach!
father:	Now Jhamuray, say "Salaam" to everyone.

(Berland, 1982, p. 101–102)

Most of these routines are based on parodies of established social roles, especially those that relate to authority and sex-role relationships. Here the child responds with patently false answers and yet gains the upper hand over the adult.

Given the egalitarian nature of Qalandar verbal interactions and the lack of sensitivity they show to unflattering verbal responses from others, there would appear to be no prescriptions against children providing noncomprehension signals to adults, or adults directing them to children, when attempts to communicate are unsuccessful. Indeed, since infants are viewed as being responsive individuals from birth, and since the verbal facility of children has economic consequences for the troup, it is likely that negotiations of meaning involving infants and young children are relatively frequent.

Because precocious development has economic rewards, the caregiving Qalandar infants receive is intensive and is provided by many different persons. Infants are the recipients of a steady stream of songs and speech, often from tentmembers other than their parents. By the time infants are 3 or 4 weeks old, they are integral members of the Qalandar camp and the diversity of their caregivers increases, for both parents and other family members are often occupied in economic activities that prohibit them providing care for the infant. Most of the custodians are women. However, older men and boys between 8 and 13 years of age also spend considerable time providing care for infants. Indeed, older siblings are given responsibility for much of the training the infant receives.

In summary, Qalandar infants are treated as competent and valued speakers. They could therefore be expected to differ from the Kaluli and barrio in the nature of the signals that are negotiated. Because Qalandar infants are likely to negotiate with a wide variety of caregivers and because siblings are the primary instructors in cultural information, they are also likely to differ from the white middle-class in the pattern of negotiation.

The Kuna, Panama

Lest the reader should conclude that only white, middle-class parents refrain from directing sexual abuse at infants and young children, the current survey ends with information concerning the Kuna Indians of the San Blas islands in Panama. The Kuna culture exerts far more stringent prohibitions against talk related to sexual matters than can be found among Western cultures.

The Kuna have developed an intricate system of speech styles and speech conventions with which children must become familiar in order to be competent speakers. However, mere competence is not the goal of the Kuna. Language abilities play a central role in the organization of Kuna society. Sophisticated speaking ability brings with it high social status. On other grounds too, language skills are viewed as worthy of the investment of time and energy. For the Kuna, speech accomplishes work (C. Cain, personal communication, December 5, 1987). It is also an activity from which they derive much pleasure, whatever the topic or context. Indeed, it could be argued that verbal skills have a more exalted position in the culture of the Kuna than they have among the white middle class in industrialized countries. Most, if not all, ritual and leadership roles in Kuna society are defined in terms of speaking. There is a focus on the acquisition and practice of verbal abilities that continues throughout the lifespan.

The Kuna use an elaborate set of distinct, yet related, linguistic varieties and styles, encompassing several subvarieties and substyles. These are differentiated by grammatical and lexical features and by the degree to which they employ metaphor and symbolism (Sherzer, 1983). There are four named Kuna linguistic varieties. The most basic of these is *tule kaya,* the everyday language of the Kuna that is accessible to all. This includes a range of speech styles, from formal to informal, and a number of specific subvarieties. Another is *sakla kaya*, the language used by chiefs during performances in the Gathering House. A third, *suar nuchu kaya*, is the language used in chants to the stick dolls and to the spirit world. The last of the major linguistic varieties is *kantule kaya*, which is used by the *ikar* knowers during puberty ceremonies.

In addition to these four major linguistic traditions are those subvarieties that are associated with particular social groups and verbal genres. Thus, for example, the "everyday" language of the Kuna *(tule kaya)* includes the language primarily reserved for the "chief's spokesman" *(arkar kaya)*, the language forms used by women in the genres they alone speak *(ome kaya)*, and the language used by all Kuna when telling stories *(kwento kaya)*.

The four major linguistic varieties are sufficiently different from one another to require specialized training. Difficulties of interpretation experienced by the unitiated are primarily due to the Kuna tradition of holding several parallel vocabularies for basic features of their environment and society. Thus, for example, the word for "woman" in everyday Kuna is *ome*, while in the stick doll language it is *walepukwa*, and in the language of the *ikar* knowers it is *yai* (Sherzer, 1983). Even within a particular linguistic variety there is considerable proliferation of lexical expressions for a single meaning. Thus, within everyday Kuna, there exists not just the basic term for crab, *suka*, but also a number of "play names" (Sherzer, 1983): *pormo yarkan* (tin can back), *kapur ipya* (hot pepper eyes), and *kampulet mali* (chair feet).

There are also day and night names for some plants and animals (Sherzer, 1983). For example, the day name for guava is *marya*, while its night name is *kaya piri* (curved mouth). The day names are taboo at night and vice versa.

The situation is further complicated by the tendency of words in one language variety to take on new meanings in others. When words taken from everyday Kuna are used in the ritualized linguistic varieties, the meaning is often figurative. These figurative relationships vary in their obscurity. For example, the word *tuttu*, meaning "flower" in everyday Kuna, is used to mean "woman" in the language of the chiefs, while the words *ipsya suli*, meaning "no eyes" in everyday Kuna, are used to mean "pieces of meat" in puberty rituals (Sherzer, 1983).

In addition to the difficulties presented to the process of negotiation by the communication system itself are others that result from more general cultural values and prohibitions. Primary among these are the taboos that exist for some words and topics of communication. Everything to do with sex is taboo. Clearly, however, it is often necessary for adults to communicate information about sexual functioning to one another. In order to comply with the prohibition, these communications take indirect forms. For example, when a woman is menstruating, she says, "I have a pain in my knee" (Nördenskiold, 1938, p. 375). Many taboos exert a similar influence over the form and function of Kuna communication. In order to comply with the taboo against the topic of hunting, for example, one says, "Tomorrow I shall gather material for weaving baskets" rather than "Tomorrow I shall go out on a tapir hunt" (Nördenskiold, 1938, p. 375).

Obviously this pattern of indirect communication further complicates the negotiation of meaning among Kuna. In particular, it is likely to hinder attempts by infants and young children to grasp their speaker's communicative intent. In the case of the sexual taboo, this is deliberate. However, at some point in the course of language development children must learn to distinguish between signals that encode actual knee pains and similar signals that do not, and signals that encode the intention to gather material for weaving and those that do not. For the child learning Kuna, the connection between signal and meaning is not only arbitrary, but also inconsistent.

One might expect, however, that problems of communication would not be restricted to young children. The negotiation of meaning, even among adults, is a complex task in Kuna society. Given the range of potential meanings, one might expect attempts to communicate to often fail. However, several distinctive features of Kuna discourse may act to minimize the difficulties of both speaker and listener. There is great redundancy in Kuna speech, whether it occurs as a ritual monologue or in the context of informal dialogue. In addition, listener feedback signalling acknowledgement appears to be unusually frequent in informal conversation (see example 37), and is "programmed" into the structure of ritualized dialogue (Sherzer, 1983).

Example 37

[Extract from the speech of an elderly Kuna man retelling a story about a boating accident to a friend]

     speaker: He told me
                It's true, ah.
                In Ukkupsenikine, a foreigner.
                He died, I tell you an American.
     friend: Ahh.
                An American died.
     speaker: An American died.
                He was speaking to me about this.

He [another person] was listening.
"There were four," he says.

friend: An American.
speaker: "They were coming in a motorboat," he says.
friend: Ah.
speaker: Probably with a sail, I think, that's my opinion.
friend: Ah.

(Sherzer, 1983, p. 44)

Other patterns in Kuna speech may also help to reduce the frequency with which attempts to communicate are likely to fail. There is a fairly direct correspondence between the rituality of a topic and the accessibility of the language associated with it. Business transactions and other necessary and everyday forms of communication are discussed in highly accessible language *(tule kaya)*. Curative chants and those relating to puberty rites are the most secret domains of Kuna knowledge and are encoded in the most obscure language. In these cases, the intelligibility of the speech to members of the village is immaterial, since they are not the ones to whom the speech is addressed.

Despite the assistance provided by such patterns of speech, the language-learning task of Kuna children is an intimidating one. It might be expected that much adult language remains unintelligible to Kuna children for an extended period. Yet the Kuna consider that language learning, like all other forms of learning, is natural and normal, requiring no special theories or training. They believe that "children just learn to talk through active participation in speech events, as speakers, listeners and audience" (Sherzer, 1983). Consistent with this belief is the policy of allowing Kuna infants and children access to almost all linguistic activities in the community. There is much informal talking to children, and a child's speech is listened to with interest and respect. Children often practice specific speech genres they have heard, and it appears that Kuna adults find the observation of this learning process both interesting and entertaining (Sherzer, 1983). Children are treated as having communicative competence. Thus, at quite early ages, they may be required to use some of the more complex verbal skills they have acquired.

It is remarkable how young children, suddenly accused of a misdeed—stealing, fighting, or bothering someone—are able to defend themselves with a long eloquent speech before an audience in the "gathering house."

(Sherzer, 1983, p. 224)

In addition to everyday Kuna, and the ritualistic speech styles, children are also exposed to speech subvarieties such as that used in story telling *(kwento kaya)*. Parents and grandparents transmit much information about the Kuna world view via this medium. In the example below, the partridge *(swirinitti)* is described as a creature created by God as food for man. The bird, who can both feel and think, reluctantly submits to a divine plan that he is powerless to fight against.

Example 38

[Extract from a story a Kuna grandfather chanted to his grandchildren]

Because Tiolele [the supreme deity] cares for us,
He provides us a well-protected home
And good food in the midst of the forest
Near Man's plantation.
Yet because God has created us for man's food,
We live in constant danger.
What a sorrowful fate.
To become food for these human beings!
Swirinitti-Swirinitti. . . .

Whenever these human beings steal our little ones,
I think to myself:
"How can they care for my little ones
As their mother does?"
Swirinitti-Swirinitti.

They will only give my little ones
Scrimpy corn meal.
Swirinitti-Swirinitti. . . .

What can I do but grieve for my fate
And the fate of my little ones?
The Supreme Deity has created us
As food for human beings.
Swirinitti-Swirinitti.

These human beings cannot care
For my little birds as I can.
They will raise them on scrimpy corn meal.

(Keeler, 1956, p. 126)

The distinctive quality of speech found in the story-telling language is echoed in another important speech subvariety. The society of the Kuna is a matrilineal one, and Kuna women are largely responsible for transmitting cultural information from one generation to another. Lullabies are a primary vehicle for this (McCosker, 1974). Males know these songs, but do not sing them to children.

From birth until 4 years of age, children are sung lullabies many times each day. In addition to quietening children, lullabies introduce them to their position within the family, the work of their parents, and the duties that will be expected of them in the future.

Despite the important role they play in the transmission of cultural information, the language of the lullabies presents difficulties of interpretation. For example, long forms of words are abbreviated, and some archaic words are used. Again, however, the high level of redundancy that characterizes other speech to children (and indeed, all Kuna communication) can easily be seen.

Example 39

[Extract from a Kuna woman's lullaby to her sons]

You are all little boys
You will go with your father to the mountains to work
You are the boys who will grow up
At the side of your father you will go to the mountains
Papa will teach you to work in the mountains
At the side of your father you are cutting down small trees
And your sisters in the house will be thinking of you
They will always greet you upon returning to the house
Your sisters will wash your clothes that you use for working
You (in my arms) are to work in the mountains
Because of this you are growing up at the side of your father
At the side of your father to cut down small trees
For this you are growing up
Alone you grow at the side of your father
                                                    (McCosker, 1974, p. 133–134)

It is obvious from the examples above that not only the forms of language addressed to Kuna infants and children, but also their content, are highly complex. Infants are seen as having a potential for understanding that would, for example, be alien to the culture of the Kaluli. Despite this, most of the speech addressed to Kuna infants and young children appears to take the form of a monologue. In the case of the Kuna, the unidirectional nature of much speech to infants appears not to reflect a belief that infants are incompetent (cf. the Kaluli) or that infants are socially inferior (cf. the barrio of Malitbog), but rather to reflect the performative quality found even in colloquial Kuna speech (see example 37).

In summary, the complexity of the Kuna signal system would suggest that attempts to communicate often fail. Despite this, currently available studies of Kuna patterns of speaking make no reference to extended negotiations of meaning. It therefore appears likely that features in the organization of Kuna discourse, such as a high level of redundancy and the expectation of frequent feedback from the listener (or of no response from the listener, in the case of the monologues), help to minimize the frequency with which attempts at shared understanding fail and the extent to which those failures that do occur are introduced as topics of conversation. Under these circumstances, the negotiation of meaning might only rarely be observable in Kuna discourse, regardless of the age of speaker and listener.

A Conclusion About Cultures

Some notion of the degree of variability in the speech environments experienced by infants can be glimpsed from the brief comparison of the Kaluli, Kuna, Qalandar and Philippino cultures outlined above. In each case the degree of training children required in order to learn language and appropriate methods of instruction are perceived differently. Similarly, the types of persons who provide care for language learning children and the variety of language forms they use also differ across the cultures. Each of these factors might be expected to impact on the way meaning is negotiated with infants and young children.

In white, middle-class families in industrialized countries, negotiations are frequent. Among the Kaluli of Papua New Guinea, they are completely absent. When negotiations do occur, the form they take is shaped by one's cultural beliefs about the development of communication skills. Thus, while the Kaluli do not negotiate meaning with their children until a relatively late age, they immediately demand clear and well-formed utterances. While white, middle-class adults carry much of the burden of communication, for example, by guessing the infant's meaning or elaborating on his signal, the Kaluli insist that the infant communicator bear this burden alone.

It is apparent, then, that the negotiation of meaning is a cultural construction. White, middle-class parents tend to ignore the obvious immaturity of their infants and treat them as though they are competent conversational partners, with something of interest to say and a means of saying it. Negotiations of meaning between adults and infants therefore result. The developmental timing and form of these negotiations are not prescribed by the biology of the infant, but by the cultural background of the adult. The beliefs adults bring to the context of communication exert a greater influence over their interpretation of infant behaviours than do the characteristics of these behaviours themselves.

Thus, there is a correspondence between cultural beliefs and the organization of communication in general, and the negotiation of meaning in particular. However, the relationship is not always a direct one. Consequently, cultures with markedly different belief systems may produce superficially similar patterns of communication, while similar cultures may produce superficially different ones. For example, much of the speech directed to both Kaluli and Kuna infants requires no response from the child. Available evidence suggests that among the Kaluli this practice reflects the belief that infants are incapable of responding, while among the Kuna it merely reflects the performative nature of many of the speech styles in their culture. Indeed, speech to Kuna infants appears to be based on the assumption that they have considerable linguistic skills.

It can be seen from the cross-cultural comparison provided here that the negotiation of meaning may be organized as a collaborative task performed by equals (as in white, middle-class populations) or as a lesson given by a more competent third party to a less competent participant (as among the Kaluli). The patterns of organization seen in the negotiation of meaning provide implicit instruction to infants about their communicative status within their cultures. However, it is also possible to explore the indirect transmission of cultural values through a detailed investigation of patterns of communication within a single culture. It is to such an investigation that this discussion now turns.

AN EMPIRICAL STUDY OF THE NEGOTIATION OF MEANING BETWEEN MOTHERS AND THEIR 8- TO 18- MONTH-OLD INFANTS[4]

The negotiation of meaning between infants and adults is a cultural construction. It involves the attribution of intentionality to infant behaviors that may or may not be intentional. It should be clear from the previous discussion, however, that no more substantial phenomena than cultural constructions are available. Different cultures may construct the psychological functioning of infants in different ways, but all are constructions. It is not useful to ask which construction is correct, or more correct than others. What may be of interest is to ask what consequences these different constructions have for the course of interactions and development.

Just as differences between cultures are reflected in the communi-

---

[4] A more detailed description of the procedure and results for this study was provided by Robinson (1988).

cation directed to infants, so too is diversity within a culture. For reasons of simplicity, cultures have earlier been referred to as though they are monolithic entities. On the contrary, however, cultural groups are loosely integrated communities embracing a variety of perspectives. The present study explores the diversity that exists in the speech directed to Australian infants by their mothers. All the mothers were white; most were middle-class.

The study focused on the emergence of negotiation skills during infancy. It should be clear that the results apply only to the culture in which the data were collected. Kaluli infants, for example, will learn negotiation skills at a different age and in a different way. Moreover, "emergence" can only be defined in culture-dependent terms.

In cultures in which infants are believed to have the capacity for intentional communication, adults will perceive that some of an infant's attempts to communicate fail. In a culture in which infant behaviors are salient, adults may provide noncomprehension signals following some or all communication failures. The provision of these signals does not necessarily reflect a belief in the infant's ability to understand the signal or to respond to it. Adults often direct speech to inanimate objects (e.g., cars, computers) without any expectation that the object will comprehend. Nevertheless, the presence of a noncomprehension signal affords the child the opportunity to respond.

Within cultures in which infants are treated as conversational partners, there are several potential sources of misunderstanding (Ryan, 1974). Firstly, the listener may have difficulty determining whether a message has been sent. This may occur when a child makes an intentional but uninterpretable noise that is without familiar intonation, gestures or any apparent relation to the setting or preceding communication. The listener must decide whether or not the child's intention was communicative. Alternatively, the child may produce noises that are not part of the adult lexicon, but are produced in such a way as to suggest to adult listeners that the infant is attempting to communicate. In this case, the listener's task lies in identifying the referent for the child's signal. A third type of difficulty arises when the infant utters a recognizable word the referent of which is apparent but the communicative intent of which is unclear. Lastly, difficulty may be encountered when a child produces the sound of a standard word, but uses it to convey an idiosyncratic meaning. Each of these sources of difficulty also arise when adults seek to interpret infants' nonverbal communications. Given this variety of sources of misunderstanding, one might expect many different types of negotiations to follow failed attempts to communicate.

Previous Research

There is a growing body of literature concerning the number and type of noncomprehension signals that white, middle-class adults direct to infants, and the types of repair responses children make in return. However, there have been relatively few studies (e.g., Golinkoff, 1986) that have examined the negotiation of meaning beyond these two conversational turns.

The frequency with which infants and very young children are exposed to noncomprehension signals appears to be influenced by many factors, including the context of communication (Golinkoff, 1986) and child characteristics (Tamir, 1980). It is not surprising, then, that there is little consensus among studies regarding this measure's developmental course. Indeed, there is currently evidence supporting the conclusions that there is an increase (Shatz, 1979), a decrease (Corsaro, 1977; Golinkoff, 1986), and no change (Cherry, 1979; Gallagher, 1981) in the frequency of noncomprehension signals with increases in child age.

Studies of the type of noncomprehension signals that middle-class adults direct to infants and very young children also show diversity. However, they suggest that adults often use relatively more requests for confirmation than requests for repetition/reformulation with younger children (Corsaro, 1977; Gallagher, 1981; Golinkoff, 1986), and use specific requests for clarification more often in speech to older than younger children (Gallagher, 1981).

By 2 years of age, children demonstrate an ability to respond appropriately to noncomprehension signals (Anselmi, Tomasello & Acunzo, 1986, Gallagher, 1981). They are able to discriminate between, and respond differentially to, specific and nonspecific clarification questions (Anselmi et al., 1986) and to repair failures of both gestural (Wilcox & Howse, 1982) and verbal communication (Wilcox & Webster, 1980). Moreover, they make such repairs selectively to noncomprehension signals and misinterpretations (Wilcox & Howse, 1982; Wilcox & Webster, 1980). From 12 months of age onwards, children's repertoire of repair skills appears to include repetitions, elaborations, rephrasings, and confirmations/disconfirmations (Golinkoff, 1986). In addition, infants show considerable persistence in their attempts to negotiate meaning (Golinkoff, 1986).

Previous research in the field has clearly sought to distill the common features of negotiations across different conversational partners. The aim has been to arrive at general conclusions regarding the frequency of behaviors, the ability levels of children of differing ages, and average developmental patterns. By doing so, they have obscured one of the main foci of the current study: individual differences in patterns of negotiation. Individual differences are central to the study of cultural influence,[5] for the locus of culture is the individual (see Valsiner, this volume).

The Conversational Sequence Under Study

The study reported in this chapter involved event sampling. The first turn in the focal conversational sequence was the infant's initiation of an attempt to communicate. The second type of turn was the listener's noncomprehension signal, which indicated that the speaker's message was not received or was not understood. The third type of turn was the infant's attempt to repair the communication failure. The optional fourth type of turn was the listener's acknowledgement that communication had been effected. The sequence may involve any number of turns and extend in duration for as long as both parties wish.

Previous research has paid little attention to infants' understanding of the negotiation of meaning—that is, whether they grasp the conversational function of noncomprehension signals and repairs. Few attempts have been made to determine the selectivity with which infants provide repair-like responses following noncomprehension signals. To overcome this limitation, the present study compared the frequency with which these responses followed noncomprehension signals with the frequency with which similar responses followed acknowledgements and "no relevant responses."

Method

A study of 70 Australian mother–infant pairs was conducted. There were 24 infants in the 8–10 month group, 32 in the 11–14 month group and 14 in the 15–18 month group. All observations were made during freeplay in a standardized playroom.

The video record for each session was viewed by observers who judged whether the infant was attempting to communicate. Such judgements were based on both the vocal and gestural behaviors of the infant. For each instance of an attempt to communicate by an infant, the mother's immediately succeeding behavior was coded either as indicating that the infant's communication had been understood (acknowledgement), a signal that the infant's communication had not been received or had not been understood (noncomprehension signal), or as

---

[5] It is clear that individual differences also reflect physical, historical, and temperamental differences, etc., between persons.

not providing any feedback regarding the success or failure of the infant's attempt to communicate (no relevant response).

Noncomprehension signals were also subject to more detailed level of analysis. They were classified as either a request for repetition/reformulation, a request for specification/elaboration, or a request for confirmation.

The child's response following each of the three types of maternal feedback was also noted according to the categories provided in Table 4.

Calculations of interobserver agreement were based on approximately 20% of data. Agreement was calculated by dividing the number of agreements by the sum of the number of agreements and the number of disagreements. Levels of agreement for the categories outlined in Figure 1 ranged between 79% and 100%.

Results and Discussion

Age differences. Because they are unable to use the standard signal system, most signals made by infants are unclear and/or incomplete. Despite this, the proportion of infants' attempts to communicate that were met with noncomprehension signals was relatively low. The highest level of noncomprehension signals for any of the age groups was a mean of 10%. Many of the mothers did not signal noncomprehension following any of their infants' attempts to communicate. In addition, noncomprehension signals accounted for a very small proportion of the total number of utterances mothers directed towards their infants. No consistent age-related patterns were found for either of these measures of the frequency of noncomprehension signals. Neither were there age-related patterns in the type of noncomprehension signals mothers provided.

Some types of conversational feedback were more likely to receive a repair-like response from infants than others (see Table 5). In each age group a Friedman Two-way Analysis of Variance was used to examine differences in the relative frequency of repetitions and reformulations following acknowledgements, noncomprehension signals and the absence of feedback. These revealed that fewer repair-like responses occurred in the absence of maternal feedback than following acknowledgements or noncomprehension signals ($x_r^2 = 16.5$, $p<.01$) for the 8- to 10-month-old infants. There were no differences in the 11–14 month group. However, among 15- to 18-month-old infants, repair-like responses were more likely to follow noncomprehension signals than either acknowledgements or the absence of feedback ($x_r^2 = 8.0$, $p<.02$).

When response patterns for individual infants were examined, it was

Table 5.   Mean Relative Frequency with which Three Types of Conversational Feedback were Followed by a Repair-like Response

Feedback	Age group (months)					
	8-10		11-14		15-18	
Noncomprehension signal	36.3	(28.8)*	37.0	(31.4)	49.1	(34.6)
Acknowledgement	27.9	(13.4)	20.3	(21.8)	9.3	(3.7)
No feedback	10.1	(10.0)	13.1	(13.5)	8.2	(6.8)
N**		18		23		12

  * Standard deviation
  ** Only infants who received at least 1 instance of each type of feedback were included.

found that many infants were selective in providing repetitions and reformulations following noncomprehension signals. For each mother-infant pair in which noncomprehension signals were observed, two z scores were calculated. These tested the strength of the association between maternal noncomprehension signals and repair-like responses, and between maternal acknowledgements and repair-like responses. Despite their appropriateness, few repetitions and reformulations were produced when mothers did not provide conversational feedback. Thus, joint consideration of the z scores for noncomprehension signals and acknowledgements provided an index of the selectiveness with which infants provided repair-like responses. Infants who provided both a greater number of repair-like responses following noncomprehension signals, and fewer repair-like responses following acknowledgements, than could be expected by chance were judged to be behaving selectively. In the 8–10 month group one infant (5.6%) met the criterion for selective responding. In the 11–14 and 15–18 month groups this was done by four (17.4%) and three (25%) infants respectively. (The level expected by chance is 0.25%).

Few infants made conversational repairs by providing "Yes/No" responses following requests for confirmation. When these responses did occur they were always accompanied by a repetition or reformulation.

The structure of negotiations. The model provided a context in which the complexity of the interactions could be examined. Lengthy negotiation episodes are of particular interest because they are unlikely to occur fortuitously. Persistence in signalling, and the substitution or augmentation of one signal by another, usually reflects some understanding of the process of negotiation.

It was found that some infants in all three groups participated in extended bouts of negotiation. Following a failed attempt to communicate, one 8-month-old and three 9-month-old infants appropriately participated in negotiations that involved six or more turns. That is, they persisted in repeating or reformulating their signal in at least two turns when their mothers failed to receive or failed to understand their messages. However, in each of these cases the infant failed to meet the criterion for selective responding (above), making interpretation of the finding difficult.

In general, there were few extended negotiations in the young group, and those that did occur often followed maternal refusals rather than maternal noncomprehension signals. Nevertheless, evidence that infants younger than 12 months of age can negotiate meaning following a failed attempt to communicate was found. A large number of complex negotiations took place between a mother and her 10-month-old son. While this infant was not typical of others in his age group, his behavior showed the level of understanding that is possible among infants of his age. A short extract from this infant's record is provided below. It contains two extended negotiations in close succession. The conversational events involved in these episodes are displayed in Figures 2 and 3. It should be noted that in Episode 2 the infant's attempt to communicate was successful, even though he was not given the object he desired. The infant met the criterion for selective responding.

Episode 1

1. Infant vocalizes "Eh" and extends his arm towards a table containing a box of facial tissues, an alphabet book, an intercom system, and a container of disposable washcloths. The infant is approximately 1.5m from the table, but does not move towards it.
2. What? This book?
3. The infant maintains his gaze on the table and continues to extend his arm towards it.
4. This book? [Spoken as the mother moves the magazine she has been holding into contact with the infant's hand.]
5. The infant pushes the magazine away while maintaining his gaze towards the table. He again extends his arm towards it, and repeats the "Eh" vocalization in a higher pitch.
6. No.
7. This one? [Spoken as the mother picks up the wash cloth container and holds it out to the infant, who does not look at it.]
8. The infant's gaze and his extended arm are directed towards the table. He vocalizes, "Nnn." The infant looks at the wash cloth container and guides his mother's hand holding the container to

the floor. He taps the container on the lid once. He then returns his gaze towards the table and vocalizes, "Eh" twice.

9. What? This? [Spoken as the mother picks up the box of tissues]
10. The infant vocalizes "Mm," smiles and lowers his arm.
11. The mother places the box of tissues on the floor next to the infant.

End of Episode 1

The infant hits the box, picks it up, examines its sides, examines its interior, then discards it. The infant explores the wash cloth container's lid briefly.

Episode 2

1. The infant glances towards his mother then extends his arm towards the table, looks towards it, and vocalizes, "Eh."
2. What?
3. The infant continues to gaze and extend his arm towards the table.
4. What now?
5. The infant stretches further towards the table, looks toward it and vocalizes, "Eh."
6. This book. [Spoken as the mother offers the alphabet book.]
7. The infant glances at the book briefly, but squirms his body away from it as it approaches, and again reaches and gazes towards the table.
8. No. You can't have that.
9. The infant maintains his reaching gesture, continues to look towards the table, and makes a giggle-like vocalization.
10. No.
11. The infant continues to extend his arm towards the table, and to look towards it, and vocalizes, "Mm."
12. No. [Said more firmly]
13. The infant looks at his mother, but continues to extend his arm towards the table. He makes a "Neh" vocalization with rising intonation.
14. No.
15. & 16.   The infant returns his gaze to the table, but lowers his arm and shortly begins to look at a magazine on the floor next to him. He turns the pages and plays contendedly by himself for some time.

The Codes (CI, NR, Ack, etc.) in Figures 2 and 3 are numbered

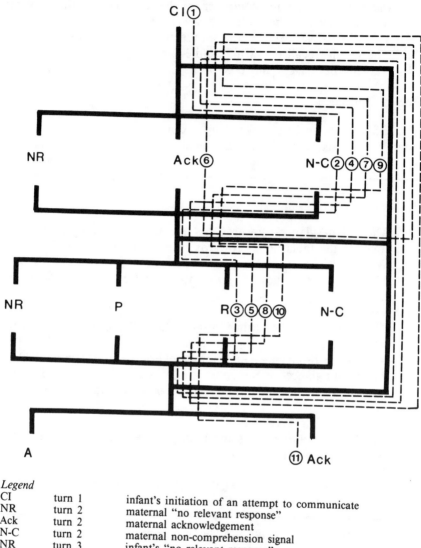

Figure 2.   A schematic representation of a negotiation episode involving a ten-month-old infant and his mother: Episode 1.

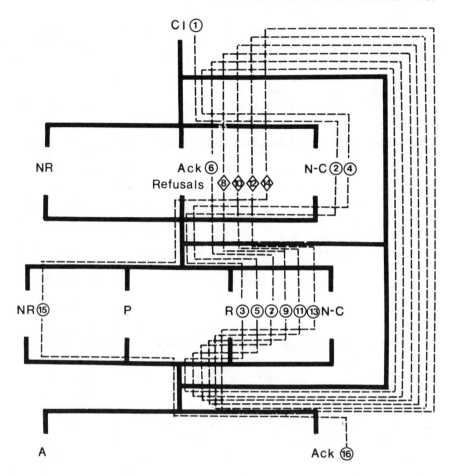

Legend

CI	turn 1	infant's initiation of an attempt to communicate
NR	turn 2	maternal "no relevant response"
Ack	turn 2	maternal acknowledgement
N-C	turn 2	maternal non-comprehension signal
NR	turn 3	infant's "no relevant response"
P	turn 3	infant's prompt for acknowledgement
R	turn 3	infant's repetition/reformulation
N-C	turn 3	infant's non-comprehension signal
A	turn 4	negotiation abandoned
Ack	turn 4	negotiation successful—usually signalled by an acknowledgement

Figure 3. A schematic representation of a negotiation episode involving a ten-month-old infant and his mother: Episode 2.

according to the sequence in which they occurred in a particular negotiation. The events in each episode can therefore be traced simply by following the numbers in order. The numbering of the events in the text (above) corresponds to the code bearing the same number in the figures.

The two examples above are of particular interest because the infant understood the process of negotiation so well that he was able to use it for other ends. Although each of the episodes began with a request for a specific object, the focus of the infant's behavior slowly shifted until negotiation itself became central, and not merely a means to an end. For as long as his mother remained a co-operative speaker, the infant was able to use the process of negotiation as a method both of sustaining interaction, and of inducing his mother to offer an assortment of interesting objects.

Individual differences. The model of the communication processes outlined in Figure 1 also provides a basis for the comparison of negotiations across individuals. In the form in which the model has thus far been presented, it is only possible to display one complex negotiation at a time. However, if the recursive loops in the model are laid end to end it is possible to display the complete set of negotiation episodes in which a mother and infant engaged on a single figure.

All the negotiations of meaning between the 10-month-old infant (above) and his mother are displayed in Figure 4. It can be seen that the 30 attempts to communicate made by the infant resulted in 14 different types of negotiations. Most of these patterns of negotiation occurred only once during the period of data collection. This was the case with the negotiation sequences labelled 1,2,3,4,5,6,7,8,9,10, and 11. Sequence 12 occurred twice, sequence 13 eleven times, and sequence 14 six times. It can be seen that more of the infant's attempts to communicate received an acknowledgment than any other form of maternal feedback. Three of the sequences, 6, 10 and 3, involved the mother providing both a noncomprehension signal and an acknowledgement within a single turn. This occurred on conversational turns 2, 6 and 6 respectively.

The negotiation episodes displayed above in Figures 2 and 3 are represented in Figure 4 as sequences 3 and 1, respectively. It can be seen that sequence 1 is the longest episode in which the mother and infant participated, while sequence 3 is the third longest.

The pattern of negotiations between this infant and his mother can be compared with those found for other pairs. For example, one mother of an 8-month-old infant had a very different style of interaction with her son. She was one of the few mothers who spent most of the session reading the magazines provided in the playroom. Her behavior allowed,

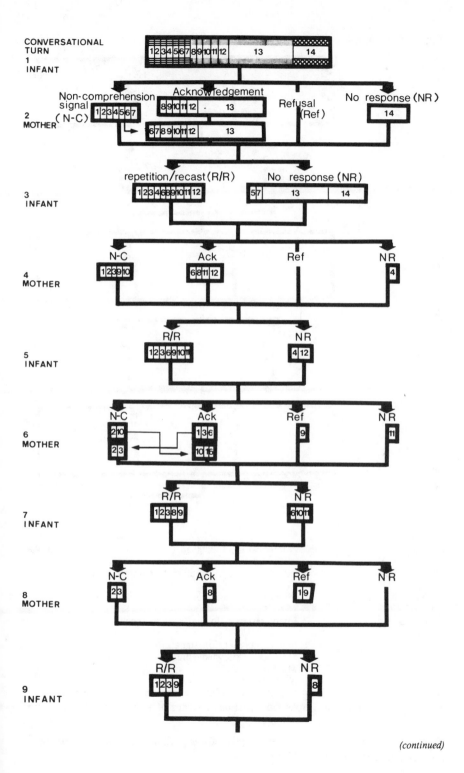

(continued)

Figure 4. (Continued)

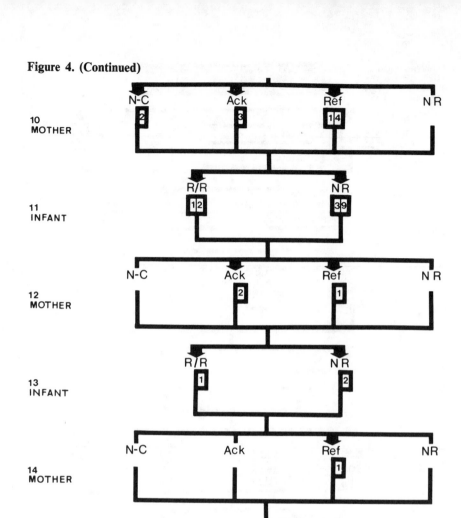

Legend

1,2,3 . . . etc. in bar graph	Numerical label assigned to all negotiations following the same path
Conversational turn 1	Infant initiates an attempt to communicate
Conversational turn 2,4,6 . . .	Maternal feedback to infant's signal
Conversational turn 3,5,7 . . .	Infant response to maternal feedback
N-C	Non-comprehension signal
Ack	Maternal acknowledgement
Ref	Maternal refusal
NR	No relevant response
R/R	Repetition or reformulation response from infant

Each 1/10 inch of the bar graphs represents one instance of a negotiation following the path indicated

Figure 4. A schematic representation of all negotiation episodes involving a mother and her 10-month-old son

indeed necessitated, independent, object-related play in her infant. Her behavior during data collection was consistent with the overall style of mothering she presented. She valued and nurtured independence in her infant, indicating, for example, that at 8 months of age he was already toilet trained. The set of negotiations in which this mother and her infant engaged are displayed in Figure 5.

Although the number of attempts to communicate made by this 8-month-old infant, 21, was almost as great as that made by the 10-month-old above, the pattern of negotiations that resulted was very different. It can be seen that most of this younger infant's attempts to communicate failed to elicit feedback from his mother. It is clear that the negotiations showed less diversity and were much briefer.

There were additional differences in the qualitative characteristics of the negotiations. It can be seen in Figure 4 that, although the infant shows persistence in signalling, and although he elaborates on his initial signal by pointing, it is the mother who carries the greatest burden in the negotiation episodes. This is not the case in Figure 5. In these negotiations, the burden of communication is borne by the infant. The mother gave requests for repetition (e.g., "What do you want?") rather than requests for confirmation (e.g., "Is this what you want?").

The differences between the patterns of negotiation shown in Figures 4 and 5 can not be ascribed solely to differences in the ages of the infant. Many mothers of 8-month-old infants had lengthy and diverse negotiations with their infants. Such patterns were found among mothers who showed an emphasis on coordination and social interaction in their dealings with their infants. The set of negotiations between one such mother and her 8-month-old daughter is represented in Figure 6. This mother described her infant as being able to talk, though of course, not using words. The egalitarian style of communication she showed in negotiations with her daughter was consistent with information she revealed about her attitude to her daughter as a conversational partner. She indicated that she spoke to her infant in the same way that she spoke to her 4-year-old son and to other adults.

It can be seen that this infant was judged to initiate more attempts to communicate than either of the two infants discussed thus far. The negotiations that resulted from these attempts showed considerable diversity, and could be quite lengthy. However, the most lengthy negotiation occurred following maternal refusals rather than maternal noncomprehension signals. In this negotiation the mother attempted to distract the infant from the forbidden object she was requesting by turning the exchange of requests and refusals into a game. After the initial interchanges, the mother leaned towards the infant and signalled her refusal by saying "No, no, no" in a playful tone after each request.

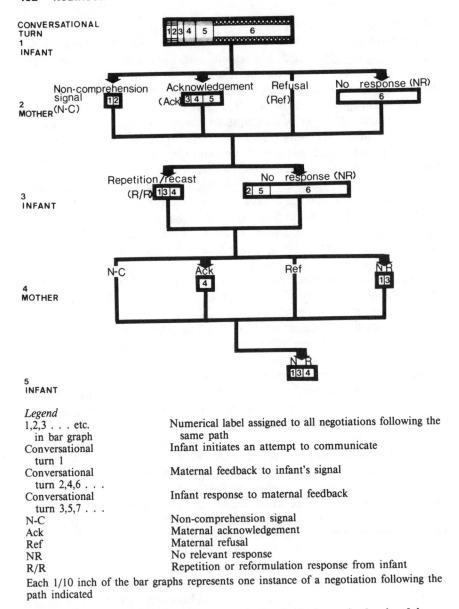

Legend
1,2,3 . . . etc. in bar graph	Numerical label assigned to all negotiations following the same path
Conversational turn 1	Infant initiates an attempt to communicate
Conversational turn 2,4,6 . . .	Maternal feedback to infant's signal
Conversational turn 3,5,7 . . .	Infant response to maternal feedback
N-C	Non-comprehension signal
Ack	Maternal acknowledgement
Ref	Maternal refusal
NR	No relevant response
R/R	Repetition or reformulation response from infant

Each 1/10 inch of the bar graphs represents one instance of a negotiation following the path indicated

Figure 5. A schematic representation of all negotiation episodes involving a mother and her 8-month-old son

The infant began to giggle in response to, and then in anticipation of, this amusing display. The infant's persistence in requesting the object became a means by which she could sustain the game. The object itself, if not forgotten, was not longer the target of the intention to communicate.

In this case, the mother attempted to transform her infant's communicative intention and the infant permitted the change. This provides a parallel to the self-initiated change in the infant's communicative intention that was observed in episode 2.

This mother and her daughter negotiate towards the goal of consensus. Negative outcomes, such as those that would result from the mother asserting her power and thwarting her child's desires, are avoided by extending the negotiation until the child agrees to change or withdraw the request. Such egalitarian styles produce lengthy negotiations precisely because their goal is consensus rather than mere resolution. Nonegalitarian patterns of negotiation are more efficient in energy and time. Totalitarian governments institute policy more quickly than democratic ones, and the same is true for parents.

It would be misleading, however, to attribute all patterns dominated by brief negotiations, for example, those found in the 8-month-old male's records, as the reflection of the mother's authoritarian style. Not only is this not an explanation, but it also fails to consider alternative maternal viewpoints that would produce similar patterns of negotiations. There is no reason for a mother to acknowledge competent behaviors from her infant (e.g., labeling) if his competence in that domain is taken for granted. Mothers of 5-year-old children do not comment on locomotor skills that they acknowledged and praised when their child was 18 months old. Conversely, very brief negotiations are also likely when mothers assume that the infant is largely or completely incapable of responding. Mothers make "no remark without remarkableness."

All the mothers discussed in the section above belonged to the same cultural group, yet the pattern of negotiations they and their infants constructed showed considerable divergence. Australian parents value both the independence of their infants and the social and co-operative behaviours they display. Both aspects of their development are fostered by parents, although some parents may tend to emphasize one somewhat more than the other. Negotiation styles reflect common enculturation processes despite these differences. This commonality is often revealed in the way contextual factors constrain different parental styles in similar ways. Negotiation sequence 8 in Figure 6, the lengthy interchange following the mother's refusal of her daughter's request, would be impossible for the same mother and infant in circumstances where there were strict constraints on the time and energy that could be invested in negotiations. Were this mother trying to supervise five infants rather than one, the negotiations may have been considerably briefer. Thus, however much Australian mothers may value egalitarian

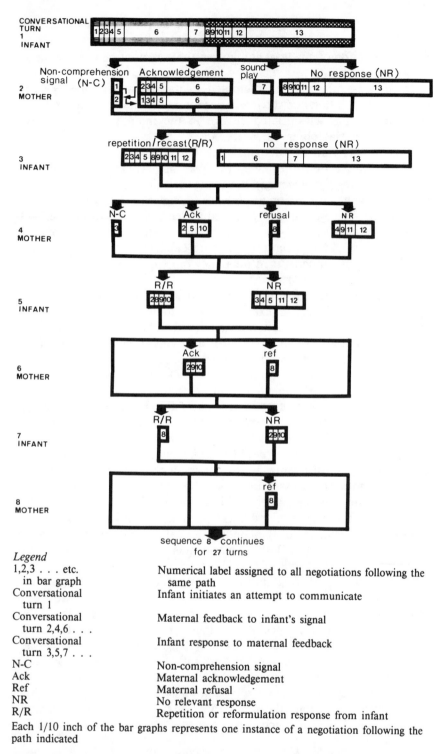

Legend

1,2,3 . . . etc. in bar graph	Numerical label assigned to all negotiations following the same path
Conversational turn 1	Infant initiates an attempt to communicate
Conversational turn 2,4,6 . . .	Maternal feedback to infant's signal
Conversational turn 3,5,7 . . .	Infant response to maternal feedback
N-C	Non-comprehension signal
Ack	Maternal acknowledgement
Ref	Maternal refusal
NR	No relevant response
R/R	Repetition or reformulation response from infant

Each 1/10 inch of the bar graphs represents one instance of a negotiation following the path indicated

Figure 6. A schematic representation of all negotiation episodes involving a mother and her 8-month-old daughter

interactions, their negotiations may necessarily be brief if their children had close birth spacing. Similarly, even egalitarian mothers of a single child are likely to negotiate meaning in an authoritarian way were the infant about to step in front of a moving car, or ingest a toxic substance. Egalitarian interactions are only possible when the infant is playing "within the rules" as the mother sees them. These rules are culturally defined, even though they too reflect some individual differences.

It is clear that that no mother will reflect one style of negotiation across all contexts. Neither does a single negotiation episode necessarily reflect only one style. Both infant and mother are strategic partners attempting to accomplish their goals. Each may modify his or her ongoing activity on the basis of the partner's line of negotiation. Any event in any turn in a negotiation episode may mark the change from one style to another. Mothers who were willing to negotiate about the refusal they have given may suddenly become adamant. Mothers who were adamant may become more flexible. Infants who were prepared to compromise following a refusal may reject the compromise and become irritable.

It can be seen that a true understanding of the boundaries cultures set on the negotiation of meaning can only be achieved if contextual and/or individual differences within a culture are explored. Cultural rules are not global but specific; they are not cloned from one generation to another, or between members of a generation; they are interpreted.

SUMMARY

Communication is a means by which the lack of understanding that initially exists between individuals may be overcome. The study of communication therefore allows one to trace the development of interpersonal understanding on a microscopic scale. The development of this understanding is accomplished through the negotiation of meaning, a process that is accessible to study when listeners initially fail to receive, or fail to understand the message. Noncomprehension signals occur whenever listeners signal that their speakers' attempts to communicate have failed. When speakers attempt to resolve these misunderstandings, their behaviors constitute conversational repairs.

However, noncomprehension signals are not always made when a listener is aware that the attempt to communicate has failed. They are not likely to occur if the message had low salience, or if providing such a signal would be culturally inappropriate or socially disadvantageous.

Familiarity between speaker and listener is often associated brief negotiations and a high motivation to achieve understanding. On the other hand, lengthy negotiations are likely to be found in conversations in which both partners know little of the signal system used by the other, or of the other's intentions, but where the partners are also highly motivated to achieve understanding. In many cultures, these conditions coexist when an adult and infant converse. Thus, conversations between parents and infants may provide a ready access for the study of the negotiation of meaning.

The structure of negotiation episodes can be investigated using a model containing four types of conversational turns: initial attempt to communicate, listener feedback, speaker response to feedback, and termination. Listener feedback may acknowledge the receipt and interpretation of the speaker's message, may signal noncomprehension, or may provide no indication as to the success or failure of the attempt to communicate. The speaker may respond to this by prompting the listener for a signal of acknowledgement, repairing the failed attempt to communicate, making no response, or signalling noncomprehension. The negotiation terminates either upon abandonment by both parties or upon communication being achieved. Whatever their length, negotiations are comprised of combinations of these four types of turns.

Cross-cultural comparisons show that the negotiation of meaning is a cultural construction which follows different paths in different cultural contexts. Thus, conclusions about the age and the way in which negotiation skills emerge in childhood are necessarily restricted to the culture in which data were collected. The patterns of negotiation adopted by white, middle-class parents appear to be very different from those used in four other cultures. A glimpse at the wide diversity of possible patterns for the negotiation of meaning can be obtained from a brief discussion of patterns of communication between adults and infants and very young children among the Kaluli of Papua New Guinea, the people of Malitbog in The Philippines, the Qalandar of Pakistan, and the Kuna of Panama. Because the pattern of communication between infants and adults reflects the culture in which the communication takes place, much information about the culture is transmitted to infants through negotiations. They learn the functions communications may legitimately serve within that culture, the meaning of particular signals in the communication system, and their status as communicative partners.

Yet cultures are not monolithic entities, and their influence cannot be studied without an appreciation of the diversity they contain. An empirical study of the negotiation of meaning between mothers and their infants revealed the different patterns of responding that are contained within the boundaries of a single culture. Cultures are lived out and transmitted by individuals, and no two individuals' experience the environment or interpret a culture in identical ways. The strength of a culture lies precisely in these individual differences. They are the foundation of many adaptations.

It is clear that all developmental research, and not only studies that explicitly address cultural issues, must attend to the influence of culture. If we are ever to arrive at explanations rather than mere descriptions of developmental patterns, commonalities across individuals, and differences between them, consideration must be given to the way cultures structure the environments in which behaviors emerge.

REFERENCES

Anselmi, D., Tomasello, M., & Acunzo, M. (1986). Young children's responses to neutral and specific contingent queries. *Journal of Child Language, 13,* 135–144.

Berland, J.C. (1982). *No five fingers are alike.* Cambridge, MA: Harvard University Press.

Cherry, L.J. (1979). The role for clarification in the language development of children. In R.O. Freedle (Ed.), *New directions in discourse processing.* Norwood, NJ: Ablex Publishing Corp.

Clark, H.H. (1985). Language use and language users. In G. Lindzey & E. Aronson (Eds.) *Handbook of Social Psychology Vol. 2.* Hillsdale, NJ: Erlbaum.

Clark, H.H., & Carlson, T.B. (1981). Context for comprehension. In J. Long & A.D. Bradley (Eds.), *Attention and Performance IX.* Hillsdale, NJ: Erlbaum.

Clark, H.H., & Wilkes-Gibbs, D. (1986). Referring as a collaborative process. *Cognition, 22,* 1–40.

Corsaro, W. (1977). The clarification request as a feature of adult interactive styles with young children. *Language in Society, 6,* 138–207.

Flavier, J.M. (1978). *Back to the barrios.* Quezon City, Philippines: New Day Publishers.

Gallagher, T.M. (1981). Contingent query sequences within adult-child discourse. *Journal of Child Language, 8,* 51–62.

Golinkoff, R.M. (1983). The preverbal negotiation of failed messages: Insights into the transitional period. In R.M. Golinkoff (Ed.), *The transition from prelinguistic to linguistic communication.* Hillsdale, NJ: Erlbaum.

Golinkoff, R.M. (1986) "I beg your pardon?": The preverbal negotiation of failed messages. *Journal of Child Language, 13,* 455–476.

Jefferson, G. (1972). Slide sequences. In D.N. Sudnow (Ed.), *Studies in social interaction.* New York: Free Press.

Jocano, F.L. (1969a). *Growing up in a Philippine barrio.* New York: Holt, Rinehart & Winston.

Jocano, F.L. (1969b). *The traditional world of Malitbog.* Quezon City, Philippines: Community Research Council.

Keeler, C.E. (1956). *Land of the moon-children.* Athens, GA: University of Georgia Press.

McCosker, S.S. (1974). *The lullabies of the San Blas Cuna Indians of Panama* (Ethnologiska Studier Series 33). Göteborg, Sweden: Göteborgs Ethnografiska Museum.

Nördenskiold, E. (1938). *An historical and ethnographic survey of the Cuna Indians* (Ethnologiska Studier Series 10). Göteborg, Sweden: Göteborgs Ethnografisks Museum.

Robinson, J.A. (1988). *The negotiation of meaning between preverbal infants and their mothers.* Unpublished doctoral dissertation. University of Newcastle, Australia.

Ryan, J. (1974). Early language development: Towards a communicational analysis. In M.P. Richards (Ed.), *The integration of the child into a social world.* Cambridge, England: Cambridge University Press.

Schieffelin, B.B., & Ochs, E. (1983). A cultural perspective on the transition from prelinguistic communication. In R.M. Golinkoff (Ed.), *The transition from prelinguistic to linguistic communication.* Hillsdale, NJ: Erlbaum.

Shatz, M. (1979). How to do things by asking: Form-function pairings in mothers' questions and their relation to children's responses. *Child Development, 50,* 1093–1099.

Sherzer, J. (1983). *Kuna ways of speaking.* Austin, TX: University of Texas Press.

Snow, C.E. & Ferguson, C.A. (1977). *Talking to children: Language input and acquisition.* New York: Cambridge University Press.

Tamir, L. (1980). Interrogatives in dialogue: Case study of mother and child 16-19 months. *Journal of Psycholinguistic Research, 9,* 407–424.

Trevarthen, C. (1979). Communication and cooperation in early infancy: A description of primary intersubjectivity. In M. Bullowa (Ed.) *Before speech: the beginning of Interpersonal communication.* Cambridge, England: Cambridge University Press.

Vygotsky, L.S. (1986). *Thought and language.* Cambridge, MA: MIT Press.

Wilcox, M.J., & Howse, P. (1982). Children's use of gestural and verbal behavior in communicative misunderstandings. *Applied Psycholinguistics, 3,* 15–27.

Wilcox, M.J., & Webster, E.J. (1980). Early discourse behavior: An analysis of children's responses to listener feedback. *Child Development, 51,* 1120–1125.

CHAPTER 6

Coping among School-Aged Children: The Influence of Development and Environment

Eve Brotman Band

Department of Psychology
University of North Carolina

Aversive life events, be they the blows of major traumas or the pin pricks of minor annoyances, occur in the lives of all people. In popular usage the concept of coping implies successful mastery or management of difficult life circumstances. It is a common notion that the effectiveness of an individual's efforts to cope with stressful life events is related to one's satisfaction and adjustment in life. The quest for greater understanding of the strategies that people use to cope has focused increased attention on the topic of coping processes.

In recent years childhood stress and how children try to cope has become an area of particular concern. Much publicity has been afforded to the notion that adult concerns, such as sexual and drug activities, are being thrust upon children in the U.S. society at an increasingly early age. As the pace of our lives continues to increase, and pressures and demands reach the youngest members of our society at an accelerated pace, several relevant questions have emerged: what events do children report cause them to feel bad, and how do children respond and attempt to make themselves feel better?

Although such questions may not be entirely new, an oft-ignored aspect to these issues is the notion that what is stressful, and how a child tries to cope, may be different for children of various ages at varying phases of development. It is intuitively sensible to presume that the processes of socialization, as well as cognitive development, may influence both *what* youngsters are likely to experience as stressful and *how* they attempt to cope at varying ages in childhood. For example, it may not be uncommon to find a child of 6 much more concerned with nightmares and the need for comfort and reassurance than with the issues of popularity at school likely to be salient for a 12-year-old youth. The possibility that various aspects of a child's development interacts with stress and coping processes bears greater elaboration. With this in mind, the following work focuses on stress and coping among children of three age levels.

In the following chapter I present and discuss the self-reports of stresses and coping behavior of 6-,9-, and 12-year-old elementary school children from a semirural area of North Carolina. In addition to illuminating the children's subjective views of stress and coping in their lives, the youngsters' descriptions depict their understanding of their individual efforts to cope as they occur in their most natural context, namely, the environmental setting which forms the backdrop for the occurrences of daily stresses in the lives of these particular children.

The chapter is organized in the following manner. Presented first are basic definitions of the concepts of stress and coping, and theoretical conceptualizations of coping processes. Second is an overview of pertinent existing research. Third, descriptive examples of the children's coping will be presented and discussed in relation to current theories. Lastly, apparent developmental, as well as socio-environmental styles evident in the children's coping efforts will be addressed.

BASIC DEFINITIONS AND CONCEPTS

In the view of theorists in the field, *coping* consists of efforts, both action-oriented or intrapsychic, to manage (i.e., master, tolerate, reduce, minimize) environmental and internal demands which tax or exceed a person's resources (Lazarus & Launier, 1978). While the concept of *stress* has received no single, unified formulation, Janis and Leventhal (1968) have offered the following perspective:

> it seems preferable to designate as a "stressful" event any change in the environment which typically—i.e. in the average person—induces a high degree of emotional tension and interferes with normal patterns of response . . . while the concept of stress is not rigorously defined, it does focus on a broad class of emotional behaviors elicited by antecedent stimulation, ranging from clear cut exposure to painful of injurious physical dangers to purely verbal statements or gestures that convey social disapproval (p. 1043).

Close examination of this definition reveals several difficulties. For one, it refers to events affecting the "average" person, who in reality does not actually exist. Secondly, the term *emotional behaviors* has an oxymoronic quality and no clear-cut meaning.

A more recent conceptualization of stress (Lazarus & Folkman, 1984) defines stress as a relationship between a person and the environment that is appraised by the person as taxing or exceeding his or her resources, and as endangering one's well-being. This latter definition, which views stress as embodied in an individual's particular transactions with his or her environment, may be more useful than the former, given that it does not rely on the fuzzy concepts of what or who may be typical or "average."

While childhood stress and children's coping abilities have emerged as a cover story on the likes of *Reader's Digest* and *T.V. Guide,* few empirical investigations have focused on the important topic of ordinary childrens' experience of everyday sorts of stresses. By directly examining childrens' self-descriptions of events they find stressful, and what they do in order to cope, we may enrich our understanding of childrens' coping efforts as well as attend to child and not solely adult perspectives.

EXISTING RESEARCH

A great deal of coping research has focused upon adults, and a more limited focus has been devoted to young children. The majority of research describing children's coping has presented generalized response syndromes based upon clinical case studies and parental report measures. Moreover, within the literature addressing children's coping abilities, the obvious threat to well-being posed by traumatic life circumstances (e.g., the death of a parent, severe illness, or physical abuse) has made the youngsters who have experienced such extraordinary events a salient group for investigation. However, concern has grown for the prevalence of multiple stresses in the daily lives of ordinary children, and recent research has suggested that the simultaneous presence of several stresses may pose a threat at least as great, or even greater, than that of one major stressor (Rutter, 1979; Kanner, Coyne, Schaefer, & Lazarus, 1981). Such findings suggest the utility of attending to the typical stresses and coping efforts of ordinary children, who have often been overlooked by those conducting research in this area.

In the existing literature, coping processes have been conceptualized along many dimensions. These have included superordinate categories such as: emotion-focused versus problem-focused coping (Folkman & Lazarus, 1980), primary control versus secondary control coping (Rothbaum, Weisz, & Snyder, 1982), active versus passive coping (Murphy & Moriarty, 1976), positive versus defensive coping (Tero & Connell, 1984), avoidant versus nonavoidant strategies (Lipowski, 1970), and facing versus avoiding strategies (Brenner, 1984). While subtle distinctions between the preceding systems do exist, there is a substantial overlap in meaning among these various dichotomies for coping behavior.

There is an additional issue worthy of note regarding various of the existing theories of coping; that is, the theoretical nature of the terms they employ (such as "denial," "facing and avoiding," or "positive and defensive") may make it difficult to know in concrete behavioral terms how these various classes of response are manifest. For example, "denial" could occur on a psychological level, implying rejection of certain thoughts, as is associated with the concept of "denial" as a psychological defense mechanism. However, "denial" may also occur in a behavioral form, perhaps involving concrete responses that contradict the apparent realities of a given situation.

STAGE THEORIES

Many early models of coping have been stage theories which delineate coping responses within the framework of a progression through a particular series of stages in response to a specific stressful event. Theorists using this approach typically have elaborated the experience of individuals facing particular traumatic circumstances, such as a divorce or the death of a close friend or relative. Such stage models, for example the well-known account of death and dying elaborated by Elisabeth Kubler-Ross (1969), have enriched our knowledge by providing detailed, qualitative descriptions of coping responses. Moreover, because severe stresses, such as death or dying, generally require an extended period of coping and adjustment, stage theorists have described and documented how coping may change over time; this embodies the view of coping as a process, rather than a static, unitary event.

PERSONALITY TRAIT VERSUS SITUATION SPECIFIC THEORIES

Polarizing the theoretical perspectives of other major theorists has been a distinction between coping conceptualized as a personality trait, and coping conceptualized as a situation-specific process. Psychoanalytically oriented theorists have commonly depicted coping as a set of ego processes which are viewed as stable personality traits (Haan, 1977; Vaillant, 1977; Menninger, 1963). In this conceptual framework it has been posited that each individual possesses a characteristic means of ego defense which comprises his or her habitual coping style. This style of ego defense is thought to be consistently employed by the individual as his or her characteristic means of coping despite varying situational demands. Thus within this perspective an individual's "coping style" may be conceived of as a personality trait, which is thought to show stability and cross-situational consistency.

Several weaknesses in the trait approach to coping are apparent. For one, a conceptualization of coping as a stable personality trait may have limited usefulness, in particular, if coping is thought of as a *process* (see Folkman & Lazarus, 1985). It has been suggested that flexibility and the range of coping behaviors comprise the most critical determinant of the outcome of stressful events (Shapiro, 1984). Worthy of note, this flexibility of response, thought of as an asset to healthy coping, is diametrically opposed to the trait-based notion of consistency of coping style. It is, therefore, not surprising that research within the trait-based framework has shown little cross-situational consistency in coping conceptualized as a personality-based style of ego defense.

More commonly, research has shown coping to vary across situations as a function of varying situational demands (Folkman, 1984). Such empirical support for the conceptualization that the form of coping efforts are a function of situational contingencies has resulted in dramatic growth in the study of coping as a situation-specific process. This perspective has maintained that strategies for coping are shaped largely by the particular demands associated with specific stressful events. For example, when faced with the prospect of a difficult upcoming mathematics test, a child may respond by studying very diligently in order to ensure a good grade. However, faced with the prospect of a highly unpleasant trip to the doctor to receive several vaccinations, the same child might respond by watching T.V. in order to distract himself or herself from his or her anticipation of a painful experience.

THE INTERACTIONIST VIEWPOINT

As in many areas, perhaps the most intuitively reasonable approach to understanding coping processes is an interactionist one, which duly recognizes a joint influence of both person and situation factors. Let us briefly extend the above coping example to illustrate this viewpoint. One particular child, a high achiever from a family of high-achieving professional parents, may study diligently when facing a difficult math exam, presumably with the expectation that his or her study will make a good grade more likely; however, another, who possesses little confidence in his or her mathematical abilities, may perceive that, regardless of his or her efforts, failure on the test is imminent, and thus respond by paying great attention to doing well in subject areas other than mathematics, as well as professing the belief that mathematics is a "stupid" subject and that he or she would rather be good at something more "creative."

The above example illustrates how personality traits (e.g., achievement motivation) may interact with the appraisal and perception of situational demands. As a result, a fine-grained examination of coping responses within a given situation is likely to reveal individual differences in the specific coping strategies employed. Thus, while coping responses may vary as a function of varying situational demands, they are at the same time shaped by personality factors, which may interact with the demands of a specific situation to produce various and complex coping efforts.

COGNITION AND COPING

Employing a situation specific viewpoint, a number of investigators (Coyne & Lazarus, 1980; Folkman, Schaefer, & Lazarus, 1979; Lazarus, 1966, 1981) have emphasized cognitive processes in stress and coping, maintaining that stress involves an individual's "cognitive appraisal," a subjective perception that environmental demands tax or exceed one's coping resources. Such appraisals may involve perceptions of "harm" (damage already done), "threat" (potential for harm), and "challenge" (potential for significant gain under difficult odds).

According to Folkman and Lazarus (1980), people respond to the stress evoked by such situational appraisals with various strategies for coping, most of which reflect "problem-focused" or "emotion-focused" modes for dealing with a specific stressful event. Problem-focused coping refers to efforts directed at doing something constructive about conditions that pose harm, threat, or challenge, whereas emotion-focused coping refers to efforts directed at regulating the emotion itself (Folkman & Lazarus, 1980; Lazarus, 1975, 1981).

Lazarus and Folkman (1984) have maintained that most people use both emotion-focused and problem-focused modes of coping in daily stressful encounters. Evidence for this assertion lies in a year-long study (Folkman & Lazarus, 1980) in which 100 middle aged men and women were interviewed and assessed with the Ways of Coping Checklist (Folkman & Lazarus, 1980), a measure containing a wide range of thoughts and actions that adults use to deal with taxing events which is designed to elicit information about the strategies a person uses to deal with a specific stressful event. Lazarus and Folkman (1984) highlighted the finding that both problem- and emotion-focused modes of coping were employed in all but 2% of 1,332 coping episodes studied; they subsequently suggested that unidimensional approaches to coping are incomplete, given that they place exclusive emphasis on one function or the other. For example, the focus of ego psychology theorists, such as Menninger (1963), Haan (1977), or Moos and Billings (1982), who have studied coping as emotional regulation or defense, or the decision-making approach of Janis and Mann (1977), who center on problem-focused functions of coping, seemingly represent only a partial aspect of the coping process. Moreover, it is worthy to consider the notion that coping is not an isolated, either/or process in which a particular response embodies solely either one function or another. It is certainly conceivable that a given coping response can have multiple functions, which may vary depending on both person and situational factors.

CONTROL AND COPING

Likewise subscribing to a largely situation specific viewpoint, locus of control theory has provided an alternate perspective for conceptualizing coping processes. Within this framework coping efforts are seen as reflecting the functions of primary control and secondary control forms of behavior (Rothbaum et al., 1982). From this perspective, *primary control* coping refers to behavior involving efforts to act upon objective sources of stress (i.e., events, circumstances, objects, or other people) in order to actively influence or modify them in such a way to enhance rewards by bringing them into line with one's wishes; *secondary control* strategies are those which aim to influence the emotional response or psychological state engendered by a stressful event (e.g., one's mood, attributions, expectations, or interpretations) so as to enhance rewards by accommodating oneself to fit existing realities of the situational context. A third dimension, *relinquished control,* denotes responses which have no apparent purpose or value in enhancing the reward or reducing the punishment associated with a stressful event.

For example, suppose a child reported getting a failing grade on an exam. The child might have responded to this stressor by studying harder to do better on the next exam (primary control), by holding to a belief that it was a very difficult test and that he or she could not have been expected to have done better (secondary control), or by "just feeling bad" but "doing nothing" (relinquished control).

Worthy of note, from the traditional perspective of locus control theory (Rotter, 1966), behaviors appearing passive or submissive are suggestive of an external locus of control orientation and perceived uncontrollability (Abramson, Seligman, & Teasdale, 1978). In contrast, the primary–secondary control model often sees such behaviors as forms of secondary control, by which individuals gain control by bringing themselves into line with existing forces (e.g., by focusing on the positive aspects of a situation). In a recent theoretical analysis of the role of personal control in stress and coping processes, Folkman (1984) has highlighted the complexity in the relationships between personal control, stress, coping, and adaptational outcomes. She has underscored that perceiving an event as controllable does not invariably lead to a reduction in stress and a positive outcome, and likewise that negative outcomes do not always follow from appraisals of uncontrollability.

Additionally, the primary–secondary control coping perspective has recognized, not only that coping responses have multiple functions, but also that any given coping response may encompass varying degrees of these various functions. For example, a child who copes with an event by crying could do so in order to elicit specific instrumental action from an adult in his or her behalf (primary control) *and/or* to "just get the feelings out" and elicit social support from an adult (secondary control). This perspective has recognized, therefore, that the functions of a given response are not necessarily mutually exclusive. A given response can serve parallel functions of primary and secondary control; the degree to which each function is represented depends upon the person and situation factors inherent in the particular incidence of the response.

PRIOR INVESTIGATION

The majority of work addressing stress and coping elaborates these processes in adults; there is a more limited scope of research to date examining stress and coping processes in children. Lacking in particular are investigations which do not confound coping processes with adaptational outcomes by allowing the latter to influence detection of the former, and studies which utilize children's self-reports of coping behavior, rather than parental or clinical measures. Additionally, given the concept of cognitive appraisal as playing a central, mediating role in subsequent coping behavior (Folkman & Lazarus, 1980; Lazarus & Folkman, 1984), a cognitive-developmental approach appears vital in order to consider how childrens' developing cognitive structure may influence their appraisal, both of the environment, and of themselves in relation to environmental events.

Children's self-reports of both cognitive and behavioral aspects of their coping attempts were gathered using a standardized, semistructured interview procedure. Seventy-three school children between the ages of 6 and 12 were interviewed individually in order to explore possible developmental differences in children's self-reports of stress and coping (Band & Weisz, 1986). The children were asked to identify some "things that make kids your age feel bad, unhappy or scared." To assess coping approaches, children were asked to tell about "a time when *you yourself* felt this way. What happened that made *you feel bad, unhappy or scared?"* Each child was asked to consider this question within six domains of experience, all suggested by previous literature as potential sources of everyday stress: (a) separation or loss (e.g., from a friend or significant person caused by moving away or moving "to a different school or class"); (b) a stressful medical event (e.g., going "to the doctor's office to get a shot"); (c) a conflict with authority (e.g., "a time when your mom, or dad, or your teacher was mad at you"); (d) peer difficulty (e.g., "a time when another kid said mean things to you"); (e) school failure (e.g., getting "a grade on an exam or your school report card that you didn't like"); and (f) physical harm (e.g., "a time when you had an accident and got hurt"). For each situation that evoked a memory, the children were asked to describe their experience, and give details about: (a) what happened (b) how it felt, (c) what they thought and did, and (d) how they thought that each thing they did would "help or make things better." Coping responses were classified as primary or secondary control coping following the primary–secondary control perspective (Rothbaum et. al., 1982). Subsequent statistical analyses focused primarily upon developmental trends in the relative use of primary and secondary control coping in the six domains of stressful experience.

A significant portion of data yielded by the above investigation was highly descriptive in nature. The richness of such qualitative data renders it particularly suitable to idiographic elaboration. Moreover, recent research has emphasized that coping with a stressful encounter is a dynamic, unfolding process, not a static unitary event (Lazarus & Folkman, 1984). Consistent with this view of coping as a complex process operating simultaneously on multiple levels, the current chapter elaborates detailed accounts related by children describing their coping efforts.

SELF-REPORTS OF COPING AMONG CHILDREN AGED 6, 9, AND 12

Developmental Differences

For most young children, the world is becoming an increasingly complex place; there is the advent of school, the need to relate to teachers and peers, as well as the necessity for mastery of new skills and demands. Expanding social roles and the growing cognitive capacity to view oneself in relation to others are inherent to the socially based stresses common in childhood (e.g., peer difficulties, conflicts with authority figures, loss/separation from important others). However, just as stressful are events that are nonsocial but which threaten physical harm (e.g., trips to the doctor or dentist, or physical accidents).

We are currently beginning to scratch the surface in the quest for understanding how children's efforts to cope with such a variety of stressful events may vary with age. One distinctive finding that has emerged from the examination of children's self-reports of coping is that younger children, (i.e., 6-year-olds), appear to rely more heavily on coping strategies of a direct behavioral nature than older children (i.e., 9- and 12-year-olds). For example, faced with the situation where her best friend moved away and went to a different school, one 6-year-old girl explained,

> I asked my mother to see if she could talk to her mother to see if she could sleep over sometimes, cause then I'd see her still . . . I made new friends too so I'd have someone to play with."

Strategies emphasizing "making new friends to have someone to play with," or "playing with others," were common in response to this situational context, being reported by 81% of the 6-year-old children. Such a response involves an instrumental means of influencing the stressful circumstance of losing an important friend, generally aiming to modify the circumstances by means of substitution or replacement. Such action-oriented strategies, which aim to directly influence stressful conditions in order to alleviate or terminate them, are consistent with the primary control conceptualization of coping elaborated by Rothbaum et al., (1982) and Weisz, Rothbaum, and Blackburn (1984a). In many coping episodes the younger children (6-year-olds) exclusively described primary control coping strategies.

Less prevalent among 6-year-old youngsters were coping strategies of a more subtle, cognitive nature. Although less frequent than behavioral responses, children of this age group did, however, describe cognitive coping efforts. The following coping episode reported by a 7-year-old girl serves to illustrate:

> When I was five my best friend moved away to her cousin's. For me it was very bad. I tried to think that she was still here, because then I'd feel happier. I pretended that I was playing with her, cause then I wouldn't be lonely. Then I made new friends.

It is evident that cognitive strategies involving thinking and imagining are central to this particular child's efforts to cope, as well as the direct behavioral activity (making new friends) predominantly described by the 6-year-old children.

In contrast to the 6-year-olds, 9- and 12-year-old youngsters appeared more likely to describe a pattern of coping characterized by either a combination of primary and secondary control coping efforts, or by secondary control coping strategies alone (Band & Weisz, 1986). Integral to this pattern are more subtle, cognitive strategies for coping. For example, a 12-year-old girl, who was going to the doctor's to receive a shot, related how it was "really scary to think about getting it," so she "tried to be brave and hold it in." She described her strategies for coping in this situation as follows.

> I tried to think of other things . . . talk to my mom or read books so I could take my mind off of it, get more relaxed and worry less. I thought about what it would be like after it was over and it made me feel better to think of the good stuff afterwards. I told myself that it happens to everybody so they don't get sick, and I thought if everybody goes through it, I can make it too.

It is interesting to note that this 12-year-old child's cognitive coping strategies included an attempt to realistically focus on the positive aspects of the situation (i.e., the "good stuff" once the shot was over, and the preventive purpose of the shot, "it happens to everybody so that they don't get sick"). In contrast, the cognitive strategies described by the younger 6-year-old child involved fantasy and "pretending" (i.e., "I tried to think that she was still here . . . I pretended I was playing with her") as opposed to the transformation of experience involved in shifting the focus to the positive aspects of the circumstances, or reinterpretation of the stressful event. The following examples of coping involving cognitive reinterpretation of a stressful circumstance were related by 11- and 12-year-old girls, respectively.

> My friend got mad and she went flying off the handle at me. She might

not have meant it, but it takes its place your heart and makes you feel really bad—unworthy of being her friend. What I did was I thought about it and told myself that I'm not those things and that what she said wasn't true.

When I found out I got a "B" on my history test I felt real bad. I usually get "A"s so I was worrying about it and talked to some friends to see how they did. They said it was a real hard test so "B" was a good grade. Then I realized that I hadn't done so bad after all and I felt better about it.

Such cognitive coping strategies are consistent with the secondary control conceptualization of coping, (Rothbaum et al., 1982; Weisz et al., 1984a) which emphasizes responding that helps the individual accommodate himself or herself to the existing situation. In addition to subtle cognitive means for adapting to existing stressful events, strategies such as distraction (keeping one's mind off of a distressing event) and eliciting social social support (telling one's feelings to a trusted friend or adult) are also consistent with the palliative function of secondary control coping. These latter strategies were related by children of all ages with comparable frequency. In the course of explaining how he attempted to cope with having received a "D" on a reading test, an 11-year-old boy described the value of distraction strategies:

I watched TV to get my mind off of it. You know, if you have a sore and you think about it it hurts, but if you don't think about it, it doesn't.

Although the 9- and 12-year-old children appeared to relate subtle cognitive modes of coping with greater frequency than the 6-year-old youngsters, cognitive coping efforts were not reported in isolation from active, behavioral modes of responding. In fact, as mentioned previously, the older children (9- and 12-year-olds) were more likely than the younger children (6-year-olds) to describe engaging in *both* secondary control and primary control efforts to cope in a given episode. The following coping episode related by a 12-year-old girl serves to illustrate.

My mom got mad. She'd told me five times to clean the litter box and I didn't. I went up to my room and banged my pillow against the bed. Its like taking your feelings and banging them and it makes me feel better. Then I went to the basement, turned on the radio and danced because then I'd forget about it for a while. Also, I told my mom I was sorry and I cleaned it because then she wasn't so mad.

The above coping episode depicts a multifacted effort to cope; the child has described a cathartic action (banging her pillow against the bed), a secondary control type of attempt to accommodate to the situation as it is (dancing in order to forget about it), and a primary control type of attempt to directly influence the stressful circumstances (cleaning the litter box and apologizing to alleviate her mother's anger).

Several possibilities may account for the greater predominance of primary control forms of coping alone observed in the younger children. For one, the secondary control responses are more subtle and invisible in form (i.e., internal cognitive and affective adjustments) than primary control behaviors. As a result, it may take longer for children to recognize secondary control mechanisms, or to see them as a viable approach for coping with stressful circumstances. Moreover, younger children (i.e., 6-year-olds) may be more likely to base their self-reports of coping behavior on concrete, observable, external characteristics (see Harter, 1983), whereas the response tendencies of older children may be based on internal psychological processes (i.e., thoughts and emotions), which are compatible with various forms (particularly cognitive strategies) of secondary control coping. A further possibility is that younger children may simply be better at applying primary control than secondary control sorts of strategies, and that the ability to use secondary control strategies effectively increases with age. If this were the case, it makes sense that young children would focus most heavily on the types of behaviors that prove most efficacious.

Situation Specificity

Thus far, our discussion has considered the general nature of children's coping without examining the influence of the six situational contexts responded to by the children. Examination of the children's self-reports of coping within the six stressful domains appeared to support the theoretical conceptualization of coping behavior as situationally determined.

Children reported engaging in primary and secondary control modes of coping in varying degrees, depending upon the situational context. The specific stressful events associated with the greatest proportions of primary control strategies (greater than 75% primary control coping) were loss/separation (79%), peer difficulties (80%), and school failure (88%), respectively. The predominantly primary control coping behavior reported in these situations may have occurred because these particular events were readily amenable to efforts for control. For example, children often reported making new friends in order to alter the loneliness engendered by loss or separation from an important playmate; children described efforts such as ignoring a taunting peer, telling the teacher, or befriending the peer in order to alter the situation of being teased by getting the other child to stop; and children related making efforts, such as studying harder after receiving a bad grade at school, in order to alter the situation by ensuring a better performance the next time. Specific examples of these common primary control types of responses are as follows.

> I made new friends after we moved so that I wouldn't be lonely (loss/separation); (6-year-old girl).

> When a girl in class was calling me names and treating me badly I tried to talk to her and get along with her so that she'd stop calling me names (peer difficulty); (7-year-old girl).

> After I got a bad grade on the math test I studied real hard so the next time I'd know the answers and do better (school failure); (12-year-old boy).

In contrast, the situations involving conflicts with authority and physical accidents were associated with more balanced use of primary and secondary modes of coping (59% and 67% primary control, respectively). This may have occurred, in part, because there is a lesser likelihood in these particular circumstances of effectively resolving stress by means of direct (primary) control activities. It seems reasonable that children may experience an event, such as conflict with an authority figure, as less amenable to direct influence than that involving conflict with a peer. Similarly, circumstances associated with physical accidents appeared to be of a less obviously controllable nature. Namely, a child might attempt to directly alter the circumstances by focusing coping efforts on promoting healing of injury or preventing future accidents, however likely to be salient are efforts at accomodating to the situation by seeking comfort from others or not thinking about the hurtful event. Examples of both primary and secondary forms of responding to these events are as follows. Typical primary control responses included:

> When my parents were mad after I hadn't cleaned my room I did stuff in the house to make mom not mad anymore (conflict with authority); (11-year-old girl).

> I was hurt and embarrassed when I fell and I decided I'd be more cautious next time so it won't happen again (physical accident); (11-year-old girl).

Common secondary control efforts concomitantly reported were:

I'd cry and get the feelings out (conflict with authority); (9-year-old girl).

I tried to get up and forget about it so I wouldn't think about it and would feel better" (physical accident); (11-year-old girl).

Attempts to resolve the stress engendered by a medical procedure revealed the lowest overall use of primary control strategies (33% primary and 67% secondary control coping strategies, respectively). This situation-specific observation may be accounted for by several factors associated with the nature of such an event for children. Namely, most young children have limited experience with medical circumstances (i.e., trips to the doctor or dentist), and, as a result, medical events present unfamiliar and uncertain conditions. Additionally, limited opportunities for direct control are seemingly inherent to medical situations, which often require that individuals undergo unpleasant procedures out of necessity. Such factors may have contributed to the higher incidence of secondary control responding observed. Secondary control types of responses commonly described included:

I talked to mom so I'd think about other things (9-year-old boy).

I told myself I'd feel better if I got the shot and it would soon be over (7-year-old girl).

Of the six specific stressful contexts described by the children, developmental differences in the use of primary and secondary control forms of coping were obvious only in the situation of a stressful medical procedure (see Table 1).

In the medical situation, 6- and 9-year-old children appeared more likely than 12-year-old youngsters to report attempting to cope by means of primary control efforts. Specifically, younger children reported

Table 1. Age Trends in the Mean Proportions of Primary Control in Six Situational Contexts (Ranges of values in parenthesis).

	Age					
	6		9		12	
Loss or Separation	82%	(0–100%)	73%	(0–100%)	82%	(33–100%)
Medical Procedure	46%	(0–100%)	40%	(0–100%)	13%	(0–50%)
Conflict with Authority	60%	(0–100%)	60%	(0–100%)	57%	(0–100%)
Peer Difficulty	87%	(0–100%)	80%	(0–100%)	73%	(0–100%)
School Failure	90%	(50–100%)	85%	(0–100%)	89%	(0–100%)
Physical Accident	70%	(0–100%)	72%	(0–100%)	58%	(0–100%)

both primary and secondary control strategies in this situation with approximately equal frequency. In contrast, older children responded almost exclusively with secondary control coping behaviors.

This finding is consistent with the hypothesis that younger children engage in an active search process in unfamiliar situations, whereby they "cast around," trying an array of strategies that may yield the outcome they desire. Conversely, older children, who likely have significant previous experience with such an event, tend to focus on a repertoire of coping responses which have previously proven helpful in this specific situation, and therefore select their strategies from this focused range of responses. This is consistent with previous research (see Stattin, 1984), which suggests that as children develop they will increasingly rely on qualities of the expected outcomes in their appraisal of anxiety-provoking situations. As a result, older children may focus on more realistic solutions, which are likely to be effective or adaptive in stressful medical circumstances. For example, older children's reports of coping behavior included the following strategies:

> It was real scary to think about getting the shot so I thought about what it would be like after it was over cause it made me feel better to think of the good stuff afterwards (11-year-old girl).

> I asked mom what would happen because then I'd be better able to anticipate what it would be like (12-year-old boy).

> I tried to make jokes with my twin sister who was there too because then we'd laugh and not think about it (12-year-old girl).

In contrast, young children frequently reported coping with a stressful medical event as follows:

> I told mom "no, no, no," to convince her I didn't need the shot (6-year-old girl).

> I tried to get mom to stop the car and told her I didn't want a shot (6-year-old boy).

> I hid in the children's corner at the office so no one would see me and I wouldn't have to get it then (7-year-old girl).

> I tried not to go (to the doctor) because I felt very scared (7-year-old boy).

These actively avoidant strategies typical of younger children appear aimed at directly altering the stressful circumstances by attempting to prevent the occurrence of getting a shot. Older children, however, seem more likely to view a medical procedure, such as a shot, as necessary; as a result, their efforts to cope appear more realistically aimed at mitigating distress associated with the impending event.

A second approach to the developmental differences observed in coping responses to a medical stressor might aim to account for the significantly greater use of primary control strategies by the 6- and 9-year-olds, and the increased use of secondary control coping by the 12-year-old subjects. From the Piagetian perspective on cognitive development, these younger subjects may be likely to yet perceive an illusory contingency between their behavior and potential outcomes, even in situations lacking in such contingency (see Weisz, 1980, 1981). As a result, these younger subjects are hypothesized to attribute greater casual powers to themselves to affect a stressful situation than the older children; hence they more often engage in primary control attempts to actively exert influence over the impending medical event. Such a cognitive-developmental hypothesis highlights the notion that children's appraisal of stressful events changes developmentally with age, and may result in concomitant changes in the relative use of primary and secondary control forms of coping.

Parallel Functions of Coping

Thus far we have explored how the form of coping may vary both as a function of developmental (age) and environmental (situation) factors. Next I would like to suggest that these two forces may interact to shape the function of a given coping activity. In short, a given coping response may embrace parallel functions of primary and secondary control, depending upon the dual influence of person and situation factors. To explore this notion, let us look at several strategies in the following coping episodes.

First, let us consider that a given coping response may serve a primary control function in a particular situation for one child; yet the same response may serve a secondary control function in another situation for another child. The following coping episodes, related by a 6-year-old girl and a 7-year-old boy, respectively, serve to illustrate this possibility.

One time I fell off a chair and I broke my arm. I went and *told my mom* because she would love it and make it feel a little better.

I was out riding by bike. Then I lost my balance and I fell. I went home

and *told my mom.* I knew she'd give me ice or a bandaid. She'd help
it get better and get well fast.

Here we see two children who, on the surface, have employed the same
essential strategy: telling their mother. However, the aim of the first
child was that her mother should "love it [her arm] and make it *feel
a little better.*" The underlying aim of this response appears to be
consistent with the function of secondary control coping—that of bringing one's subjective experience in line with existing conditions. This
particular child looks to her mother in order to "love it and make it
feel better" apparently to increase her comfort in her present situation.
There is no indication that this action will help her arm heal, or
influence the objective condition that her arm is broken. In contrast,
the second child, also physically hurt, tells his mother so that she will
"help it get better and get well fast." In the case of this second child,
the response "tell your mother" appears consistent with the function
of primary control coping behavior. In particular, the strategy appears
to aim to directly influence the objective event by bringing about
healing of the physical damage.

The above example illustrated the notion that a given response may
serve a primary control function in one instance, and a secondary
control function in another. An additional possibility is that a particular
strategy can serve parallel primary and secondary control functions in
a given coping episode. Consider the following coping incident reported
by 7-year-old boy.

I fell and hit a rock and busted my knee. I went to mama. I knew she'd
help me fix it. And I knew that she would make me feel a lot more
better.

In this episode, the child's response of going "to mama" appeared to
serve dual primary and secondary control aims. Specifically, the child
related that he knew that his mama would "help fix it"—consistent
with the primary control aim of directly influencing the objective
condition of physical damage. In addition, the child specified that he
"knew that she would make me feel a lot more better"—consistent
with the secondary control aim of influencing the subjective experience
of emotional distress.

SUMMING UP: THE INTERACTIONIST POSITION

In essence, the interactionist viewpoint appreciates the complexity of
the coping process. Person and situation factors combine to influence

an individual's response to stressful events. At the same time, multiple functions of coping (e.g., primary and secondary control-based coping efforts) are intertwined within the same person and within the same coping episode. To best appreciate the richness and complexity of the topography of coping, I shall now elaborate the coping efforts of one particular child in response to several stressful experiences. The following is the transcript of a 9-year-old boy who first described how he responded to the death of a close family friend. Enclosed in brackets are the interviewer's queries.

[Sometimes kids have a good friend or a neighbor or someone they really like to play with. And then that person moves away and you don't see them anymore. Has something like that ever happened to you?]

"Something worse than that. See I had this friend Joe, and he was married and everything. He was older than me. I don't know how old he was. I would always like to go down there, and one night my mom had to, and some nights I'd go over there and spend the night with him, and they would babysit for me. And I would take toys and stuff and transformers and stuff like that. And then one day my mom told me that Joe was in the hospital of cancer. I was real sad about it. And then a few days later he called me and said he was feeling a lot better. And then, I'm not sure, but he died. I'm not sure when. And we went to his funeral and everything and I was just real sad about it. Because he was a good friend of mine. I felt pretty sad, very bad because I like him a lot.

[Do you remember all the things you did and thought then at that time?]

"My mom, she said to me, "Do you want to stay here at Ronnie's house," he lives beside me and he's a friend of mine too, "or do you want to go to Joe's funeral with Dad and I?" I said, "I want to go to Joe's funeral because he was a good friend of mine," so I decided to go to his funeral.

[What else did you do? Did you try to think about it, or did you try to not think about it]

I tried to get the idea that it already happened and there was nothing I could do. My sister, she didn't want to go, because her friend named Tina was Joe's daughter. She didn't want to go the funeral . . . I guess she just didn't like funerals that much.

[Did you talk to anybody about it?]

To my Dad, he's my very best friend.

[How did you think that deciding to go the funeral was going to help, or make things better?]

Well, I thought it would make me better because I'd be able to see him once more before he'd be buried. You know, I'd be able to see him again. Then I'd be able to visit him. I sort of knew he was always in my heart. He may not be on this earth, but he's, you know, somewhere in my heart because I remember him. After the funeral I felt relieved that it was over and done with. And now I can talk about it, you know, and not even worry because I'm so used to the fact that there was nothing I could do.

[So another thing you did was tell yourself there was nothing you could do about it. How did you think that that was going to help you or make things better?]

Well, at first, well I'm sure that when you were little you thought something may have been your fault, you know, . . . and I sort of thought that it was my fault that I didn't, wasn't able to go the hospital and visit him because my mom wouldn't let me go in there. I sort of thought that it was my fault. So thinking that there was nothing I could do helped me feel it wasn't my fault. It helped a lot.

[You also said that you talked to your Dad. How did you think that that was going to help or make things better?]

Well, my Dad and I are very, very close. We're best friends really. And, umm, he has a way with words, he's got a real way with words and he sort of told me what to think, it wasn't my fault, and he made me feel a lot better.

[So you talked to him mainly because you knew he'd make you feel better?]

Uh humm.
[Now when this happened did you think something could be done to change the situation?]

Well, nothing could be done because he had had cancer for a long, long time."

[But did you think that you could do something to make yourself feel better?]

There wasn't much I could do.

[Did it work out?]

Yea, it worked out after a while. I got used to the fact that it, well that it took time.

The above episode presents diminished possibilites for personal control over the objective event itself—the death of a friend from cancer. Consistent with such an appraisal of the event, the child's coping responses do not appear to have the primary control intent of influencing the objective circumstances. The child appears to have employed secondary control coping efforts to influence his subjective experience of the death and help himself adapt to the existing situation. Central to his attempt to modify his subjective experience, the child focused on: (a) retaining the memory of his friend and (b) the belief that there was nothing he could have done to change what happened.

The child's secondary control behavior can be seen as indicative of perceived uncontrollability with respect to the objective event. Nevertheless, the child described how he thought that he was somehow guilty, that it was "his fault," as if some primary control coping action should have been a viable possibility. In fact, primary control coping behavior would likely have been less effective given the circumstances. In this episode, the child's acceptance of the idea that there was nothing he could have done to change the situation was indeed adaptive. Such accurate perception of noncontingency allowed the child to more productively focus his coping efforts on adaptation to the event. However, as this child readily disclosed, he did not fully perceive the noncontingent nature of the event without his father's assistance. As he related, he relied on his father's instruction that there really was nothing he could have done about his friend's illness and death. Clearly illustrated herein is the influence of person factors, such as the child's cognitive maturity, upon the situational appraisal of controllability and contingency central to subsequent coping behavior.

Next, let us examine how this 9-year-old boy described his efforts to cope with an accident that resulted in a trip to the hospital.

I had to go to the hospital on Christmas Eve. What a time. You see I had been playing around in some water and I had this test tube and I pushed it into my hand and it broke and shattered and I had to get stitches for it and get the glass out of my hand. I was real scared. I was about six years old when it happened. I remember I yelled and screamed, "I don't want to go the hospital," but my Daddy told me, "You got to go to the hospital or you'll lose a lot of blood." I said, "I don't want to die either." So I went to the hospital and they said to me, "This shot will hurt a lot." I think they said this to get me used to it. So the nurse said, "I'm going to go out of here and the doctor will come in and he'll examine you and give you a few shots." It turned out I had to get a whole bunch of shots. At first I felt real bad, but afterwards they gave me some sort of shot so I'd go to sleep you know.

[So, when all this happened, one of the first things you did was say that you didn't want to go to the hospital. And when you got there it was scary because the nurse told you you were going to get shots that were going to hurt. What did you do then?]

Well, the nurse, she told me this joke you see about a big, ole football player who walked into the hospital one day and he said, "Oh, I've broken my leg, I've broken my leg." And he had broken his leg, and they took an X-ray and sure enough his leg was broken. And they had to give him a shot and he screamed and he yelled and cried, "waahh," and he didn't like the shots at all. And I don't know if this really was true or false, but he didn't like the shots at all. And then at the operation he was sitting there crying. And then that sort of got my confidence up because I thought, "I can be bigger than that football player."

[So you listened to this story or joke and . . .?]

Yea. And I then I told myself that I can do better than that, be bigger than that football player was. It helped me to feel braver.

[Okay. Now you told me that at first you didn't want to go to the hospital. How did you think that telling your Dad that you didn't want to go was going to help or make things better?]

Well, I thought then he wouldn't take me there. But I know now that it wouldn't make anything better for me to not go. I was hurt and crying but I wasn't really worried about my thumb, I just didn't want to go to the hospital.

In contrast to the episode which involved the death of his friend, the above incident presented the child with a more ambiguous situation with respect to the possibility for personal control over the objective event. The event described took place when the child was reportedly 6 years of age. Like many children of 6, he first responded in a primary control fashion, resisting the stress provoking trip to the hospital. This can be seen as an attempt to influence one aspect of the stressful circumstance—namely, the necessity for going to the hospital or to see a doctor. However, at his current age of 9, the child was able to reflect that not going to the hospital "wouldn't make things better." On the other hand, many 6-year-olds, caught up in their attempt to exert control over the dreaded event, may be likely to focus exclusively on avoiding the trip regardless of the circumstances. Beyond his initial primary control-based response, however, the child appeared to expend the bulk of his coping energies on secondary control efforts to cope with the stressful medical proceedings at the hospital. Given the essential unworkability of primary control in the face of the medical circumstances, the child's ultimate focus on secondary control coping appears likely to be adaptive in this situation.

CONCLUSION

In recent years the study of coping has spawned diverse theoretical approaches. While various theorists have highlighted different facets of coping, it is clear that coping is a multidimensional process which does not occur in isolation from the dual influence of both person and situation.

Unlike personality influences, which are internally based and to varying degrees externally expressed, situations present an external structure in-and-of themselves with which individuals must cope. If we look at coping from a perspective emphasizing each individual's efforts at exerting personal control, either by acting to alter objective circumstances (primary control), or by acting to alter subjective experience to accommodate to existing circumstances (secondary control) (Rothbaum et al., 1982, Weisz et al., 1984a,b), the exigencies of the environment which shape the individual's potential for gaining control are undeniably important. In particular, environmental circumstances can be viewed in terms of the structure they present with respect to potential controllability or uncontrollability. Coping with a situation which presents diminished possibilities for control over objective circumstances is essentially different from coping with a situation which is clearly amenable to attempts to influence the objective stressful event. Thus, although situation *content* is often considered the crucial shaper of coping behavior, stressful content may be more productively viewed in tandem with the *structure* a situation presents with respect to potential controllability.

Given this viewpoint of stressful situations as presenting a blend of content and structure, how might we best understand children's attempts to cope with the various stressful events they encounter? The coping efforts exerted by children in various situations appear shaped by their appraisals of environmental exigencies, both content and structure. Similarly to views of coping in adults (Lazarus & Folkman, 1984), cognitive processes appear central to children's appraisals. The manner in which children appraise events in their environment will obviously affect their evaluation of the kind of coping behavior befitting various circumstances. However, unlike adults, children present a mental structure that is actively growing and changing in its cognitive capacities. As a result, children's appraisals of both the content and structure of environmental events may change with increasing cognitive development. In particular, appraisal of the structure of situations with regard to potential controllability may evidence change with increasing cognitive maturity. Parallel to such developmental change in perceptions of control, the actual coping behavior of children of various ages may differ with respect to the relative use of primary control and secondary control modes of coping (Band & Weisz, 1986).

However, while developmental change in childrens' understanding of the structure of situations with respect to controllability appears to occur, this does not occur in isolation. Children's responses to the content of stressful situations is equally subject to the influence of development. In particular, as children mature, the social environment takes on increasing importance. Concomitantly, as situations of a social nature grow in import with age, the specific content of children's coping activities may also change with development. Driven by the motor of socialization, the content of children's coping may be filled in by many different specific activities. Moreover, above and beyond changing perceptions of structure and controllability, secondary control coping activities emphasizing cooperation with existing forces may take on greater importance in the face of broader social demands.

Major or minor, daily or yearly, aversive life events are inherent to lives of all people. As life pressures and demands continue to reach the youngest members of the U.S. society at an accelerated pace, stress and coping among children is likely to remain a source of concern. Child stress and coping cannot occur in a vacuum. Children learn to cope against the socio-environmental backdrop which gives rise to the occurrences of stress in their lives. Concomitantly, as children develop and change, children's coping appears molded by the interplay between the forces of development and environment.

REFERENCES

Abramson, L.Y., Seligman, M.E.P., & Teasdale, J. (1978). Learned helplessness in humans: Critique and reformulation. *Journal of Abnormal Psychology,* *87,* 49–74.

Band, E.B., & Weisz, J.R. (1986). *What feels bad and how to feel better:*

Children's perspectives on everyday stress and coping. Manuscript submitted for publication.

Brenner, A. (1984). *Helping children cope with stress.* Lexington, MA: D.C. Heath.

Coyne, J.C., & Lazarus, R.S. (1980). Cognitive style, stress perception, and coping. In I.L. Kutash & L.B. Schlesinger (Eds.), *Handbook on stress and anxiety: contemporary knowledge, theory and treatment.* San Francisco, CA: Jossey-Bass.

Folkman, S. (1984). Personal control and stress and coping processes: A theoretical analysis. *Journal of Personality and Social Psychology, 46,* 839–852.

Folkman, S., & Lazarus, R.S. (1980). An analysis of coping in a middle-aged community sample. *Journal of Health and Social Behavior, 21,* 219–239.

Folkman, S., & Lazarus, R.S. (1985). If it changes it must be a process: A study of emotion and coping during three stages of a college examination. *Journal of Personality and Social Psychology, 48,* 150–170.

Folkman, S., Schaefer, C., & Lazarus, R.S. (1979). Cognitive processes as mediators of stress and coping. In V. Hamilton & D.M. Warburton (Eds.), *Human stress and cognition: An information processing approach.* London: Wiley.

Haan, N. (1977). *Coping and defending.* New York: Academic Press.

Harter, S. (1983). Developmental perspectives on the self-system. In P.H. Mussen (Ed.), *Handbook of child psychology* (Vol. 4). New York: John Wiley & Sons.

Janis, I.L., & Leventhal, H. (1968). Human reactions to stress. In E. Borgatta & W. Lambert (Eds.), *Handbook of personality theory and research.* Chicago, IL: Rand Mcnally.

Janis, I.L., & Mann, L. (1977). *Decision making.* New York: Free Press.

Kanner, A.D., Coyne, J.C. Schaefer, C., & Lazarus, R.S. (1981). Comparison of two modes of stress measurement: Daily hassles and uplifts versus major life events. *Journal of Behavioral Medicine, 4,* 1–39.

Kubler-Ross, E. (1969). *On death and dying.* New York: Macmillan.

Lazarus, R.S. (1966). *Psychological stress and the coping process.* New York: McGraw-Hill.

Lazarus, R.S. (1975). The self-regulation of emotion. In L. Levi (Ed.), *Emotions: Their parameters and measurement.* New York: Raven Press.

Lazarus, R.S. (1981). The stress and coping paradigm. In C. Eisdorfer, D. Cohen, A. Kleinman, & P. Maxim (Eds.), *Models for clinical psychopathology.* New York: Spectrum.

Lazarus, R.S. & Folkman, S. (1984). Coping and adaptation. In W.D. Gentry (Ed.), *Handbook of behavioral medicine.* New York: The Guilford Press.

Lazarus, R.S., & Launier, R. (1978). Stress-related transactions between person and environment. In L.A. Pervin & M. Lewis (Eds.), *Perspectives in interactional psychology.* New York: Plenum.

Lipowski, Z.J. (1970). Physical illness, the individual and the coping process. *International Journal of Psychiatry in Medicine, 1,* 91–102.

Menninger, K. (1963). *The vital balance: The life process in mental health and illness.* New York: Viking.

Moos, R.H., & Billings, A.G. (1982). Conceptualizing and measuring coping resources and processes. In L. Goldberger & S. Breznitz (Eds.), *The handbook of stress.* New York: Free Press.

Murphy, L.B., & Moriarty, A.E. (1976). *Vulnerability, coping and growth.* New Haven, CT: Yale University Press.

Rotter, J.B. (1966). Generalized expectancies for internal versus external control of reinforcement. *Psychological Monographs, 80,* (1, Whole No. 609).

Rothbaum, F., Weisz, J.R., & Snyder, S.S. (1982). Changing the world and changing the self: A two-process model of perceived control. *Journal of Personality and Social Psychology, 42,* 5–37.

Rutter, M. (1979). Protective factors in children's responses to stress and disadvantage. In M.W. Kent & J.E. Rolf (Eds.), *Primary prevention of psychopathology: Social competence in children* (Vol. 3). Hannover, NH: University of New England.

Shapiro, J. (1984). Family reactions and coping strategies in response to the physically ill or handicapped child: A review. *Social Science Medicine, 17,* 913–931.

Stattin, H. (1984). Developmental trends in the appraisal of anxiety-provoking situations. *Journal of Personality, 52,*(1), 46–55.

Tero, P.F., & Connell, J.P. (1984). *When children think they've failed: An academic coping inventory.* Manuscript submitted for publication.

Vaillant, G.E. (1977). *Adaptation to Life.* Boston, MA: Little, Brown.

Weisz, J.R. (1980). Developmental change in perceived control: Recognizing noncontingency in the laboratory and perceiving it in the world. *Developmental Psychology, 16,* 385–390.

Weisz, J.R. (1981). Illusory contingency in children at the state fair. *Developmental Psychology, 17,* 481–489.

Weisz, J.R., Rothbaum, F.M., & Blackburn, T.F. (1984). Standing out and standing in: The psychology of control in America and Japan. *American Psychologist, 39,* 955–969.

Weisz, J.R., Rothbaum, F.M., & Blackburn, T.F. (1984). Swapping recipes for control. *American Psychologist, 39,* 974–975.

PART THREE

Culturally Structured Environments for Children: Canalization of Child Development

INTRODUCTION:

In the final part of this volume, the issue of children's development within culturally structured environments is addressed by representatives of disciplines neighboring traditional child psychology—anthropology and education. Child psychologists have largely overlooked the potential that analyses of child-related historical artifacts has for better understanding of the processes of child development. The contribution by Norris Brock Johnson (Chapter 7) reminds about the possibility of linking socialization of adolescents with culturally structured environments that are mostly thought of in connection with art history—the Paleolithic European decorated caves. The analysis of children's and adults' footprints in conjunction with the paintings located in hard-to-approach parts of the caves leads to the possibility that decorated caves were used as specially structured environments for the purposes of conducting adolescent initiation rituals. The decorated caves, of course, are an example pertaining to child development in historical times quite removed from our own. Contemporary developmental psychology has largely overlooked the opportunities that remain hidden in the study of historical records pertaining to child development. Undoubtedly, such study is a complicated endeavor, in which the extraction of "basic facts" from historical records poses methodological problems that psychologists are rarely ready to handle. Anthropologists and ethnographers, in contrast, have had to solve these problems in their own ways. Johnson's ethnographic analysis of "historically remote" places of child socialization should encourage contemporary developmental psychologists to be more alert to the ways in which contemporary environmental settings—homes, schools, psychology laboratories, play-

225

grounds, etc.—are constructed in their fixed-feature spatial organization with definite socialization functions in mind.

The contribution of Uwe Zänker (Chapter 8) brings the reader back from prehistory to our contemporary times, and to psychological phenomenology closely tied to socio-political realities of the modern world. It makes the ideological embeddedness of applied developmental psychology in any society very obvious. The author's analysis of the "secondary socialization goals" of textbooks used in East German schools after the Second World War is a dramatic illustration of how children's environment is purposefully structured with definite ideological goals in mind. An analysis of the secondary socialization processes that are embedded in school curriculae may bring to surface similar structuring of students' learning environments in any country, although perhaps not to the same extent. Such ideological guidance might not appear in the physics and mathematics textbooks, but in those of other disciplines. For example, an American readers who are familiar with the heated controversy in the 1980s about the inclusion or exclusion of ideas of evolution in biology textbooks used in U.S. schools may recognize a rather familiar issue at stake, which is only perhaps more accentuated in the case of the East Germany. Analysis of socialization goals embedded in cultural messages for children that are communicated to them via significant objects that dominate their learning environments is a powerful, albeit underused, research strategy for contemporary developmental psychology.

CHAPTER 7

Prehistoric European Decorated Caves: Structured Earth Environments, Initiation, and Rites of Passage

Norris Brock Johnson

Department of Anthropology
University of North Carolina

Culture is a fairly integrated pattern of behavior, ideology, and artifact extant within human society. Animals other than human beings systematically manipulate "things," but human beings are the only animals to do so with respect to a conscious ideology. Material artifacts are component elements of culture, and culture is the structured environment framing human society. Material culture is concretized ideology, and the environments human beings create for themselves in turn condition human sensibilities. People make structured social and cultural environments; then structured environments help make people social and cultural.

Psychological approaches to sociocultural conditioning emphasize study of people's mental rules for behavior as well as study of the interactions, patterned encounters, and transactions occurring among people. An assumption is that sociocultural conditioning is a process by which people transact "equivalences of meaning . . . in the course of recurrent encounters of each member of the group with some other . . . cultural transmission consists of such transactions and equivalences in certain encounters, principally of nonadults with adults and each other" (Gearing, 1973, p. 1). The encounters important to the sociocultural conditioning of children are assumed confined to dyadic, face-to-face interchanges occurring among individuals. It is taken for granted that social and cultural information is stored within individuals and remains the exclusive property of persons.

Theoretical approaches to the process of sociocultural conditioning are limited in two important ways: (a) by overidentification of sociocultural conditioning with the cognitive and behavioral aspects of culture, and (b) through near-exclusive focus on the synchronic, ethnological study of sociocultural conditioning occurring in existing human societies.

Psychological approaches to the study of sociocultural conditioning rarely acknowledge the manner in which material culture, artifact, and structured environments are implicated in the process of making children social and cultural beings. A conceptual and analytic focus on cognition and behavior, on adult/child dyadic interaction, distorts the complexity of the mechanisms by which sociocultural systems condition children. Psychological approaches to the study of sociocultural conditioning, further, are rarely cross-cultural; when studies are cross-cultural, the societies chosen for comparison invariably are historical or existing ethnographic societies. Prehistoric, paleontological, and archaeological case studies rarely appear in the literature on child conditioning. Paleontological and archaeological evidence, though, yields insight into the ways prehistoric peoples constructed environments to store and display sociocultural information, thereby suggesting methods of child sociocultural conditioning archetypal in the human experience.

Prehistoric European cave painting and engraving are well known. Prehistoric European cave paintings and engravings are variously interpreted as aesthetic phenomena (Ucko & Rosenfeld, 1967, pp. 117–122), as graphic instructions about hunting strategy and totemism (Ucko & Rosenfeld, 1967, pp. 123–138), as a prearithmatic notation and mnemonic system (Boroneant & Frolov, 1979; Marshack 1972), and as a complex sign system expressing presumably universal principles of male/female complementary opposition (Leroi-Gourhan, 1967, pp. 106–157, 1968). Interpretations of the human activity in prehistoric caves are for the most part based on structural and symbolic study of cave paintings and engravings rather than on material and environmental study of the caves in which the paintings and engravings occur. To decorate a cave through painting, drawing, or engraving is, in fact, to structure an environment, and we neglect to consider the importance to prehistoric people of the structured environment of the cave itself. Archaeological evidence, in the form of human handprints and footprints, indicates that the people visiting the decorated caves were mainly preadolescent children. Archaeological evidence implies that prehistoric peoples structured specific environments as settings for specific child experiences.

This article initially presents evidence of human activity in several decorated caves from prehistoric Europe. The evidence is the child footprints found in several upper Paleolithic Magdalenian period caves in the Pyrenees region of south central France: Montespan, Niaux/ Reseau Clastres, and Les Trois Freres/Le Tuc d'Audoubert (see Figure 1).

My interpretation of the evidence is that these particular decorated caves were structured environments, settings for child initiation and rites of passage. I find the spatial character of the Pyrenees caves congruent with a spatial model of rites of passage generated from my comparative study of several ethnographic cultures. A conclusion is that the cave environment itself was as important, if not more im-

1. NORTHERN AND EASTERN FRANCE.   2. CHARENTE, PÉRIGORD.   3. QUERCY.   4. PYRENEES.
5. CANTABRIAN SPAIN.   6. CENTRAL AND SOUTHERN SPAIN.   7. LANGUEDOC, RHONE, PROVENCE.
8. ITALY.

Figure 1.   Location of Principal Decorated Caves.

portant, to prehistoric peoples than were the wall paintings and engravings the caves contain. Ucko and Rosenfeld (1967, p. 224) claim that "until it is known what exactly Paleolithic man was doing inside caves, apart from painting and engraving on their walls, all interpretations . . . can only be tentative hypotheses." We will never know, as there are no prehistoric Europeans to tell us, the indigeneous meaning of cave paintings and engravings. But through comparative spatial analysis of cave forms, we can infer the purposes of the cave as a structured environment. Child footprints and the spatial configuration of several Pyrenees caves are "things" deciphered more literally than are the symbolic and semiotic meanings of cave paintings and engravings. The prehistoric decorated cave is content as well as context. Marshall McLuhan reminded us that the medium is the message, a principle of communication and experience of which prehistoric Europeans seemed conscious.

Study of three prehistoric European decorated caves and the child footprints they contain, provides cases supporting the proposition that encounters with other human beings are a sufficient but not exclusive means of childhood sociocultural conditioning. Sociocultural conditioning in every human society occurs, in part, through the interactions of people with socioculturally charged environments. The "keepers" of sociocultural information are not limited to people themselves. Environments, structured human environments, are sociocultural information and knowledge. Sociocultural systems are integrated wholes, and children, in particular, are conditioned to society and culture at the level of structured environment and material artifact as well as at the level of verbal language and interpersonal exchange.

PEOPLE, CULTURE, AND SOCIETY IN THE EUROPEAN UPPER PALEOLITHIC

The *Paleolithic,* meaning old stone age, is an archaeological designation for the time period in which the emergence and development of human society and culture takes place. The Paleolithic period is from about 3,000,000 B.C. to about 8,000 B.C. Fossil hominid (human) groups such as the Australopithecines, Homo Habilis, Homo Erectus, Neanderthals, and Cro-Magnon are associated with the Paleolithic period. The Old World Paleolithic is divided into lower (c. 3,000,000–100,000 B.C.), middle (c. 100,000–40,000 B.C.), and upper (c. 40,000–8,000) sequences with respect to forms of tool technology and associated sociocultural developments such as firemaking among Homo Erectus populations or systematic ritual burials of the dead among Neanderthals.

The Paleolithic is succeeded by the *Mesolithic* (c. 12,000–8,000 B.C.) and *Neolithic* (c. 8,000 B.C.–3,500 B.C.) periods.

The period of the European Upper Paleolithic is from c. 32,000 B.C. to 8,000 B.C. The culture and society of the peoples of the European Upper Paleolithic was quite diverse (cf. Campbell, 1976, pp. 363–377; Hadingham, 1979, pp. 59–84; Poirier, 1977, pp. 331–351), and prehistoric archaeologists distinguish four major sociocultural traditions within this period: (a) the *Aurignacian* tradition, from c. 32,000–27,000 B.C., was widespread across Europe and is associated with mobile bands of people hunting herd animals such as mammoth and reindeer with a varied assemblage of finely worked stone tools; (b) the *Gravettian* culture, from c. 27,000–19,000 B.C. and located primarily in eastern and central Europe, is associated with tent dwelling peoples using ivory from mammoth tusks to carve the famous "Venus" figurines of females; (c) the *Solutrean* tradition, from c. 19,000–15,000 B.C., is associated with cold-adapted glacial dwellers famous for their aesthetically rendered leaf-shaped spear points; (d) the *Magdalenian* tradition, from c. 15,000–8,000 B.C. in western Europe, is associated with elaborate cave painting and engraving. Andre Leroi-Gourhan (1967, pp. 188–202), extending an initial chronology for the Upper Paleolithic offered by the Catholic priest and prehistoric archaeologist Abbe Henri Breuil (1952b), suggests a correlation between the diachronic development of styles of cave decoration and technology/sociocultural traditions in the Upper Paleolithic (see Figure 2).

The Style I period is associated with monochromatic outline drawings of animals and abstract line compositions on cave walls, portable ivory and bone sculptures of horses, and scattered petroglyph rock engravings. Style II designates a later period of more abundant and more complex renderings of animals, and the greater occurrence of portable small carvings such as "Venus" figurines. Style III is associated with a period of decline in sculpture and a period of elaboration in painting and engraving. Style IV designates a period characterized by elaborate polychrome painting and drawing in comparatively elaborate cave settings. Leroi-Gourhan's Style IV stage overlaps the Magdalenian period, noting the emphasis Magdalenian people placed on ritual experiences in caves.

The prehistoric humans in the Upper Paleolithic are termed Cro-Magnon, so named for the discovery, in 1868, of the first fossil from the group at the site of Cro-Magnon near Les Eyzies in the Dordogne region of France. Cro-Magnon peoples occupied what is now Hungary, the Soviet Union, the Middle East, North and South Africa, China, Southeast Asia, Australia, and North America, as well as the geographic area of concern here: southwestern France. The fossil record reveals that Cro-Magnon people are physically similar to contemporary human

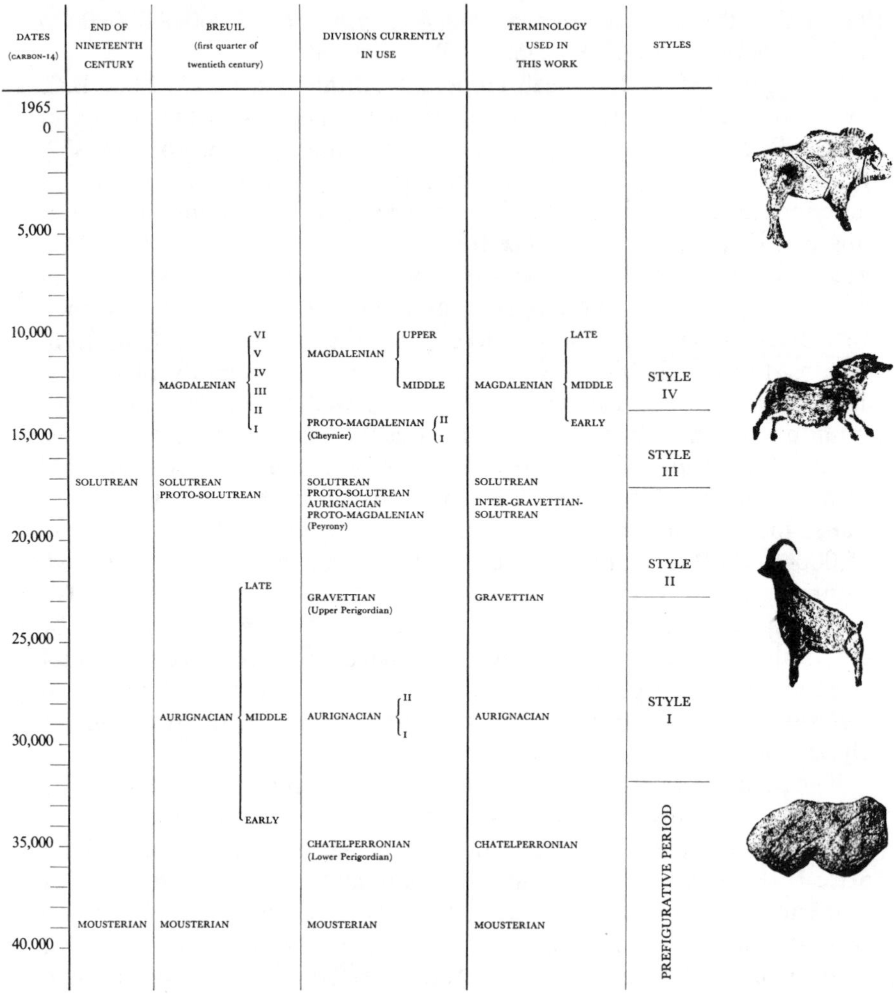

DATES (CARBON-14)	END OF NINETEENTH CENTURY	BREUIL (first quarter of twentieth century)	DIVISIONS CURRENTLY IN USE	TERMINOLOGY USED IN THIS WORK	STYLES
1965 / 0					
5,000					
10,000		MAGDALENIAN VI, V, IV, III, II, I	MAGDALENIAN { UPPER, MIDDLE }	MAGDALENIAN { LATE, MIDDLE, EARLY }	STYLE IV
15,000	SOLUTREAN	MAGDALENIAN; PROTO-MAGDALENIAN (Cheynier) II, I; SOLUTREAN PROTO-SOLUTREAN	PROTO-MAGDALENIAN II, I (Cheynier); SOLUTREAN PROTO-SOLUTREAN AURIGNACIAN PROTO-MAGDALENIAN (Peyrony)	SOLUTREAN; INTER-GRAVETTIAN-SOLUTREAN	STYLE III
20,000					STYLE II
25,000		LATE	GRAVETTIAN (Upper Perigordian)	GRAVETTIAN	
30,000		AURIGNACIAN { MIDDLE }	AURIGNACIAN { II, I }	AURIGNACIAN	STYLE I
35,000		EARLY	CHATELPERRONIAN (Lower Perigordian)	CHATELPERRONIAN	PREFIGURATIVE PERIOD
40,000	MOUSTERIAN	MOUSTERIAN	MOUSTERIAN	MOUSTERIAN	

Figure 2. Chronology of The Upper Paleolithic.

populations. An appropriately clothed Cro-Magnon couple would go unnoticed in a contemporary urban population. The skulls from Cro-Magnon are anatomically modern (Brace & Montagu, 1977, pp. 347–57). Cro-Magnon skulls possess a chin, high forehead, even rows of teeth, and oral and nasal cavities suggesting a developed capacity for vocalization. Alexander Marshack (1972) and Boris Frolov (1978) are researching the manner in which the high cognitive and intellectual abilities of Cro-Magnon peoples associated with their "art" and material culture.

Cro-Magnon peoples living during the Magdalenian period in south-western France faced an environment pleasant but increasingly de-manding in several critical respects. By environment, I mean human-made sociocultural systems as well as naturally occurring fauna (animal life) and flora (plant life). The fourth major glacial period in world history, the Würm glacial period, predominated during the mid- to late Paleolithic period. From about 25,000 B.C. to 14,000 B.C., much of Europe was glacial. In southern France and Spain, however, glacial conditions were less extreme than in northern and central Europe. Ice sheets covered what is now Scandinavia and most of the British Isles. Britain, Germany, and Belgium were unoccupied from 25,000 B.C. to 14,000 B.C. (Mellars, 1974; Bordes & de Sonneville-Bordes, 1970). The Würm glacial broke at the foothills of the Pyrenees and the Cantabrian mountain range in southern France and northern Spain, respectively. Michael A. Jochim (1983, pp. 214–216) notes that these variations in glacial conditions generated a comparatively great degree, and kind, of faunal and floral diversity in the area between the Cantabrian and Pyrenees mountains. People living there during Magdalenian times in this sense did so in a favorable food environment within a comparatively pleasant temperate living area. Jochim says that the severity of Würm glacial conditions north and west of this area encouraged the migration of both people and other animals into southwestern France, and left the remainder of Europe nearly unpopulated during this time. The middle to late Upper Paleolithic period in southwestern France, then, witnessed what probably was a disturbing increase in population num-bers and density (cf. Hadingham, 1979, pp. 85–105; Pfeiffer, 1982, pp. 53–72; Sieveking, 1979, pp. 7–26). The traiditon, begun in the Aurig-nacian period, of painting and engraving in caves is predominant in the Magdalenian period. There is an association, then, between height-ened Magdalenian activity in caves and regionally increasing population numbers and population density.

The Pyrenees region in southwestern France is critical to the history of Europe. Prehistoric cave painting and engraving are widely distrib-uted, but are a predominant activity in southwestern France. There are, further, two major types of prehistoric decorated caves: what Annette Laming-Emperaire (Ucko & Rosenfeld, 1967, pp. 221–223) terms *daylight* caves and *deep* caves. Daylight caves and rock shelters, such as La Grèze and Pair-Non-Pair in France, are comparatively shallow, and paintings and engravings occur near entrances and in several cases are exposed to the daylight. These types of caves exhibit comparative ease of access to the wall paintings and engravings. On the other hand, deep caves, such as the ones described for the Pyrenees, contain paintings and engravings only experienced with considerable difficulty. It is not so much that Magdalenian people in the Pyrenees painted and engraved in caves, but that the caves selected for painting and engraving are of a particular kind. Rather than the paintings and engravings themselves, I suggest that the spatial characteristics of several decorated caves in the geographically critical Pyrenees region were of utmost concern to the Magdalenians.

Following are descriptions of the form and spatial layout of three important Pyrenees caves, and descriptions of the child footprints found in the deep recesses of these caves. From these case descriptions, I interpret the Pyrenees caves as both content and context with respect to the initiation and rite of passage activity in the caves. Attention is then given to the symbolic significance of caves in several cultural settings, and then to the relationship between painting and engraving, initiation, and rites of passage. The conclusion restates the significance of the study of archaeological and prehistoric evidence of child activity to understanding of the mechanisms for the sociocultural conditioning of children, and the significance of structured environments and "things" to the process of sociocultural conditioning.

THREE PYRENEES CAVES AND THEIR PREHISTORIC FOOTPRINTS

Montespan

The cave at Montespan (Haute Garonne) is 2.5 kilometers long and contains the underground part of the Houantou river system running between the villages of Ganties and Montespan. The cave was initially discovered by Louis Trombe (Trombe & Dubuc, 1947), then systematically studied in 1925 by Norbert Casteret and H. Godin, who offered interpretations of the significance of its wall engravings and clay statues of bison. In 1926 Felix Trombe and G. Dubuc crossed interior lakes on rafts to discover wall paintings, drawings, and engravings in the deeper chambers of Montespan. The cave is a network of intricate passages and is entered through a hillside opening, presumed to be the prehistoric entrance, south of the village of Montespan. A second, smaller entrance to the cave is alongside the Houantou river at the location where the river flows through the village of Ganties. Leroi-Gourhan (1967, pp. 370–373) dates the wall paintings and engravings in Montespan to the middle to late Magdalenian period.

The spatial configuration of the Montespan cave makes for a difficult entrance and subsequent passage. The ceiling of the cave is quite low near the entrance, and a ridge of rock projects downward from the ceiling, serving, during periodic flooding, to nearly stop the inflow of water from the Houton river. Often, the water level is close to the ceiling of the cave, and one is forced to swim underwater to enter the main chambers of the cave. The banks of the cave floor bordering the center river channel are wide, and mobility is undemanding when the water level is low but difficult when the water level is high.

At about 72 meters from the Montespan entrance to the cave, the roof lowers to within 1 meter from the water in the central cave channel. Beyond this point, access to the rich clusters of wall paintings and engravings is quite difficult. The first group of paintings and engravings is 58 meters beyond this point and 130 meters from the Montespan entrance to the cave. The Casteret Gallery, named after the scholar/explorer Norbert Casteret, contains several clay statues of bears and high relief wall engravings of horses with human-made (spear point) holes in their sides (see Topographic Map 1).

Prehistoric human footprints at Montespan occur deep in the cave system at points where the river banks partially are covered with flood water. One wonders at the original number of footprints left by children, footprints obliterated by the seasonal ebb and flow of the Hountou river. Entrance to the important decorated chamber here, the Trombe Dubuc Gallery, is difficult. The roof of the cave near the Trombe Dubuc Gallery in places is as low as 87 centimeters. The decorated chamber is entered by squeezing through a cleft in the wall, then crawling on one's hands and knees. One travels in this fashion for about 30 meters before seeing any wall decorations. A panel of engravings on the left wall, about 60 centimeters high by 3 meters long, contains a frieze of horses with small holes in their flanks, interpreted (Ucko & Rosenfeld, 1967, pp. 131, 187–189) as made through the ritual killing of the animals depicted (cf. Topographic Map 5). A group of human footprints, children's footprints measuring 17.9 centimers, are seen near this frieze of horses.

Niaux/Reseau Clastres

Niaux is one of several caves in the vast cavern of La Calbiere. The studies of Emile Cartailhac and Abbe Henri Breuil in 1908 brought the cave system to the attention of scholars (Cartailhac & Breuil, 1908; Breuil, 1950, 1952a). Niaux, about two kilometers in length, is a partially desiccated river cave containing the remnants of several large underground lakes fed by the Ariege river. Access to the cave is difficult and the present entrance to Niaux is 90 meters above ground level, demanding a half-hour climb to reach. Three hours are required to pass through the cave of Niaux. On the basis of the style of wall paintings

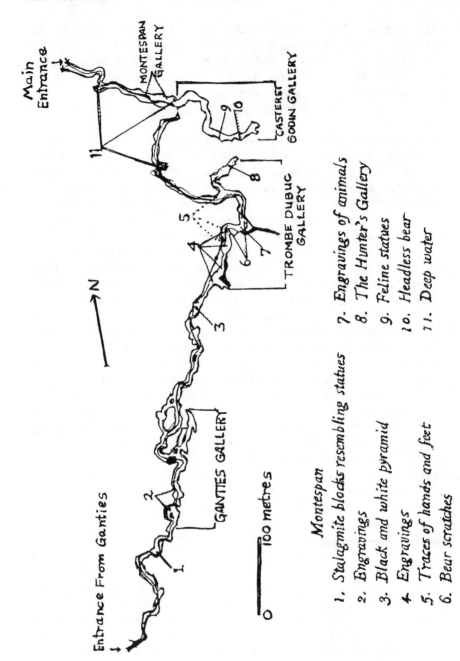

Topographic Map 1.

and engravings, Leroi-Gourhan (1967, pp. 362–365) dates human activity in Niaux to the middle Magdalenian period.

Paintings, drawings, and a few engravings begin about 450 meters inside the cave. The principal group of wall decorations is found in the Salon Noir, named with respect to the dramatic black-outlined wall paintings of bison, horses, and extinct ibex found there (see Topographic Map 2).

Intact human footprints are found in a rear area of the main cave channel in Niaux, and a section of the Reseau Clastres chambers intersecting Niaux (Pales, 1976). Niaux and the Reseau Clastres chambers have been studied most recently by Professor Jean Clottes (Clottes & Simonnet, 1972), and the human footprints dramatically described by John Pfeiffer (1982, p. 184):

> The gallery is one of the most difficult to explore in this or any other cave. It is blocked off by three lakes, the first of which was crossed on a raft during a winter dry spell in 1925. An even more impassable lake frustrated explorers until 1940, while lake number three was finally crossed in December 1970 after pumps had been brought in to lower the water level. That opened the way to about 3,000 feet of new passages, currently sealed off by a protective wall. But they contain about 500 footprints, more than have been found in all other caves combined . . . one small area alone includes 120 to 140 footprints. Three children were walking on a sand dune close to the wall, side by side. One cannot help imagining that they were holding hands. Their footprints are 18 to 20 centimeters long, so we estimate that they must have been eight to ten years old.

Difficult territorial movement, either over or through the earth, is a common world-wide feature of childhood initiation and rites of passage. A group of children's footprints occur near the right side wall in the main corridor of the Reseau Clastres system (see Figure 3). On this wall are three bison and a horse outlined in black manganese and charcoal. A group of children walked near these wall images, and I later discuss the importance of the presence of the children in conjunction with the wall images. The central part of the sand bank close to what once undoubtedly was a stream flowing in the cave, apart from where the children were standing, exhibits the prints of an adult human. The children, not the adult, moved toward, then away from, the wall paintings (see Figures 4 and 5).

Other prints in this area suggest that at least two groups of people, separated by a long period of time, by how much time presently is not known, followed each other into and out of the cave. Deep sediments of calcite lie in the first group of prints, thereby permitting relative

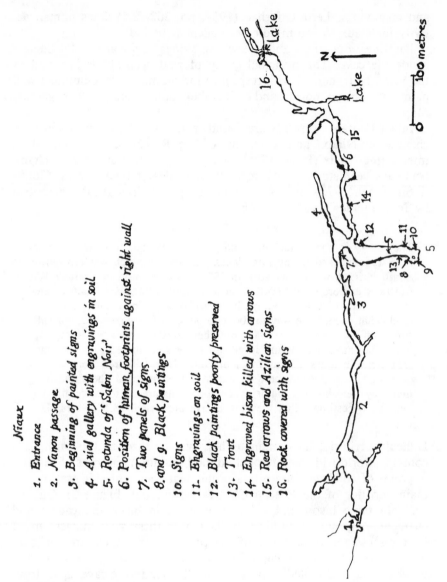

Niaux

1. Entrance
2. Nanon passage
3. Beginning of painted signs
4. Axial gallery with engravings in soil
5. Rotunda of 'Salon Noir'
6. Position of human footprints against right wall
7. Two panels of signs
8. and 9. Black paintings
10. Signs
11. Engravings on soil
12. Black paintings poorly preserved
13. Trout
14. Engraved bison killed with arrows
15. Red arrows and Azilian signs
16. Rock covered with signs

N

Lake

Lake

0   100 metres

Topographic Map 2.

dating with samples of sediment taken from floor areas in other areas of the cave. The child footprints in the Pyrenees caves are not contemporary or even historical. There is no evidence that the child footprints do not exist in temporal association with the wall paintings and engravings.

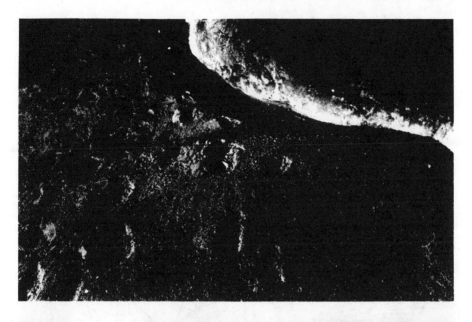

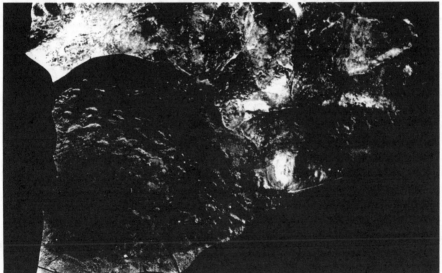

Figure 3.   Footprints at Niaux.

Le Tuc d'Audoubert

The cave of Le Tuc d'Audoubert is under a mountain through which flows the Volp, a tributary of the Garonne river. Les Trois Frères is

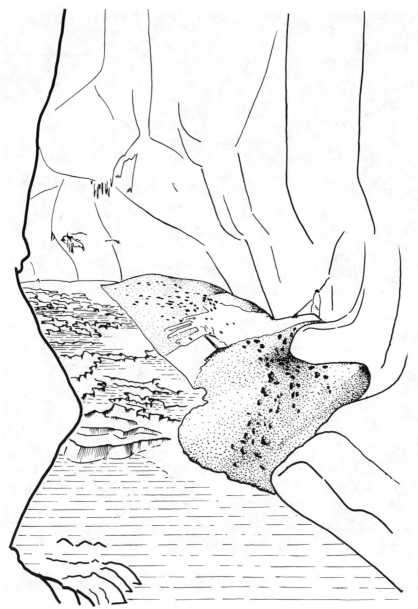

Figure 4. The Sandbank in Niaux.

quite close to Le Tuc d'Auboubert, although they were not connected in prehistoric times. The probable prehistoric entrance to Les Trois Frères is through a hole in its ceiling that is on the slope of a hillside bordering the Garonne river. The probable prehistoric entrance to Le

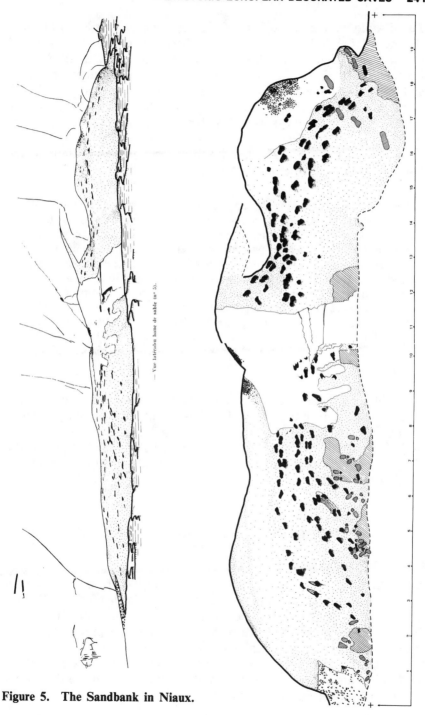

— Vue latérale banc de sable (n° 5).

Figure 5. The Sandbank in Niaux.

Tuc d'Audoubert is through a hillside opening on a hillside above a channel of the Volp. Le Tuc d'Audoubert was explored in 1912 by Count Henri Bégouën and his sons (Bégouën & Bégouën, 1928, 1931; Bégouën, 1912). Le Tuc d'Audoubert is about two kilometers in length, and the extant human footprints are found in that cave system. Leroi-Gourhan (1967, pp. 366–368) dates human activity in the cave system, in association with the style of wall painting and engraving, to the middle to late Magdalenian period (see Topographic Map 3).

Sieveking (1979, p. 197) describes the location and pattern of the human footprints in Le Tuc d'Audoubert.

> The sanctuary containing the clay bisons is in the upper galleries of the cave, which are reached up a chimney at the far end from the entrance to the main hall. . . . On the left wall at the top are two small engravings, the head and shoulders of two animals, perhaps cows, which are said to be guarding the entrance to the sanctuary. A tunnel facing the engravings leads into the upper galleries, several hundred yards long, containing a large number of halls, in one of which, just before reaching a second lake, is a series of human footprints. On the right-hand side of the gallery there is a low alcove containing traces of what is interpreted as a children's initiation ceremony. The floor of the alcove, composed of fine clay, has preserved a series of deep heel marks belonging to five or six children, apparently dancing in a semicircle.

As at Niaux/Reseau Clastres, human footprints occur in conjunction with a small number and group of wall paintings and engravings reached after a difficult journey (cf. Topographic Map 8). The 50 or so footprints at Le Tuc d'Audoubert are 20–21 centimeters in length and, on the basis of size and proportion, Sieveking concludes they were made by preadolescent children.

PREHISTORIC CAVES: STRUCTURED EARTH ENVIRONMENTS

Other than those described, prehistoric human footprints are extant in only a few other caves (Aldene, Fontanet, and Pech Merle in France; Ojo Guarena in Spain; Toirano in Italy) (Clottes & Simonnet, 1972). Why is the footprint evidence of human activity in prehistoric caves concentrated in the Pyrenees region of southern France?

During the middle to late Magdalenian period, Cro-Magnon populations in Europe began to socially and culturally respond to the retreat of the Würm glacier. Within the delimited geographic areas of south-

Le Tuc d'Audoubert Les Trois Frères

1. Drawings
2. Gallery of the clay bisons
3. Heel imprints
4. Bisons
5. Henriome
6. Owls
7. Human figure
8. Engraved lions
9. Bison bones

10. Lioness
11. Dots
12. Hands
13. Hands
14. Black bison
15. Excavations
16. Horse
17. Red lines
18. Red dots

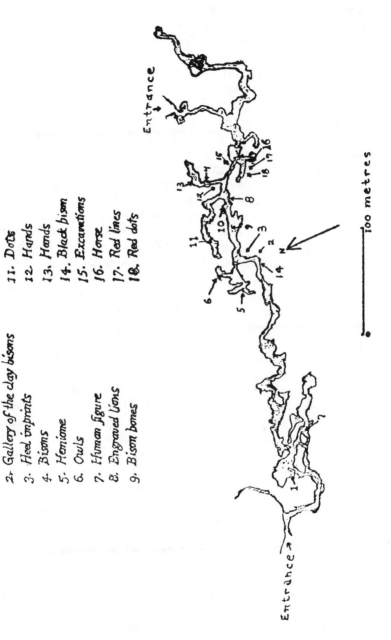

100 metres

Entrance

Entrance

Topographic Map 3.

western Europe, the refuge influx of peoples from the north and west resulted in competition for flora and fauna resources (Jochim, 1983, pp. 216–219). As early as 17,000 years ago, resource depletion began to occur in the Pyrenees region (Pfeiffer, 1982, p. 72). The puzzle is this. Painting and engraving in caves occur from the Aurignacian through the Magdalenian period, but painting and engraving in comparatively long and deep underground caves in the Pyrenees are associated with the middle to late Magdalenian period. Painting and engraving in deep caves are associated with an overexploited, competitive subsistence environment. Magdalenian populations, it appears, did not resort to violence as a means of solving the subsistence problems accompanying population increase, but turned to structuring earth environments decorated with paintings and engravings as part of their response to a critical sociological and ecological problem. There is no archaeological evidence of intragroup conflict during the Magdalenian period. The chosen solution to this still persistent human problem of balancing population size and density, subsistence resources, and environment appears to be intragroup cooperation rather than conflict.

During the middle to late Magdalenian period, hunter gatherer social organization increased in complexity, and cross-regional contacts and associations developed between local groups of people (Campbell, 1976, pp.363–395; Hadingham, 1979, pp. 85–105; Pfeiffer, 1982, pp. 191–209). Increasing regional-level population density, and decreasing subsistence fauna, encouraged the development of regional-level sodalities; for example, more extensive cross-group marriage arrangements, associations for trade in commodities, and management organizations regulating the hunting of animals to make for efficient exploitation of fauna and flora resources (Jochim, 1983, pp. 214–215).

The uses to which painting, drawing, and engraving were put might have been intended to be another innovation reinforcing regional-level group relationship. While painting and drawing are at least as old as Neanderthal culture (Hadingham, 1979, pp. 34–58; Pfeiffer, 1982, pp. 88–101), they find new applications in the European Upper Paleolithic. Geographically central sites, such as the decorated caves in the Pyrenees, appear important to the territorial and regional-level organization of local groups of Magdalenian people.

The sociocultural context of the Pyrenees footprints suggests that the function of cave painting and engraving was more political and ecological than aesthetic. My interpretation of the evidence is that Magdalenian children from differing territorial regions and subgroups living in the Franco-Catabrian mountain valleys were periodically brought together in the Pyrenees to ritually experience these caves. Exploration of the caves resulted in regionally heterogeneous groups of children from areas now called Germany, Britain, France, and Spain receiving a common ritual experience and a common body of esoteric, restricted knowledge—whatever the knowledge concretized in the cave wall paintings and engravings. The Magdalenian period witnessed the development of relationships and sociocultural identities more regional than local. As a consequence, some people had to very early be trained to think and behave at levels of concern beyond that of the local group. The midcontinent placement of the Pyrenees decorated caves, within the mountain range between Spain and France, is a geographic fact associated with the postulated function of the caves in enhancing the regional-level sociocultural organization of Magdalenian peoples. The Pyrenees caves can be interpreted as sites for gathering children from various local groups together for a common identity-binding ritual experience.

Initiation and Rites of Passage

None of the human footprints extant in upper Paleolithic caves indicate the primary presence of adults. All of the footprints, particularly within the Pyrenees caves, either are of groups of children or of a group of children accompanied by an adult. Child footprints average 16–17 centimeters in length, adolescent prints average 18–23 centimeters, and adult prints average 24–26 centimeters by present-day (European/ EuroAmerican) standards (Clottes & Simonnet, 1972; Garcia, 1979; Robbins, 1985). The point of significance is not the fact of prehistoric peoples visiting the Pyrenees caves, but the fact that the majority of the Magdalenians visiting the Pyrenees caves were children (Hadingham, 1979, pp. 172–196; Garcia, 1979; Pfeiffer, 1982, pp. 174–190). Though made by adults (because of style of rendering and technique of execution), the Pyrenees cave paintings and engravings were intended to be experienced by children.

The prehistoric footprints in the Pyrenees caves were made by preadolescent children, most probably male children. The footprints occur in sets. The caves, and their wall decorations, are not intended to be experienced by single individuals or by large groups of people. The linear and directional quality of the footprints suggest a procession of several children and an adult. The footprint evidence, additionally, reveals that the Pyrenees caves were visited only a few times each.

A few caves have footprints in sand or mud, but at Niaux, for example, in the Reseau Rene Clastres these belong to a few adults and children exploring on one occasion only, whereas one might have expected the floor to be trampled with hundreds of superimposed footmarks. . . . The evidence we have in this context suggests little use. When interpreters of Paleolithic art talk of mine and dances enacted in front of the painted friezes they should consider how often they assume this to have happened over the millennia, how many torches were carried and how many people participated. (Sieveking, 1979, pp. 102–103)

Signs of intensive occupation and habitation do not occur in the Pyrenees caves. People did not live in these caves, as they did seasonally at Lascaux and at Altamira (Leori-Gourhan, 1982b; Straus, 1977). Further, it seems that, the deeper and less accessible a cave, the scantier is the evidence of frequent visitation.

This fact, along with the relative scarcity of footprints in many areas, suggests that prehistoric expeditions to the innermost sanctuaries were as arduous and rare as they are today. . . . That both children as well as adults penetrated into these deep and tortuous galleries seems certain, but the possibility of regular ceremonies . . . seems improbable. (Hadingham, 1979, p. 183)

Why decorate caves only to have comparatively few people, and children at that, visit them?

My suggestion is that the children visiting the Pyrenees caves were age cohorts organized into initiation groups to experience what we term *initiation* and *rite of passage*. Initiation, as conceptualized by Mircea Eliade (1957, pp. 190–228, 1958), signals the beginning stages in a process of sociocultural conditioning and marks the points in a person's life, whether child or adult, when he or she is ushered to new levels of expected participation in a sociocultural system. Rites of passage, as conceptualized by Arnold Van Gennep (1960, p. 3), are "ceremonies whose essential purpose is to enable the individual to pass from one defined position to another defined position which is equally well defined . . . by passing through several stages and traversing several boundaries." Rite of passage gives sociocultural meaning to the biological transition from child to adult, while initiation reveals the sacred meaning of ordinary life. My interpretation of the matter is that the Pyrenees cave footprints were made by a few high status children from various regions and local groups of people from France, Spain, and northern Europe who together experienced a common initiation and rite of passage.

Initiation and rite of passage are associated with the (status and prestige) differential distribution of sociocultural knowledge and experience, and with reinforcement of the status and prestige associated with the knowledge gained through initiation and rite of passage.

Material culture evidence of status and prestige ranking occurs very early in human history. Neanderthals are the first hominids to bury their dead, and the skeletons of buried Neanderthal children often bear the remnants of clothing and jewelry (Pfeiffer, 1982, pp. 99–102). Artifact indicators of social ranking are very old, and are elaborated in Upper Paleolithic cultures.

The prevailing ethnographic model for the interpretation of Upper Paleolithic cultures are egalitarian foragers and hunters such as the aboriginal Australians. Though most probably structured in band units of about 20 to 40 people, Magdalenian bands were not as mobile or as independent as aboriginal Australian band units. The prehistoric evidence from southwestern France suggests that bands of people moved from seacoast settlements to inland settlements in a regular seasonal pattern (Hadingham, 1979, pp. 220–238; Jochim, 1983; Sieveking, 1979, pp. 133–138). Further, these bands of people appear to have been forging regional-level patterns of relationship with respect to trade and exchange, ideology and belief, kinship, and social organization. Among existing groups of people, this pattern is parallel to traditional Innuit (Eskimo) seasonally seminomadic band life and the cultural ecology of semisedentary, territorially interdependent foragers and hunters of the North Pacific coast of North America, for example, the Kwakiutl, Tinglit, and Tsimshian. The sociocultural situation among Northwest coast peoples is especially appropriate, for here we find food collectors *not* reflecting principles of egalitarianism customarily associated with huntering and gathering peoples such as the aboriginal Australians. Magdalenian people are similar to the people of the Northwest coast with respect to status consciousness and status ranking. John Pfeiffer (1982, p. 64) argues that, in the Upper Paleolithic, we see "the first signs of a departure from egalitarian principles that seem to have prevailed over thousands of previous millenniums." Pfeiffer (1982, pp. 67–68) discusses the burials of children at the 20,000-year-old sites of Sungir near Moscow, the Grottes des Enfants in Italy, and La Madeline in southwestern France.

> The boys, aged seven to nine and twelve to thirteen, respectively, were buried face up in the same narrow trench in a head-to-head position, with an impressive array of grave goods—some 8,000 ivory beads, arctic-fox canine teeth, assorted rings and braclets, and sixteen spears, darts, and daggers. . . . A set of graves excavated in the Grottes des Infants on the Italian Rivera also included two young children with large clusters of perforated shells around their midsections, presumably the remains of decorated clothing. . . . A child about seven years old was buried at the La Madeline rock shelter, powdered with ochre and decorated with rings

of strung-together shells on its head, neck, elbows, wrists, knees, and ankles.

Every Cro-Magnon child was not buried in this manner. The question is whether these children had done anything (achieved status) to merit such observation upon their burial, or whether these are the burials of children from families of means (ascribed status). I suspect both are probable. On the northwest Coast, the children of nobility and of chiefs (ascribed status) from many geographic areas participate in winter *Tseyka* ceremonies, go through primarily male initiations into *Hamatsa* clans (achieved status), and are incorporated into society as special people as a result of ritual experiences not available to children of lesser status. On the Northwest coast, the children from local groups of chiefs and the nobility receive similar ritual experiences and come to have more in common with each other than they do with children of lesser status within their local groups. Northwest coast male initiations and rites of passage are intended sociocultural conditioning for regional-level identity and for the maintenance of regional level sociocultural integration.

My feeling is that the Pyrenees footprints mark the passage of high status children being exposed to a common body of comparatively restricted information and knowledge. As in many other sociocultural situations, exposure to a common body of information reinforces in children, especially in the socioculturally heterogeneous situation, a common supralocal identity, status, and role. Magdalenian children probably were unequal with respect to other children, but equal with respect to each other by virtue of a common ritual experience in the caves. The few children to experience the Pyrenees caves had to be selected on some basis. My political interpretation has it that the experience of the caves for these few Magdalenian children both conferred status and was a result of status. The subsequent supralocal role of the comparatively few children experiencing the Pyrenees caves most likely included political leadership, economic resource management, and shamanic training.

Leroi-Gourhan's (1967, 1982a) research stops short of suggesting that differences in the style and location of cave paintings and drawings, compared over wide geographic areas across the European/Eurasian continent, is associated with the spatial ranking, if not the stratification, of knowledge. The knowledge of the existence of the Pyrenees caves, knowledge of their location, and knowledge of what is contained in the caves, would be esoteric rather than common knowledge. The decorated caves of the Upper Paleolithic did not serve similar sociocultural functions. There were spatially accessible caves for the storage and display of comparatively common information and knowledge, such as Lascaux in France and Altamira in Spain, as well as spatially inaccessible deep caves for the storage and display of comparatively esoteric information and knowledge in the Pyrenees mountain range between France and Spain. "Difficulty of access," Sieveking (1979, p. 160) reminds us, "is a characteristic of the sanctuaries of the later Magdalenian." Esoteric information and knowledge always are comparatively inaccessible (Bourdieu 1973; Bourdieu & Passeron, 1977). Information and knowledge are property, often valuable property, and upper Paleolithic social and cultural information and knowledge appear as differentially ranked and distributed, with respect to age and sex and social status, as it is in modern sociocultural systems.

Structured Spatial Environments and Rites of Passage

Out of all the caves that could have been used by the Magdalenians, only a few, about 200, contain paintings, drawings, and engravings. Why did people choose some caves over others to decorate for various child activities?

The Pyrenees caves consciously or unconsciously were selected over other caves, I feel, because of their spatial configuration. Form follows function, according to the architect Louis Sullivan. The spatial configuration of the Pyrenees caves is congruent with the spatial settings for initiation and rite of passage occurring among existing groups of people. In comparing rites of passage in a variety of sociocultural settings, Van Gennep (1960, pp. 15–25) emphasizes the recurrent spatially lineal quality of the settings for children the passage through which is symbolic of transition from one sociocultural status to another. The point is literal. Rites of passage comprise a spatial movement from one place to another place to mark analogous movement from one status and role to another status and role.

The major status/role phases and associated spatial movements comprising rite of passage are *separation* from one's customary social and cultural group, *transitional* experiences often involving trial and ordeal and conditioning to a new way of thinking and being, and final *incorporation* into a new level of society and culture (Gluckman, 1963, pp. 1–52; Leach, 1976, pp. 77–79; Van Gennep, 1960, pp. 1–13). Rite of passage is associated with the symbolic death of a former status and role and the symbolic birth of a new status and role. The sexual metaphor of birth and rebirth is not literal but is symptomatic of a primal principle of regenerative renewal Van Gennep felt is archetypically expressed in every society, thereby accounting for the universal occurrence of rites of passage. Several examples from existing cultures illustrate rite of passage as *spatial* separation, transition, and incorporation.

The Ndembu live in Zambia, south central Africa. Victor Turner has detailed aspects of Ndembu culture and society, in particular, the structure and symbolism of Ndembu ritual and rites of passage (Turner, 1962, 1964). The important Ndembu rite of passage for preadolescent males is termed *Mukanda*. A special place, the "place of dying," termed *ifwilu*, is ritually prepared by male officials. The site is considered sacred, and is prohibited for uninitiated males and all females. The site is formed around three special trees, each of a different species: a *mudyi* tree (Diplorrhyncus mossambicensis), a *muyombu* tree (Kirkia acuminata), and a *mukula* tree (Pterocarpus angolensis). The rite of passage is spatially organized with respect to these three symbolic trees. Young males are circumcised under a naturally occurring *mudyi* tree, carried over a transplanted *muyombu* tree, then placed on a freshly cut log from a *mukula* tree until their initiation wounds cease to bleed (Turner, 1962, p. 126). Each tree is said to represent a "place" or "state of being" in the male passage from social infancy to social maturity. At each tree distinctive rites are performed, and each tree is associated with symbols designating the boys' separation from a female social world and incorporation into a male social world.

> The positional meaning of the three station-symbols may be shortly summarized by stating that the boys are taken away from the sphere where both sexes interact, passed over the *muyombu*, representing the continuity through males of universal Ndembu values, and joined together in a community of male age-mates, who together bleed, heal, and receive nourishment from the generation of their fathers. (Turner, 1962, p. 169)

Mukula means "to grow," and the spatial passage from tree to tree marks a ritual death and rebirth insuring the continuity both of individual Ndembu males and of Ndembu society.

The Ndembu *Mukula* rite of passage is composed of distinct phases of separation, transition, and incorporation. These three phases are congruent with the three spatial areas marked by symbolic trees. The prehistoric caves in the Pyrenees appear to have been similarly structured for the spatial passage of preadolescent males initially separated from the outside world and society, subjected to the physical and psychological trials accompanying passage through caves, then incorporated into society on new levels of status, role, and expected participation by adult mentors responsible for their sociocultural conditioning. I later suggest that the sparse but spatially organized panels of painting and engravings in the Pyrenees caves functioned similarly to the tree stations among the Ndembu. Cave painting and engravings, as well as sociocultural knowledge to be experienced, can be interpreted as station markers on the transitional ritual passage through the caves. As with the Ndembu, the evidence suggests that prehistoric cave rites of passage in the Pyrenees were age-graded and composed of small groups of adolescent children, most probably male children.

There is an association between sex and physical space in initiation and rites of passage. The cross-cultural pattern is that rituals for males invariably occur in groups within confined areas distant from habitation and domestic spaces, involve physically and psychologically difficult tests and trials, and exhibit content emphasis on origins, the mythic history of society and culture, and emphasis on the metaphysical structuring of relationships between self (either individual or social) and others. Female initiation and rite of passage rituals invariably occur dyadically, in spaces overlapping habitation sites and domestic areas, tend not to involve tests or trials, and exhibit content emphasis on childrearing and households. Females learn they are creators and maintainers of life, says Eliade (1958, p. 45), while males learn they are implicated in the creation and maintenance of society. Eliade's (1958, pp. 41–47) cross-cultural review of female initiation and rite of passage rituals emphasizes their individualistic nature as against the collective nature of male rituals (cf. Brown, 1963; Young, 1962, 1965). The footprints in the Pyrenees caves are evidence of collective, not individualistic or dyadic, activity and support the interpretation of primarily male activity in the caves.

Descent into the earth as a component of male rites of passage occurs among Pueblo native Americans, both prehistoric and contemporary, of the southwestern United States. *Kivas,* found in every pueblo village (Dozier, 1970, pp. 140–141; Driver, 1969, pp. 184–185), are semisubterranean ceremonial adobe structures. The great *kivas* of New Mexico, such as Casa Riconada, date from the 11th century A.D. Jennings and Reed (1956, p. 86) note that ceremonial earth chambers in the New World date to 25,000 years ago (cf. Ellis & Hammack, 1968), somewhat older than the Old World Pyrenees caves. The *kiva* at Casa Riconda "is located atop an isolated portion of a natural ridge, formed of sandstone and a series of carbonaceous shale layers. The major part of its height was sunk through the shale layers into the knoll" (Vivian & Reiter, 1965, p. 9). Entrance to a *kiva* is similar to entrance to a prehistoric Pyrenees cave. First one goes up, then one descends down into a series of subterranean chambers interconnected by narrow passageways. Benches are cut into the earth chambers of the *kiva,* and altar platforms line south-facing walls.

Ascent is an archetypal image of separation from the ordinary world.

This initial phase of a rite of passage is spatially expressed in temple (Paul, 1976) and church (Marc, 1977) architecture as well as in ideas recurrent in the world's cultures of mountains, such as the Pyrenees mountains, as spiritual places (Eliade, 1959, pp. 37–41; Yetts, 1919). A rite of passage is a spatial movement, and that spatial movement often is vertical as well as horizontal. Descent into the earth in many cultures is equated with a return to the telluric womb, to the place of the origin of things. Descent into the earth also is death as well as birth. To enter into the earth then return from the earth is to die yet be reborn (Eliade, 1958, pp. 57–60; Jung, 1980, pp. 111–147; Van Gennep, 1960, p. 65–115).

The word *kiva* also refers to the initiation society associated with these structured earth environments (Bunzel, 1932; Dozier, 1970, pp. 154–176). Kiva groups are associated with the *katcina*. *Katcina* are spirits associated with rain, fertility, and group well-being. There are many types of *katcina;* some are animals such as the owl, eagle, or bear, while others are found in water, in a tree, or in the wind. *Katcina* are represented at ceremonials by adult masked dancers who are the guardians of the life-enhancing knowledge associated with the supernaturals. To gain access to this knowledge, one must be initiated into a *kiva kachina* group (Eggan, 1956; Thompson, 1945). Initiation groups are formed every 4 years. Between the ages of 6 and 9, young people are initiated into a *katcina* society and undergo physical and psychological trial during rite of passage through a *kiva*. The rite of separation occurs during the night, when male children are taken from their mothers by masked men, led to the *kiva* where they are forced to observe silence and a period of fasting, then expected to withstand severe whippings with branches from a sacred *yucca* tree. The darkness of the *kiva* is punctuated by flickering torchlight. *Katcina* dolls line the altars in front of the stone benches where the boys huddle in terror. Water and corn pollen are sprinkled on the boys' initiation wounds. After a time the masked adults tell the boys they now are men, and that they have been made transformed from boys to men by the *katcina*. The adults unmask, revealing they are *katcina* and that the *katcina* now live in the initiates as well. The adults depart and, after a time, so do the initiated young males now incorporated into society one new levels of status, role, and expected participation.

Generational difference always characterize participants in initiations and rites of passage. The Pyrenees footprints are of one or several adults with a group of children, yet another sign of initiation and rites of passage.

The Symbolism of the Cave

Decorated caves such as the famous ones at Lascaux and at Altamira are comparatively short, lack rivers and water, exhibit signs of seasonal occupation by fairly large groups of people, and wall paintings and engravings occur close to the entrance of the caves. Caves such as these spatially conform to Conkley's (1980) idea of "aggregation" sites deliberately chosen to accommodate large habitation groups of people for specific (seasonal) ritual activities. The decorated caves in the Pyrenees, on the other hand, are comparatively long and narrow river caves exhibiting no sign of habitation and containing wall paintings and engravings occurring deep within the earth. The spatial configuration of these Pyrenees caves conforms to the spatial settings characteristic of contemporary initiations and rites of passage.

Prehistoric evidence suggests the conclusion that the earth itself, here in the form of the cave, is a primal environment for human psychological and sociocultural development. Caves, the earth, are prototypic settings for generative, transformational activity. The mythic birthplace of Zeus is deep within the Kamares cave on Mount Ida in Crete, and prehistoric kamare pottery is associated with the origin and development of religious activity on Crete. Christian spiritual transformations hinge on belief in the death of Jesus Christ, His entombment in a cave, and subsequent emergence from the earth. Japanese legend says that Ama-no-Iwato, a rock shelter in southern Japan, is the place in the earth into which the Sun Goddess Amaterasu-o-mi-Kami retreated in disgrace at the disruptive behavior of her brother Susa-no-ono-Mikoto. Literally, the sun went out and the world was plunged into darkness and confusion. Amaterasu-o-mi-Kami was eventually lured out of the earth by spirits who placed a mirror in front of the cave at Ama-no-Iwato so that the Sun Goddess would investigate a radiance equal to her own. The daily rising of the sun, depicted in the Japanese national flag, is reminiscent of the light that filled the sky upon the rising of Amaterasu-o-mi-Kami from the earth. Plato chose to use the cave as a metaphor for speaking of the relationship between shadow appearances and the blinding light of ultimate reality.

The relationship between the idea and symbolism of the cave and the idea and symbolism of the temple is manifested in the cave temples of prehistoric India and China. The shrine of Lomas Rishi in India dates to the 3rd century B.C., and is literally carved into the Barabar hills. In the 6th century A.D., Chalukyan Hindu carved an elaborate temple to Siva in the side of a mountain at Elephanta. At Tun-huang in north central China, beginning about the 5th century A.D., over 300 shrines and temples were cut into rock cliffs. The walls and ceilings of the cave temples in India and China are systematically decorated with paintings and engravings, just as paintings and engravings decorate the prehistoric caves of Europe. Temples and cave temples in each case are sacred spaces and express a much earlier human belief in the cave itself as a sacred space. It is not surprising that, except for two footprints in Fontanet, all of the footprints in the Pyrenees caves are of unshod, bare feet. Magdalenian children removed their footwear before entering the caves, a still universal behavior accompanying entrance into a sacred space.

PAINTING AND DRAWING IN INITIATION AND RITES OF PASSAGE

From the spatial characteristics of the Pyrenees caves as a structured environment, I infer the caves as settings for initiation and rite of passage. There remains the matter of accounting for the practice of decorating prehistoric caves with wall paintings and engravings. The following interpretation of the decorations in the three Pyrenees caves under consideration is by way of analogy with the uses of painting and engravings in existing rite of passage initiation rituals. Painting and engraving, image making to be precise, are intimately associated with initiation and rite of passage (Forge, 1970; Lewis-Williams, 1981; Munn, 1973). There are three concerns here: the subject matter and nature of the images in the Pyrenees caves; the spatial relationship of the cave paintings and engravings to the lineal spatial configuration of the Pyrenees caves; and the evidence of the behavior of the Magdalenians experiencing the caves, with respect to the location of the cave paintings and drawings.

Image Making in Initiation and Rite of Passage

The paintings and engravings on the walls of the Pyrenees caves are of animals, primarily bison and horses. The occurrence of animal images in the context of initiation and rites of passage is quite common. The Innuit (Eskimo) people of Alaska and the Arctic Circle make images depicting the manner in which animals come to help and accompany them on vision quests (Butler & Bridge, 1977; Eber, 1971). Animal spirits claim particular human beings and human beings during initiation and rite of passage come to know their animal helper, how to contact the animal helper, and the powers the animal helper is willing to share with them. Plains Indian people such as the Sioux speak of sacred animals, the buffalo and the horse, that come to help and accompany them on vision quests or through ordeals like the Sun Dance ritual (Niehardt, 1961, pp. 20–47). Youths returning from vision quests or from other rites of passage customarily paint on their tipi images of the animals appearing to them during fast-induced altered states of consciousness. Among the Kwakiutl people on the northwest coast of North America, during traditional times there occurred a winter rite of passage ceremony termed *hamatsa* (Holm, 1972, pp. 9–11; Macnair, 1977). The *hamatsa* ceremony functioned to publically validate and legitimize claims to status by the male children of chiefs and the nobility. Preadolescent males claimed special status by experiencing a ritual believed to bring them into contact with animal helpers existing since the beginning of things. Association with these animal spirits confer special status. During the *hamatsa* ceremony, age-graded groups of young males forgo their customary names, are stripped of their customary clothing, and are expected to spend 4 months in the deep of the cedar woods in training with senior *hamatsa*. In the timeless woods lives Baxbakualanu Xsiwae, the cannibal at the north end of the world. Initiates, during this transition period, must defeat Baxbakulanu Xsiwae by braving cold and dark and fear. From the first of times Baxbakulanu Xsiwae has sought the flesh of humans, and the survival of the Kwakiutl people depends on initiates continuing to defeat Baxbakualanu Xsiwae. Friendly animal spirits such as the beaver and the whale accompany initiates during their ordeal. The young boys return to tell invited guests from many villages of their ordeal, and of the animals that appeared to them. Initiates to the *hamatsa* clan perform a stage ceremony, each dressed in the image of the animal who helped them. The young boys are incorporated into society as special people, ascribed the experience of participating in the continuing defeat of forces seeking the continual destruction of human beings in general and the Kwakiutl in particular.

In each ethnographic instance, image making in the form of painting and drawing is an intimate part of initiation and rite of passage. The making of an image is an act of evocation; the representation calls into being that which is represented (cf. Munn, 1973; Newcomb & Reichard, 1975; Young, 1985). Images of animals, then, are more than the image of animals (Rawson, 1977). Images of animals in each case refer to the transcendental, to the transformation of consciousness, and to individual psychological as well as to sociocultural well-being. To make an animal image in this context is to cancel time and space, and to *in illo tempore* experience the beginning of things. Animal images assist in the process of renewal and regeneration, both for the individual and for society. Further, to make an image is to participate in the beingness of that which is represented. One is both animal and human, or to refer to Levi-Strauss's (1963) theory of totemism, the animal images characteristically associated with initiation and rite of passage encourage children to think about what it means to be an animal, a Magdalenian, an Inuit, or a Kwakiutl.

Image making is what sociocultural anthropologists term *sympathetic magic*. Sympathetic magic is the widespread belief that one can enter into relationship with something through participation in its image likeness. There are primarily animal images, as against other sorts of predominant images, on the walls of the Pyrenees caves, because the purpose of the caves was initiation and rite of passage and animal images are common in male initiation and rites of passage.

Cave Painting and Drawing, and Cave Architectectonics

The paintings and drawings within Montespan, Niaux/Reseau Clastres, and Le Tuc d'Audoubert are not evenly distributed along the great length of the caves but occur in periodic clusters within delimited wall areas disappearing into vast blank spaces of rock. Paintings and engravings are not presented in museum fashion, strung along the wall in an even but often unrelated display. The three Pyrenees caves in this respect exhibit interesting design similarity (see Topographic Maps 4, 5, and 6).

Comparison reveals a way-station organization to the placement of the paintings and drawings in the four Pyrenees caves, a linear organization reminiscent of the spatial placement of sacred trees in Ndembu rite of passage ritual. Leroi-Gourhan's (1967, pp. 106–157) comparative study of about 60 upper Paleolithic caves found that the paintings and drawings throughout an entire cave are related to each other in terms of complementary opposed subject matter (bison/horse, for example) placed in complementary opposed areas of the cave, in particular the front and rear areas of the cave (Ucko & Rosenfeld, 1967, pp. 143–148). Paintings and drawings are displayed with respect to the linear space and spatial configuration of caves. It is probable, then, that the paintings and drawings in the Pyrenees cave were designed as a sequence of related images to be experienced in sequential fashion as one moved through the caves.

Paintings and drawings are related to the caves in another important manner. Think of a museum. Museum paintings and drawings are a display set against the backdrop of a neutral setting. Museum paintings and drawings, except for experimental displays, are not part of the museum setting itself. In the Pyrenees caves, on the other hand, paintings and drawings are part of the cave itself. A cave wall is not like a museum wall. A cave wall sweats, glistens in torchlight, ebbs and

PREHISTORIC EUROPEAN DECORATED CAVES 257

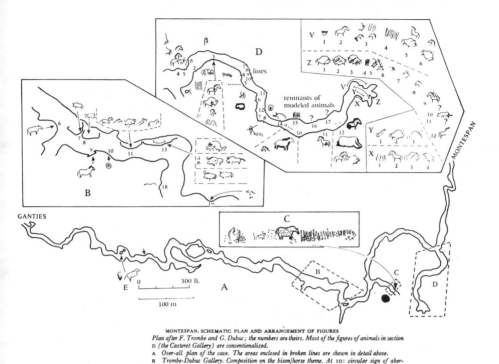

MONTESPAN. SCHEMATIC PLAN AND ARRANGEMENT OF FIGURES
Plan after F. Trombe and G. Dubuc; the numbers are theirs. Most of the figures of animals in section
D *(the Casteret Gallery) are conventionalized.*
A *Over-all plan of the cave. The areas enclosed in broken lines are shown in detail above.*
B *Trombe-Dubuc Gallery. Composition on the bison/horse theme. At 10: circular sign of aberrant type. At 11: bird (?).*
C *"Hunting scene" panel.*
D *Casteret Gallery. As the inventory of figures shows, the over-all theme is bison/horse/ibex.*

Topographic Map 4.

flows in contours revealed as one passes between narrow passages, seems without beginning or end, is both warm and cold to the touch, provides a welcome passage through the dark, and spatially dictates the often frustrating and emotion-ridden manner of one's passage (cf. Bordes, 1972; Casteret, 1938, 1954; Penton, 1986). Sound emanates from everywhere and from nowhere. Time is erased and space is distorted, as there is no customary perspective frame of reference. The paintings and engravings in the Pyrenees caves are fitted to this type of surface and environment. The face of a bison is painted on the projecting face of a rock such that the shape of the rock in fact is the shape of the bison. The face of the bison is the first thing unexpectedly encountered as you move in flickering torchlight through narrow walls. The effect is three-dimensional and quite startling. Is there a bison there? You move on, slowly, the body of the bison appearing from the darkness in subtle shades of red and brown and black. John Pfeiffer (1982, pp. 132–152) speaks of the anamorphic aliveness of cave painting

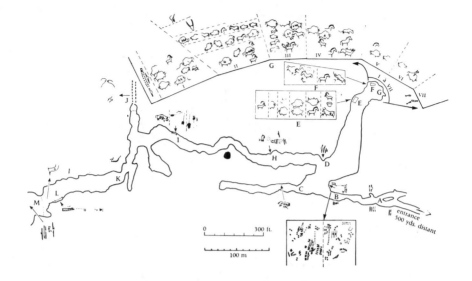

NIAUX. SCHEMATIC PLAN AND ARRANGEMENT OF FIGURES

The animal figures in the Black Salon (E, F, G) have been conventionalized. (Plan after Commandant Molard.)

A Entrance strokes, paired signs in a recess on the right.
B More strokes, large panel of signs on the right at the turning into the gallery, rows of dots.
C Secondary gallery (Gallery of Cave-Ins) with one ox figure engraved on the ground.
D Strokes and paired signs opposite group B.
E Engravings on the ground at the entrance to the Black Salon: one ox/ibex/isolated-sign composition, and a bison/horse/ibex composition.
F Engravings on the ground in the Black Salon. The first group includes a horse and a rhinoceros (very doubtful), the second a complete composition: bison/ horse/paired-signs + ibex.
G The full set of panels in the Black Salon. Note the paired claviform signs at the two sides (I and VI), and the recurrence of the basic bison/horse/ibex theme in

each panel. On panel II, painted on a recessed part of the wall having several plane surfaces, note that the signs are repeated in clear-cut fashion on each of these; note also the stag and the human figure (?) at the very back. Concerning the composition as a whole, note the stag and feline at the end of the continuous sequence I-II-III-IV, and the fish at the very end of the entire sequence (VII).
H Red panel: "the dying bison." The animal is drawn vertically, and there are dots, claviform signs, and strokes.
I Bison engraved on clay floor, marked with paired signs; horse and barbed signs in red on the wall.
J Figures located on the other side of "Green Lake." Facing ibexes and ox, painted black.
K Upside-down horse's head, making use of an irregularity of the wall.
L Composition at the terminal lake: lattice sign of untypical character, dots, and strokes. Headless ibex without forelegs, marked with a red dot.
M On the far side of the terminal lake: paired signs.

Topographic Map 5.

and drawing. It is the play of light, dark, and the movement of people past the paintings and engravings that transforms the image of a bison into a bison. Magdalenian children going through the ordeal of a mile-long passage through a narrow cave at that moment would be comforted, owing to feelings the children undoubtedly associated with bison and other animals, by the image presence of a bison. The children were not alone on their passage through the cave, just as animals continue to accompany children on rites of passage in cultures not then existing. The children move on past a station dense with animal images floating from the cave walls, go through another quarter mile of darkness to be relieved by yet another cluster of animal images, and so on. If there is semiotic knowledge in the wall images, then the children can only

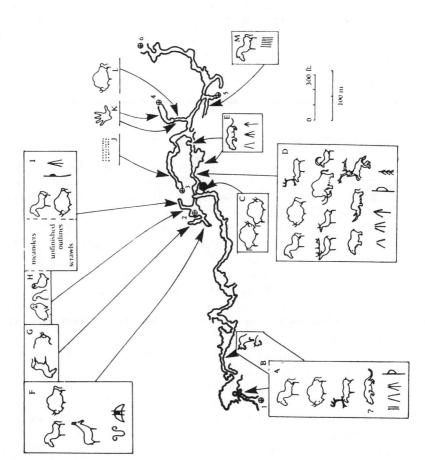

LES TROIS FRÈRES AND LE TUC D'AUDOUBERT.
Schematic plan of the caves and arrangement of subjects After H. Bégouën and H. Breuil; the layout of the figures is conventionalized.

A Side gallery at the entrance to Le Tuc d'Audoubert. Composition on the basic bison/horse + reindeer theme. Paired signs and a problematic feline.

B "Monsters" marking the end of the front part of Le Tuc.

C Bison modeled in clay, at the point where Le Tuc overlaps Les Trois Frères.

D Conventionalized inventory of the themes in the so-called Sanctuary. Except for the ox, all mammals "normal" in Paleolithic art are represented (felines are near by).

E Felines.

F Figures in the "Gallery of the Wild Ass." Bison/horse theme.

G Bison and horse in the intermediate gallery.

H "Owls."

I The "Aurignacian" Gallery. Group comprising horses, bison, and signs in Early Style IV.

J, K, L, M Isolated figures, the relation of which to the rest has not yet been clearly established.

1 Entrance to Le Tuc d'Audoubert. 2 Highly probable former entrance to Les Trois Frères in the "Entrance Chamber." 3 Mass of fallen earth masking a possible entrance. 4 Present-day entrance. 5 Entrance through which the discovery of Les Trois Frères was made. 6 Entrance to the Enlène cave.

Topographic Map 6.

be taught that knowledge by experiencing the images in their planned sequential context; that is, only if the children complete the passage through the cave. The Pyrenees caves under consideration are long and narrow, and exhibit the spatial configuration of a labyrinth (cf. Matthews, 1970). Wall paintings and engravings are apprehended only after a long and arduous journey. The difficult journey in darkness is a theme recurring in the initiations and rites of passage in many cultures (Eliade, 1957, pp. 155–189). Often, youths must cross dangerous bodies of water such as still occur deep within the Pyrenees caves, a sign of disconnectedness from society as well as a near-universal symbol of the purification attending passage to a new level of sociocultural or spiritual being (cf. Eliade, 1959, pp. 129–132; Jung, 1980, pp. 17, 222, 322; Van Gennep, 1960, p. 90). Analogy with contemporary initiations and rites of passage suggests that Magdalenian children did not know what they would encounter in the Pyrenees caves. My feeling is that, like the young males experiencing the Kwakiutl *hamatsa* ritual ceremony, Magdalenian children would be expected to report what they had seen and experienced. In this respect, the passage through the Pyrenees caves probably was a test. Children would perform differently on the test, see different things, exhibit different behaviors, the consequence of which would be a basis for deciding social roles.

Cave Painting and Drawing as Participatory Experience

A prevailing interpretation of the footprint evidence is that Magdalenian children walked along sand banks deep within caves from biological intentions rooted in "play impulses." "One must wonder," says Leroi-Gourhan (1967, p. 181), "whether this does not simply attest to the fact that children like to step on places where the foot sinks in . . . the children were carefree enough, however solemn the attending circumstances may have been, to play around in mud puddles." The paintings and engravings in deep caves are the product of increasing leisure in Upper Paleolithic society. This activity is personal expression, and the fact of children being in caves only supports the idea that art as painting and engraving is rooted in play. This "play" thesis (Ucko & Rosenfeld, 1967, pp. 165–173), though, does not acknowledge the significance of Magdalenian behavior toward the images part of childhood initiations and rites of passage.

Initiation and rite of passage in many cultures are felt to be the reality of life itself. The pattern of movement through initiation and rite of passage *is* the movement of life. Initiation and rite of passage are matters of utmost seriousness and sacredness. Ritual order and ritual meaning are too much a characteristic of initiation and rite of passage to permit a "play" thesis in accounting for elements of particular ceremonies, be they marriage ceremonies, funeral ceremonies, or the prehistoric status and role ceremonies I argue occurred in several Pyrenees caves.

Initiation and rite of passage are participation in the movement pattern of life and the images associated with life. The Magdalenian children in the Pyrenees caves, at Niaux for example, intentionally brought themselves into proximity to the wall paintings and drawings (see Figures 4 and 5). They touched them. The paintings and drawings on the walls were meant to be touched. Touching is participation. Touch is a way of knowing, just as sight is a way of knowing. Sociocultural anthropologists term the behavior contageous magic, the widespread belief that contact with a thing permits sharing the nature of the thing touched. We touch the Bible with a belief in contageous magic, the Wailing Wall, the ring of the Pope, the faded picture of a deceased loved one. The children at Niaux crossed the sandbank bordering the center river stream of the cave I feel to touch the images of the animals on the wall and to participate in whatever sensibilities they felt lived in those animals.

The famous sandpaintings of the Navaho are images meant to attract the wandering spirits of Holy Man and Holy Woman, ancestral beings who created the world and the Navaho people (Newcomb and Reichard 1975). Attention to detail and aesthetics in rendering images of people and animal helpers in the dry paintings is important so that spirits are attracted and, similar to the case of Amaterasu-no-mi Kami in Japan, move closer to investigate the mirror-like image of their own beauty. The Navaho believe spirits can be attracted to reside in the images of spirits, so that the image and the subject of the image momentarily become one. Navaho dry paintings are used for a variety of purposes, a predominant purpose being the restoration of psychological and spiritual well-being. After a long and complex ritual ceremony people, often children, are brought into the Hogon and told to lie on the carefully prepared image of Holy Woman or Holy Man. The image, the subject, and the person through contageous contact become one and I suggest this also was momentarily the case when Magdalenian children touched cave paintings and engravings. As the Holy People know no illness or disturbance, so contact with the Holy People negates any illness or disturbance. The many designs for sandpaintings, the ritual knowledge of drawing and painting with sand, and the power to relate images to people are secret to male shamans who experience special initiations and rites of passage. Sand paintings are destroyed after use, as their images are sacred and powerful. While not destroyed, the Pyrenees paintings and engravings are effectively hidden underground in caves the locations of which undoubtedly were not public knowledge. In both cases here, the earth itself is the context for the joining of people and images through contageous association. The earth is the setting for rituals of human transformation, both prehistoric and contemporary.

CONCLUSION: ALL THE WORLD'S A STAGE

We do not know what information was explicitly transmitted in the Pyrenees cave initiations and rites of passage. There is both prehistoric and contemporary evidence, though, that (1) Magdalenian cave environments were structured for specific childhood experiences, and (2) the architecture and spatial structure of Magdalenian cave environments support a position that the purpose of these structured cave environments was initiation and rites of passage. There is a consistency relationship and high degree of redundancy between the ideological, behavioral, and material aspects of culture. The ideas and behaviors at work in the Pyrenees caves, such as initiation and rites of passage, can to some extent be read from the material environment of the caves. Initiation and rites of passage are an archetypal form of sociocultural conditioning, and appear in both prehistoric and contemporary cultures (cf. Johnson 1983, 1985, 1987).

The keepers of sociocultural information are material "things," such as structured environments for child sociocultural conditioning, as well as people themselves. Verbal language is a necessary but not sufficient condition for child sociocultural conditioning. The averbal imprinting of ways of thinking, feeling, and behaving is strongly conditioned by human relationship to material culture and structured environments.

Initiation and rites of passage are ritual, ritual is performance, and performance "is the proper finale of an experience" (Turner 1982:13). If the world indeed is a stage, as Shakespeare tells us, then life is a performance with raw experience as its subject. Life is the performance of experience. This is a probable lesson, a timeless, archetypal lesson of sociocultural conditioning, I believe imparted in the child initiations and rites of passage in the prehistoric Pyrenees caves.

REFERENCES

Bégouën, H. (1912). *Une nouvelle grotte à gravures dans l'Ariège: la caverne du Tuc d'Audoubert* [A new cave and engravings in Ariège: The cave of

Tuc d'Audoubert]. Geneva: Congrès International d'Anthropologie et d'Archéologie Préhistorique.

Bégouën, H., & Bégouën, L. (1928). Découvertes nouvelles dans la caverne des Trois-Frères à Montesquieu-Avantès (Ariège) [New discoveries in the cave of Trois-Frères and the front of Montesquieu] *Revue Anthropologique, Anne 38,* 358–364.

Bégouën, H., & Bégouën, L., (1931). *Notre campagne de fouilles dans la caverne des Trois-Frères* [Our excavations in the cave of Trois-Frères]. Geneva: Congrès International d'Anthropologie et d'Archeologie Préhistorique.

Bourdieu, P., & Passeron, J.C. (1977). *Reproduction in education, society and culture.* London: Sage.

Bourdieu, P. (1973). Cultural reproduction and social reproduction. In R. Brown (Ed.), *Knowledge, education, and social change* (pp. 71–112). London: Tavistock.

Bordes, F. (1972). *A tale of two caves.* New York: Harper and Row.

Bordes, F., & de Sonneville-Bordes, D. (1970). The significance of variability in Paleolithic assemblages. *World Archaeology, 2,* 61–73.

Boroneant, V., & Frolov, B.A. (1979). On Upper Paleolithic symbol systems. *Current Anthropology, 20,* 604–608.

Brace, C.L., & Montagu, A. (1977). *Human evolution: An introduction to biological anthropology.* New York: Macmillan.

Breuil, H. (1950). Les peintures et gravures parietales de la caverne de Niaux (Ariège). *Préhistoire et Spéléologie Ariégeoises, 5,* 9–34.

Breuil, H. (1952a). La caverne de Niaux, complements inédits sur sa decoration [The cave of Niaux, previously unpublished matters concerning its decoration]. *Préhistoire et Spéléologie Ariégeoises,* [Ariège prehistory and cave exploration] *7,* 11–35.

Breuil, H. (1952b). *Four hundred centuries of cave art.* Montignac and Paris: Centre d'Etudes et de Documentation Préhistoriques [Center for Prehistoric Study and Documentation].

Brown, J. (1963). A cross cultural study of female initiation rites. *American Anthropologist, 65,* 837–853.

Bunzel, R.L. (1932). Introduction to Zuni ceremonialism; Zuni origin myths; Zuni ritual poetry; Zuni katchinas: An analytical study. In *Forty-Seventh Annual Report of the Bureau of American Ethnology for the Years 1929–1930* (pp. 467–1086). Washington, DC: Government Printing Office.

Butler, K.J., & Bridge, K. (1977). My uncle went to the moon: An informal conversation with K.J. Butler. In A.T. Brodzky, R. Danesewich, & N. Johnson (Eds.), *Stones, bones, and skin: Ritual and shamanic art.* (pp. 122–126). Toronto, Canada: Society for Art Publications.

Campbell, B. (1976). *Humankind evolving.* Boston, MA: Little, Brown.

Cartailhac, E., & Breuil, H. (1908). Les peintures et gravures murals des cavernes Pyrénéés III, Niaux (Ariège). [Cave mural paintings and engravings]. *L'Anthropologie,* [Anthropology] *19,* 15–46.

Casteret, N. (1938). *Ten years under the earth.* New York: Greystone Press.

Casteret, N. (1954). *The darkness under the earth.* New York: Henry Holt.

Clottes, J. (1985). Conservation des traces et des empreintes [Preserved tracks and footprints]. *Histoire et Archaeologie* [History and Archaeology], *90*, 40–49.

Clottes, J., & Simonnet, R. (1972). Le réseau René Clastres de la caverne de Niaux (Ariège). [The René Clastres system of the cave of Niaux]. *Bulletin de la Société Préhistorique Française* [Bulletin of the French Prehistoric Society], *69*, 293–323.

Conkley, M. (1980). The identification of prehistoric hunter-gatherer aggregation sites: The case of Altamira. *Current Anthropology, 21*, 609–630.

Dozier, E.P. (1970). *The Pueblo Indians of North America.* New York: Holt, Rinehart & Winston.

Driver, H.E. (1969). *Indians of North America.* Chicago, IL: University of Chicago Press.

Duday, H., & Garcia, M. (1983). Les empreintes de l'homme préhistorique [Prehistoric human footprints]: La grotte du Peche-Merle à Cabrerets (Lot): Une relecture significative des traces de pieds humains [The cave of Peche-Merle in Cabrerets: The significance of the tracks of human feet]. *Bulletin de la Société Préhistorique Française,* [Bulletin of the French Prehistoric Society], *80*, 208–215.

Eber, D. (1971). *Pitseolak: Pictures out of my life.* Seattle, WA: University of Washington Press.

Eggan, D. (1956). Instruction and affect in Hopi cultural continuity. *Southwest Journal of Anthropology, 12*, 347–370.

Eliade, M. (1957). *Myths, dreams and mysteries: The encounter between contemporary faiths and archaic realities.* New York: Harper & Row.

Eliade, M. (1958). *Rites and symbols of initiation: The mysteries of birth and rebirth.* New York: Harper & Row.

Eliade, M. (1959). *The sacred and the profane: The nature of religion.* New York: Harcourt, Brace, & World.

Ellis, F.H., & Hammack, L. (1968). The inner sanctum of Feather Cave, a Mogollon sun and earth shrine linking Mexico and the Southwest. *American Antiquity, 33*, 25–44.

Forge, A. (1970). Learning to see in New Guinea. In P. Mayer (Ed.), *Socialization: The approach from social anthropology* (pp. 269–291). New York & London: Tavistock.

Frolov, B.A. (1978). Numbers in paleolithic graphic art and the initial stages in the development of mathematics. *Soviet Anthropology and Archaeology, 16*, 142–166.

Garcia, M. (1979). Les silicones elastomères R.T.V. appliqués aux relevés de vestiges préhistoriques: Art, empreintes humaines et animales) [Plastic silicone RTV applied to the prehistoric footprints: art, human footprints, and animals]. *L'Anthropologie,* [Anthropology], *83*(1), 5–42, *83*(2), 189–222.

Gearing, F. (1973). Where we are and where we might go: Steps toward a general theory of cultural transmission. *Council on Anthropology and Education Newsletter, 4*, 1–10.

Gluckman, M. (1963). *Essays on the ritual of social relations.* Cambridge, England: Cambridge University Press.

Hadingham, E. (1979). *Secrets of the ice age: The world of the cave artists.* New York: Walker and Company.

Holm, B. (1972) *Crooked beak of heaven.* Seattle, WA: University of Washington Press.

Jennings, J.D., & Reed, E.K. (1956). Seminars in archaeology. The American Southwest: A problem in cultural isolation. *American Antiquity, 22,* 2.

Jochim, M. (1983). Paleolithic cave art in ecological perspective. In G. Bailey (Ed.), *Hunter-gatherer economy in prehistory: A European perspective* (pp. 212–241). Cambridge, England: Cambridge University Press.

Johnson, N.B. (1983). School spaces and architecture: The social and cultural landscape of educational environments. *Journal of American Culture, 5,* 77–87.

Johnson, N.B. (1985). *West Haven: Classroom culture and society in a rural elementary school.* Chapel Hill, NC: University of North Carolina Press.

Johnson, N.B. (in press). Zen Buddhist meditation gardens and the training of Zen Buddhist priests. In M.W. Coy (Ed.), *Anthropological perspectives on apprenticeship: Theory and method.* Buffalo, NY: State University of New York Press.

Jung, C.G. (1980). *The archetypes and the collective unconscious.* Bollingen Series XX, Volume 1, Part 9. Princeton, NJ: Princeton University Press.

Leach, E. (1976). *Culture and communication: The logic by which symbols are connected.* Cambridge, England: Cambridge University Press.

Leroi-Gourhan, A. (1967). *Treasures of prehistoric art.* New York: Abrams.

Leroi-Gourhan, A. (1968). *The art of prehistoric man in Western Europe.* London: Thames & Hudson.

Leroi-Gourhan, A. (1982a). *The dawn of European art: An introduction to paleolithic cave painting.* New York and Cambridge, England: Cambridge University Press.

Leroi-Gourhan, A. (1982b). The archaeology of Lascaux cave. *Scientific American, 246,* 104–112.

Levi-Strauss, C. (1963). *Totemism.* Boston, MA: Beacon Press.

Lewis-Williams, J.D. (1981). *Believing and seeing: Symbolic meanings in Southern San Rock paintings.* New York: Academic Press.

Macnair, P.L. (1977). Kwakiutl winter dances: A reenactment. In A.T. Brodzky, R. Daneswich, & N. Johnson (Eds.), *Stones, bones, and skin: Ritual and shamanic art* (pp. 62–81). Toronto, Canada: The Society for Art Publications.

Marc, O. (1977). *Psychology of the house.* London: Thames & Hudson.

Marshack, A. (1972). *The roots of civilization.* New York: McGraw Hill.

Matthews, W.H. (1970). *Mazes and labyrinths: Their history and development.* New York: Dover.

Mellars, P.A. (1974). The paleolithic and the mesolithic. In C. Renfew (Ed.), *British prehistory* (pp. 41–99). Park Ridge, NJ: Noyes Press.

Munn, N. (1973). The spatial representation of cosmic order in Walbiri iconography. In A. Forge (Ed.), *Primitive art and society* (pp. 193–220). London: Oxford University Press.

Newcomb, F.J., & Reichard, G.A. (1975). *Sandpaintings of the Navaho shooting chant.* New York: Dover.

Niehardt, J.G. (1961). *Black Elk speaks: Being the life story of a holy man of the Oglala Sioux.* Lincoln, NE: University of Nebraska Press.

Pales, L. (1976). Les empreintes de pieds humains dans les cavernes [The footprints of human beings in caves]. Les empreintes du Réseau Nord de la caverne de Niaux (Ariège). [The footprints of the North System of the cave of Niaux]. *Archives de l'I.P.H., 36,* Masson édition.

Paul, R. (1976). The Sherpa temple as a model of the psyche. *American Ethnologist, 3,* 131–146.

Penton, Elizabeth. (1987). The cave setting as key to the interpretation of European Upper Paleolithic cave painting, drawing, and engraving. M.A. Thesis, Department of Anthropology, University of North Carolina, Chapel Hill.

Pfeiffer, J.E. (1982). *The creative explosion: An inquiry into the origin of art and religion.* New York: Harper & Row.

Poirier, F.E. (1977). *In search of ourselves: An introduction to physical anthropology.* Minneapolis, MN: Burgess.

Rawson, J. (1977). *Animals in art.* London: British Museum Publications Limited.

Robbins, L.M. (1985). *Footprints: Collections, analysis, and interpretations.* Springfield, IL: Charles C. Thomas.

Sieveking, A. (1979). *The cave artists.* London: Thames and Hudson.

Straus, L.G. (1977). The upper paleolithic cave site of Altamira (Santandar, Spain). *Quaternaria, 19,* 135–148.

Thompson, L. (1945) Logico-aesthetic integration in Hopi culture. *American Anthropologist, 47,* 540–553.

Trombe, F., & DuBuc, G. (1947). *Le centre préhistorique de Ganties—Montespan (Haute Garonne)* [The Prehistoric Center of Ganties Montespan]. Paris: Memoire 22, Archives de L'Institut de Paléontologie Humaine.

Turner, V. (1962). Three symbols of passage in Ndembu circumcision ritual: An interpretation. In M. Gluckman (Ed.), *Essays on the ritual of social relations* (pp. 124–173). Manchester, England: Manchester University Press.

Turner, V. (1964). *The forest of symbols: Aspects of Ndembu ritual.* Ithaca, NY: Cornell University Press.

Turner, V. (1982). *From ritual to theatre: The human seriousness of play.* New York: Performing Arts Journal Publications.

Ucko, P.J., & Rosenfeld, A. (1967). *Paleolithic cave art.* New York: McGraw Hill.

Van Gennep, A. (1960). *The rites of passage.* Chicago, IL: University of Chicago Press.

Vivian, G., & Reiter, P. (1965). *The great Kivas of Chaco Canyon, and their relationships.* Monograph 22. Albuquerque, NM: The School of American Research, University of New Mexico Press.

Yetts, P.W. (1919). Chinese Isles of the Blest. *Folklore, 30,* 35–62.

Young, F.W. (1962). The function of male initiation ceremonies: A cross-cultural test of an alternative hypothesis. *American Journal of Sociology, 67,* 379–391.

Young, F.W. (1965). *Initiation ceremonies: A cross-cultural study of status dramatizations.* New York: Bobbs Merrill.

Young, M.J. (1985). Images of power and the power of images: The significance of rock art for contemporary Zunis. *Journal of American Folklore, 98,* 1–48.

CHAPTER 8

Teaching Ideology via Science: Direction of Child Socialization through Mathematics and Physics Curriculae in East German Schools*

Uwe Zänker

Oberer Eichweg 43
D-3550 Marburg
Federal Republic of Germany

The present chapter is aimed at describing the secondary socializing role of school curriculae (aside from their primary education for the content matter), using the case of East German schools as a representative example. I follow the lines set up by Emile Durkheim who, at the turn of this century, defined education as *methodical socialization*. The selection of the example of mathematics and physics curriculae may at first seem a poor choice—but only from the perspective of readers who are used to the educational plurality of Western democratic countries where the socializing aspect of the "hard sciences" in schools may be minimized. However, the socio-cultural context of child socialization in East Germany is quite different from that of the West in this respect, and it is exactly the special example of East Germany that reveals the "secondary socializing" role of school curriculae par excellence.

---

* The present author is very grateful to Jaan Valsiner for his editorial recommendations and friendly help in the writing of this article. He is also grateful to Olaf Zänker for his help with translation of the original manuscript into English.

THE SOCIAL-POLITICAL CONTEXT OF GERMAN
EDUCATIONAL SYSTEMS AFTER WORLD WAR II

Socio-culturally structured environments for child development come into being over time. Therefore, any understanding of their current state requires a historical analysis. The general political situation in Germany after the Second World War was complicated. As a result of the lost and long-lasting war, most German people were resigned and exhausted. Another reason of their disappointment was the shock about the Anglo-American bomb attacks, which had destroyed their towns.

A minority of ancient democrats and communists, who were emigrants and adversaries of the Nazis, wanted to start with the reconstruction of daily life and with the rebuilding of a new political system. The kind of democracy and the way to realize it depended on the political party, or rather on the political opinion of the occupying power.

The U.S.A., Great Britain, and France gave permission to political parties and democratic groups for constructing and creating a democracy, which was influenced by the occupying powers. However, the Soviet Union was interested in two possible scenarios for East Germany (see also Churchill, 1960):

> *First:* They thought that the other occupying powers would leave their zones. Afterwards they could influence these zones, and later on the whole country would be controlled by them.
> *Second:* If the other occupying powers wanted to stay in Germany, only the Soviet-occupied zone would be controlled by the USSR.

The Soviet occupying power started with the following policy: first, groups of communists in exile returned from the Soviet Union and started the reconstruction of daily life in East Germany and Berlin. In conformity with the occupying power this reconstruction was described by following slogan: "Maintaining the pretence of democracy, but actually we (the communists) must be the rulers!" (Leonhard, 1955, p. 365). As a consequence of this, the first steps taken concerning school policy were the following ones:

- Dismissal of all teachers and administrators who had been members of the Nazi party or Nazi organizations.
- Institution of "new teachers courses of instruction". This meant that many young people were speedily prepared for school teaching.
- Production of new books. In 1946 a central publishing agency for

the text-books was founded: "Volk und Wissen Verlag" [Publishing house "People and knowledge"]. (This publishing agency remains the only producer of textbooks in East Germany/GDR at present).

• The school reform concerning the reform of the curriculum and the school organization. This reform was named "the democratic school-reform" and was introduced in May 1946, by the "Law for democratization of the German schools."

Accompanying measures included the following ones:

• The youth organization Freie Deutsche Jugend ("FDJ") [Free German Youth] was founded in March 1946. (This was a communist youth organization, and one of its first leaders was Erich Honecker.) And in December 1948 it was followed by the children organization Junge Pioniere [Young Pioneers]. (One of the first leaders of this organization was Margot Feist, now E. Honecker's wife and minister for education in GDR.)

• In the universities and institutes the fight against "bourgeois sciences" started. It means that many scientists and researchers in all scientific disciplines were expected to consider their work as if the Germany of Hitler never existed. They should be bound to the traditions which existed before 1933. This fight was a very embittered one, especially in the social sciences, because the new power intended to introduce Marxism in these kinds of sciences. In the beginning of 1948, for example, the professors of philosophy received a special questionnaire with 15 well-founded questions about marxist philosophy on it. They had to prove their ability for being able to research and teach this philosophy (Baske & Engelbert, 1966, p. 210).

• A declaration above the entrance of the universities at the end of 1945 and in July 1947. Only a small part of former Nazi organizations' members could receive the opportunity for higher education. It is important to keep in mind that most young people had been forced by the Nazis to join the HJ or BDM, but despite this fact they didn't get a chance of studying at universities in East Germany (Baske & Engelbert, 1966, pp. 10–12).

EAST GERMAN EDUCATIONAL POLICIES IN THE POST-WAR PERIOD

Quite predictably, the particular decisions made by the leadership of the post-war East Germany educational system were in line with the ideological directions of the Soviet-sponsored "new Germany."

The real situation in schools can be characterized with following remarks:

- After the lost war, the majority of school buildings were destroyed, many teachers had been dismissed, and the production of textbooks and exercise books was minimal.
- The Soviet occupying power was interested in beginning as soon as possible with school education along the lines that fitted the new political system.
- The German communists had to fulfill the wishes of the Soviet occupying administrators.

In 1946, the "Law for democratization of German schools" was introduced. In it was written that the "new German democratic school" has to impart a well-founded knowledge to all the children. The school system had to be organized in a standardized way with the meaning of standard school for all pupils. This school education lasts 8 years, from age 6 to 14. The majority of pupils were to leave school at 14 and start apprenticeships. Some academically superior students were admitted to secondary school, which lasted 4 years and ended with the "Abitur" exam. This exam was needed for entry into an university. For the elementary school a standard curriculum was proposed by the law with instruction in the following subjects (from Baske & Engelbert, 1966, pp. 8–9):

- German language and literature;
- native country knowledge;
- biology;
- chemistry;
- foreign languages;
- arts and practical works;
- history;
- geography;
- physics;
- mathematics;
- music;
- sports.

Russian became the first foreign language (the school children in GDR at present start learning it in the 5th grade). A number of subjects (history, "knowledge of the native land," German language and literature, geography) were reorganized in accordance with new curriculae that reflected the world view of the new political power. The school subjects were supposed to support the socialization of young East Germans for loyalty to the new system.

The first steps taken concerning socialization for the new loyalty started with the help of the introduction of the reformed curriculum in July 1946. It was oriented towards total re-education of the youth. Instructions for teaching physics were required to be helpful for establishing the new ideology in the children's minds.

The terms *democratic education* and *re-education of the youth* were very cleverly and flexibly interpreted by the leaders of the educational administration. For example, Paul Wandel delivered a speech on the "First Pedagogical Congress" in East Berlin (August 15–17, 1946) with 800 invited teachers from the Soviet occupation zone and 175 guests from Berlin:

> The solution of our social and economic problems can be found only in the construction of a democratic Germany and on the basic of socialist righteousness. (Wandel, 1946)

Of course, behind the slogan of *construction of democratic Germany* and *socialist righteousness* was a complex social-political scheme (see Leonhard, 1955). The democratization of the German school started in the Soviet occupation zone with the issues pertaining to teachers. The old teachers who had not been Nazis were remaining on school faculties, and most of the young new teachers were subjected to direct social-political guidance. Under these circumstances they had to learn to work and think along the lines prescribed and expected by the state.

Since many older and experienced teachers had been dismissed under alleged connections with the Nazi ideology during the Third Reich, there were not enough teachers in East German schools. Therefore, new teachers were prepared quickly and under careful idological guidance. Furthermore, many totally unprepared pedagogues became teaching in the school system. Their main qualification may have been their "contact with the working class" or "wholesome sensibleness" rather than preparedness to teach school subjects (see Lindner, 1946). It is particularly the "hard science" curriculae, including physics and mathematics, that suffered most from such lack of qualified teachers.

Thus, already in the latter half of the 1940s, the plans of the new East German leaders and the reality of everyday educational practice started to differ on a vast scale. That difference did not go unnoticed. In 1950, many East German school principals claimed that the planned change of curriculae could not be implemented, due to the lack of teachers for physics, chemistry, and biology (Moller-Krumbholz, 1950a). The curriculae for physics and mathematics were thus at the intersection of two diametrically opposite social demands. On the one hand, the new leadership of East Germany (which in 1949 was announced as the "German Democratic Republic"—as a politically separate state within the Eastern European economic and military system) demanded a full-scale use of all school subjects for purposeful socialization of young German children in directions specified by them. On the other hand, there were very few qualified teachers of physics or mathematics who would willingly accomplish the socialization task prescribed to them. There were, of course, quite a few unqualified teachers who were all too happy to make the socialization for loyalty into a prominent task in East German schools. How, then, did that situation resolve itself in East Germany?

SOCIALIZATION FOR LOYALTY THROUGH TEACHING NATURAL SCIENCES: THE HISTORY OF EAST GERMAN CASE

The East German leaders of school education were interested in changing all the points of view, especially those, concerning the natural sciences and mathematics. The new term was *partisanship*. Some examples of such a "partisan point of view" were given in a journal called *Mathematics and Natural Sciences in the New School,* which was published especially for teachers. On the pages of that journal, East German teachers were told different stories that related events and inventors in the area of "hard" sciences to social-political perspectives that were preferred by the East German and Soviet world views. Also, cases of German scientists who publicly repented for their past views and glorified Soviet (and, by proxy, East German) political views were reported in that journal for teachers. The following list provides a glimpse of the themes represented in those stories:

- The story about "Russian Marconi"—Alexander Popov, the "ingenious inventor of wireless telegraphy." The Italian Marconi had "stolen" the Russian's invention! (Kauffeldt, 1950)
- The story about the "French fighter for peace," Frederic Joliot-Curie. This scientist and member of the peace movement disagreed with the development of the French atomic bomb. In 1951 the "Stalin prize" of the Soviet Union was awarded to Joliot-Curie for his political activities. (Joliot-Curie, 1951)
- The story about "Joseph Stalin's transformation of the nature." This meant planned constructions of hydroelectric power stations and channels in European and Asian parts of the Soviet Union. These

constructions should be remarked as "testimony of the better society under the leadership of sage Stalin." ("Die Grossbauten," 1951)

- The story of "the self-critical natural philosopher Georg Klaus." He is a marxist philosophical writer who declared in 1950 that his own "point of view" was not scientifically founded because he had not studied Stalin's fundamental ideas of 1906. Only these ideas—added to the philosophical utterances of Friedrich Engels—could be used as a "sharp weapon against the so-called philosophical systems of the american nonopolists" by Marxist philosophers. (Klaus, 1950)

One of the further steps was the changing of school curriculae. In 1949 a 2-year plan of economic reconstruction was put into practice. It was the beginning of planned economy in East Germany. In 1948, the introduction of new curriculum included social reflections of this plan. What that meant in real terms was the introduction of "positive examples" of workers who had been made into models for the others who participated in "socialist construction." In the Soviet Union, the best-known case of that kind was that of the "shock-worker" miner Alexey Stakhanov, who overfulfilled the official work norms in excess in 1936 and was glorified as a model for everybody. A similar example for others was also created in East Germany—in the case of the miner A. Hennecke who in 1948 was glorified by the East German mass communication media along similar lines. The example of Hennecke was introduced into school textbooks on mathematics so young children could calculate the percentages by which this ardent worker overfulfilled production norms, thus (it was hoped) becoming ready to follow on similar tracks (Lüders, 1950).

In the teaching of physics, a similar modeling of young children's world views along Soviet models could be seen. For the most part, the achievements of Soviet physics were emphasized, whereas the results of "capitalist" physics were downplayed (Renneberg, 1949).

The strong emphasis on "partisanship" was evident all through the East German educational reforms of the late 1940s. Reports from teacher's conferences, published in these years, illustrate it well:

The following report about this teachers-activists-conference in Leipzig should demonstrate the "new quality" concerning educational work: All the participants were members of the United Socialist Party of Germany ("SED"). They all felt obliged to educate the young generation in accordance with the political program. Paul Wandel remarked, that the main question for every teacher could be formulated like this: "What do you think about the Soviet Union?"—to which the required answer was: "Only the Soviet Union is able to protect peace and to achieve social progress." The Soviet professor of educational sciences Mitropolskij claimed, that school cannot exist separately from politics and he added that the pedagogical fight is a political one, too. (*Lehreraktivisten tagten,* 1949, pp. 2–5)

This kind of attitude could also be noticed in the way of teaching natural sciences. The political "partisanship" was dominant in textbooks and teaching materials. The didactic journals gave many examples— and the school lessons were loaded with political viewpoints.

> Many progressive teachers (in mathematics-UZ) proposed to change calculation with square-root slide rule for progressive political calculation in context with planned economy.
>
> Concerning the physics lessons they proposed to demonstrate the peaceful using of nuclear science in the Soviet Union in opposite to the way of using it in U.S.A.: The american imperialists want to use nuclear power just for a war of mankind-annihilation. (Lüders, 1950, pp. 547–555).

As a consequence of the East German educational reform in natural sciences, the new direction of education can be summed up like this:

> All children get a modern scientific point of view on the most progressive science—the dialectical materialism. (Siebert, 1951, pp. 449–460)

What was the everyday reality behind the emphasis on "dialectical materialistic" teaching of physics and mathematics in East German schools? How were particular topics in the curriculae used for socialization purposes? In the East German case, that everyday reality of school practice took the form of covert direction of pupils' thinking along the "right" (i.e., favorable to the state) *and* aggressive lines.

"PATRIOTIC MILITANCY" IN THE MATHEMATICS AND PHYSICS CURRICULAE OF EAST GERMAN SCHOOLS

Ideology, politics, and moral standards are the basic values of loyalty, as leadership and teaching are the main methods for inculcating patriotic feelings; consequently, the pupil will be able to be a "good socialist soldier." Being a socialist soldier is the most sublime of feelings concerning loyalty—killing in the name of the socialist fatherland, in case of emergency even one's own West German brother. Here are some examples, which illustrate the "obvious militarism" in schools:

1. A foreword, written in a mathematics textbook in 1962, concerning the chapter of quadratic equations and functions: "The socialistic countries are equipped with the best weapons. E.g., a modern Soviet supersonic bomber" (with illustration -UZ) (*Mathematik*, 1962, p. 93). Another example in the same book includes calculations of power and power-functions that are illustrated with a trench mortar and five GDR-soldiers.
2. A number of examples from a 10th-grade physics textbook of 1965:
   a) repetition of the "Popov versus Marconi" controversy (as described above; cf. also Kauffeldt, 1950);
   b) a story on the peaceful nature of Soviet nuclear research;
   c) an emphasis that the television was invented by a *Russian* engineer (albeit living in the U.S.A.);
   d) discussion of the use of radar equipment in war situations;
   e) description of the use of prism-binoculars by soldiers;
   f) the development of nuclear weapons (*Physik*, 1965).

The way in which the development of nuclear weaponry is described in that textbook is illustrative of ways in which socialization goals are interwoven with educational information:

During the time of the Second World War the Nazi-Germany and the U.S.A. founded research teams for developing atomic weapons. The imperialistic Germany was close to getting the atomic-bomb. That's the reason why A. Einstein and other famous scientists helped the American imperialists to produce this bomb. Although being victorious, the U.S. Air Force dropped two atomic bombs on Hiroshima and Nagasaki. They wanted to present their new weapon to all the world. (*Physik*, 1965, pp. 185–189)

The issue of the use of the nuclear bomb is exploited to equate American "imperialism" with the militaristic goals of former Nazi Germany:

[Nazi] Germans wanted to have "the bomb", in reality Americans had it and used it!
Who is a greater war criminal?
The best defense against American imperialists and "the bomb" is the Soviet fight for peace and disarmament! *Physik*, 1965, pp. 185–189)

An analysis of different educational literature from the East German education system has revealed a widespread use of military content in the process of teaching basic physics and mathematics to school children (see further evidence in Darr & Zänker, 1985).

Some further examples from "teaching help-books" from East Germany would make the socialization aims of the examples even more evident, since these books are meant for *teachers,* whom they inform about expected psychological effects:

I. Physics teaching in the 9th grade (Source: *Unterrichtshilfen. Physik. Klasse 9,* 1982a)
    1. The pupil has to report about Galileo. He has to put emphasis on the similarity of Galileo's working method and "our materialistic method" (p. 41).
    2. In context with the chapter "the oblique throw": The teacher shows the difference between the throw-parabola and ballistic curve. He calculates ballistic curves and demonstrate the importance of ballistic for pupils future as soldiers. The scientific technology must be comparable to artillery and "Sputnik-rockets" with the aim of producing "a partial feeling or opinion concerning the pupil" (pp. 45–46).
    3. What is the importance of "artificial space satellites"?
        – connection between the socialistic system and research;
        – the position of GDR in Comecon;
        – possibility of finding answers for scientific and technical problems by their own means in socialistic countries;
        – collective cooperation between the socialistic countries in the space exploration;
        – a "partial point of view" for the understanding of the significance of Soviet satellites.
        These are the fundamental "educational aims" in knowledge about "artificial satellites" (p. 92).
    4. In the context of the topic "magnetism," one pupil has to give an example of military uses of the compass (pp. 135–137).
        When applying all physical knowledge to practice, pupils get ready to execute planned behavior and abilities (pp. 231 ff.).
        [That meant that the practical exercise in the end of the school year demonstrates the realization of "educational aim": physical knowledge as a means for developing pupil's loyalty].
II. Physics teaching in the 10th grade (Source: *Unterrichtschilfe. Physik. Klasse,* 10., 1982b):
    1. Teaching about "nuclear sciences" gives the same well-known point of view as the textbook [see the point above on atomic weapons]:
        "Only the existence of imperialistic countries, first of all of the U.S.A. would be the base for using nuclear weapons. That's why all socialist countries are forced to develop nuclear weap-

ons too. The example of Oak Ridge (U.S.A.) in 1945 showed, that the imperialists would be wasting much resources producing the bomb only with the aim "to rule the world" (p. 28).

2. The topic "waves": "The knowledge has to serve as a base for ideological interpretation with the following educational aim: The pupil will work as wireless operator. He will be well-qualified in premilitary training and help to defend the socialist fatherland" (p. 147).

The mathematics "teaching help-books" show more general recommendations than those for physics. Compared to physics, mathematics teachers have to coordinate the individual chapters and the curriculum that "demands ideological education." The following examples are of interest in that respect:

I. Grade 9 (Source: *Unterrichtshilfen. Mathematik. Klasse 9,* 1980): "Mathematics serve as a solution-means for problems and processes in nature, technics and society. . . . Mathematical knowledge especially in the way of applied mathematics will be helpful for pupils to find solutions in connection with the demands of socialist society" (pp. 73, 144).

II. Grade 10 (Source: *Unterrichtshilfen. Mathematik. Klasse 10,* 1979): Mathematical tasks have to be coordinated with applied mathematics by the teacher in the following fields:
   – Socialist economy: e.g., statistics; production methods and results in industry and agriculture (p. 42).
   – Socialistic technology: e.g., work of machines (pp. 96–97).
   – The military field: e.g., bomb-attacks; speed calculations for fighter-bombers, fighters, helicopters, tanks, and military vehicles; topographical survey, etc. (pp. 103–105).

MESSAGES TOWARDS CHILDREN IN THE EAST AND WEST GERMANIES: A DIRECT TEXTUAL COMPARISON

The implicit socializing message of East German mathematics textbooks becomes particularly clear if it can be compared with texts meant for sale to the West—for the schools of German Federal Republic. Usually, such comparisons are rarely possible, since parallel "East" and "West" versions of the same book hardly ever exist. However, in the case of mathematics textbooks, such a comparison is possible. A special "Mathematics Survey" for 8th–10th grades was published in East Germany first for the consumption of the educational system of GDR (*Mathematik in Übersichten,* 1973). Three years later, a parallel version of the same textbook was published in GFR for West-German schools (*Mathematik in Übersichten,* 1976).

The following *corresponding* places from these texts that represent the way the history of mathematics is presented to students are illustrative of the goals of "secondary socialization":

A. The East-German version:
"1829: Russian mathematician, N. Lobatschewski found interesting research results about special geometry (geometry by Euclid). At the same time you can find similar results in the work of the Hungarian Janos Bolyai and Carl Friedrich Gauss" (pp. 259–262).
B. The West-German version:
"1829: Carl Friedrich Gauss developed the proof about the parallel-axiom.
Russian mathematician N. Lobatschewski and Hungarian Janos Bolyai developed a geometry without this axiom" (pp. 259–262).

Another example:
The special "Physics Survey" (*Physik in Übersichten,* 1970 and 1976)—same publishing forms as "Mathematics Survey"—show different facts about the moon-landing in 1969.

A. In GDR-Survey:
"1970. Landing of the movable laboratory 'Lunochod' on moon. Research of moon, Moon-stone was brought to the earth." (Physik in Übersichten, 1970, p. 242).
B. In GFR-licence-published Survey:
"1969/70: Research of the moon. Firstly men set Feet on the moon." (Physik in Übersichten, 1976, p. 242).

CONCLUSIONS

Educational systems in all countries reflect the social-political context that dominates the given country at the particular historical period. The East German educational system has been molded in accordance with the political ideology of that state since the end of the Second World War. In this chapter, the ways in which socialization for loyalty has been embedded in the context of mathematics and physics curriculae in the schools in East Germany (GDR) were briefly analysed. The core of the socialization process in the "objective" or "hard" science curriculae in East Germany is the axiom that no science exists outside its ideological context—there is no "objective science" separate from the social ideology of the given society. Based on that axiom, the principle of "partisanship" of science—all science has to be in service of the "right" perspective—is advocated. Given that, it is not surprising that the teaching of mathematics and physics in East German schools is aimed at two goals in parallel—on the one hand, it is to provide children with basic knowledge (which, by virtue of its fundamental nature, is universal and impartial to any social context). On the other hand, the content matter of real-life examples is set up so as to promote the idea of in-group/out-group separation and conflict. The latter is accomplished first by explicit emphasis on the advancements of Soviet and "German socialist" science. In parallel, many of the examples in physics textbooks are given in the context of military activity—thus connecting the study of basic science with the potential use of it in the military context whenever the social-political system decides to call its citizens up for demonstrating their loyalty in practice.

REFERENCES

Baske, S., & Engelbert, M. (Eds.). (1966). *Dokumente zur Bildungspolitik in der sowjetischen Besatzungszone Deutschlands* [Documents about the educational policy in the Soviet occupied zone of Germany.] Bonn and West Berlin, West Germany: Bundesministerium für Gesamtdeutsche Fragen. [Publ. by the Department for all-German affairs.]

Churchill, W. (1960). *Der Zweite Weltkrieg* [The Second World War.] Berne, Switzerland—Stuttgart, West Germany: Alfred Scherz.

Darr, H.-J., & Zänker, U. (1985). "Rechnen" zwischen Schützengraben und Kernwaffenstrahlen: Physik und Mathematik im Dienste des DDR-Militarismus ["Calculations" between trench and nuclear-weapons-rays. Physics and mathematics helping by GDR-militarism.] *Pädagogische Rundschau* [Pedagogical Review], *39*, 349–363.

Die Grossbauten der Stalinschen Epoche. (1951). [The grandiose constructions of the Stalin epoch.] *Mathematik und Naturwissenschaften in der neuen Schule* [Mathematics and natural sciences in the new school], *3*, 249–266.

Joliot-Curie, F. (1951). Ein hervorragender Friedenskämpfer und Wissenschaftler erhielt den Stalinpreis [A prominent peace-fighter and scientist became the Stalin-price]. *Mathematik und Naturwissenschaften in der neuen Schule* [Mathematics and natural sciences in the new school], *3*, 305–308.

Kauffeldt, A. (1950). Die Geschichte der Entdeckung der drahtlosen Telegraphie [The history of discovering of wireless telegraphy]. *Mathematik und Naturwissenschaften in der neuen Schule* [Mathematics and natural sciences in the new school], *2*, 324–335.

Klaus, G. (1950). Die Bedeutung des "Anti-Dühring" für die moderne Natur-wissenschaft [The importance of "Anti-Duhring" for modern natural sciences]. *Mathematik und Naturwissenschaften in der neuen Schule* [Mathematics and natural sciences in the new school], *2*, 505–519.

Lehreraktivisten tagten. (1949). [Teachers-activists meeted.] *die neue schule* [the new school], *4*, 2–5.

Leonhard, W. (1955). *Die Revolution entlässt ihre Kinder* [Revolution dismisst their children]. Cologne, West Germany: Kiepenheuer und Witsch.

Lindner, J. (1946). Die Gestalt des NEUEN Volkslehrers [The figure of the NEW people's teacher]. *die neue schule* [the new school], *1*, 14–15.

Lüders, R. (1949). Aktivistenbewegung und progressiver Leistungslohn. Ein Beispiel für die Behandlung im mathematischen Unterricht [Activist movement and efficiency wage. An example for mathematics instruction]. *die neue schule* [the new school], *4*, 17–21.

Lüders, R. (1950). Der Fünfjahrplan zur Entwicklung der Volkswirtschaft der Deutschen Demokratischen Republik und der mathematisch-naturwissen-schaftliche Unterricht [The five-year-plan for the economical development of the GDR and the instructions of mathematics and physics]. *Mathematik und Naturwissenschaften in der neuen Schule* [Mathematics and natural sciences in the new school], *2*, 547–555.

Mathematik. Lehrbuch für die Oberschule. Klasse 9. (1962). [Mathematics. Textbook for the 9th grade]. East Berlin, East Germany: Volk und Wissen Verlag.

Mathematik in Übersichten. Wissensspeicher für die Klassen 8 bis 10. (1973). [Mathematics Survey. Collected knowledge for grades 8 to 10]. East Berlin, East Germany: Volk und Wissen Verlag.

Mathematik in Übersichten. Wissensspeicher für die Sekundarstufe I. (1976). [Mathematics Survey. Collected knowledge for secondary schools]. Cologne: Aulis Verlag Deubner & Co KG.

Möller-Krumbholtz, D. (1950 a). Aufgaben des naturwissenschaftlichen Unter-richts [Tasks of the natural-sciences instruction]. *Mathematik und Naturwissenschaften in der neuen Schule* [Mathematics and natural sciences in the new school], *2*, 1–4.

Möller-Krumbholtz, D. (1950 b). Die Zentralfachkurse für die mathematisch-naturwissenschaftlichen Fächer [Central teaching-courses for mathematics and natural sciences instructions]. *Mathematik und Naturwissenschaften in der neuen Schule* [Mathematics and natural sciences in the new school], *2*, 5–8.

Physik. Lehrbuch für die Oberschule. Klasse 10. (1965). [Physics. Textbook for secondary schools. 10th grade]. East Berlin, East Germany: Volk und Wissen Verlag.

Physik in Übersichten. Wissensspeicher für die Klassen 9 und 10. (1970). [Physics Survey. Collected knowledge for grades 9 and 10]. East Berlin, East Germany: Volk und Wissen Verlag.

Physik in Übersichten. Wissensspeicher für die Sekundarstufe I. (1976). [Physics

Survey. Collected knowledge for secondary schools]. Cologne: Aulis Verlag Deubner & Co KG.

Renneberg, W. (1949). Physikalische Chemie und Zweijahresplan im Unterricht [Physical chemistry and two-year-plan in instruction]. *die neue schule* [the new school], *4,* 84–86.

Siebert, H. (1951). Fünf Jahre demokratische Schulreform im naturwissenschaftlichen Unterricht [Five years of democratic school-reform in instructions of mathematics and physics]. *Mathematik und Naturwissenschaften in der neuen Schule* [Mathematics and natural sciences in the new school], *3,* 449–460.

Unterrichtshilfen Mathematik. Klasse 10. (1979). [Teaching help-book: "Mathematics". 10th grade]. East Berlin, East Germany: Volk und Wissen Verlag.

Unterrichtshilfen Mathematik. Klasse 9. (1980). [Teaching help-book: "Mathematics". 9th grade]. East Berlin, East Germany: Volk und Wissen Verlag.

Unterrichtshilfen Physik. Kasse 9. (1982a). [Teaching help-book: "Physics". 9th grade]. East Berlin, East Germany: Volk und Wissen Verlag.

Unterrichtshilfen Physik. Klasse 10. (1982b). [Teaching help-book: "Physics". 10th grade]. East Berlin, East Germany: Volk und Wissen Verlag.

Wandel, P. (1946). Schlusswort zum Pädagogischen Kongress. [Summary on pedagogical congress]. *die neue schule* [the new school], *1,* 335–336.

EPILOGUE

Ontogeny of Co-Construction of Culture within Socially Organized Environmental Settings

Jaan Valsiner

Department of Psychology
University of North Carolina

The core idea that unifies the contributions to the two volumes of *Child Development within Culturally Structured Environments* is straightforward: child development takes place within environments that are physically structured in accordance with the cultural meaning systems of the people who inhabit these environments. Volume I dealt mainly with the reasoning of parents and their conduct in interaction with children. Contributions included in that volume led to the need for viewing child development as a *constructive* social process, in which the contributions of both the developing child and his or her caregiver(s) leads to the emergence of novel psychological phenomena in the course of ontogeny.

Contributions to the present volume addressed the issue of social co-construction of child development in more specific ways. Not surprisingly, theoretical concerns dominate in this volume (especially in the first five chapters). Constructivist perspectives on development are rare in existing literature on child development, partially because the theoretical basis of developmental psychology is notoriously underdeveloped at the present time. It is therefore a rather complicated intellectual task to try to conceptualize development as a co-constructivist process. The contributors to the present volume try to proceed in that direction, offering rather variable solutions to the problem. None of the solutions offered need to be in any way "final," since the construction of a theoretical perspective is a complicated process where first solutions rarely turn out to be the best.

Taken together, the present volume outlines a co-constructivist approach to the study of child development that emphasizes the interdependent participation of both the parents and the children in the latters' development. Such an approach has been only rarely advocated in developmental psychology (Wozniak, 1986). It emerges from the traditions of interactionist (Bell, 1979; Bell & Harper, 1977; Cairns, 1979; Sears, 1951) and transactionist perspectives (Sameroff, 1975, 1982). It sets the adult–child reciprocity into an environmentally structured context (Bronfenbrenner, 1979, 1986), where the regulation of child–environment relationships is the main role that adult–child interaction plays. It is of interest to elaborate on some generalizations about the environment-supported social process of child development. Two issues are of particular interest here:

1. What is the meaning of "culture"—as it provides guidance for the ontogeny of particular individual children? How does the variability between children in their culturally structured childhood "life courses" relate to the shared aspect of "culture" that is common to all families of those children?
2. What are the ways in which culture is transmitted from parental generation to that of children? How do both the "transmitters" (parents, teachers, caregivers) and the "recipients" of that transmission (children and their peers) participate in the transmission process?

Both of these two problem domains are closely intertwined with the co-constructivist emphasis of the present volume. First, high interpersonal variability of forms of social interaction (i.e., the process through which culture transmission takes place) was demonstrated in a number of contributions. Furthermore, similarly high variability was observed in the products of transmission (e.g., children's self-reported coping strategies in middle childhood), and in the cognitive processes of caregivers. At the same time, the populations to which the respective samples of subjects belonged could be described as "sharing" the "culture" of the particular ethnic group. Secondly, the interest of the majority of the contributors to this volume is in the study of the process of cultural transmission between adults and children. That process itself is a phenomenon that occurs in a high variety of forms. Furthermore, particular episodes of adult–child interaction process may be of limited consequence for the general outcome of the culture transmission (i.e., it is impossible to find direct, elementaristic causal links between a certain form of adult–child interaction in a particular situation as an antecedent, and the long-term "success" in the child's enculturation). At the same time, that high variety of forms of social interaction process is oriented towards the goals of child socialization within the culture. How, then, does the cultural transmission process (in general) function in a sufficiently robust way, if it is to be composed from a high variety of context-bound episodes of social interaction, which (each in particular) are of little long-term consequence? These questions are in need to be addressed explicitly if we desire to understand the processes that are responsible for children's development under guidance of their social environments.

TWO PERSPECTIVES ON CULTURE: COLLECTIVE AND PERSONAL

There are two facets of culture that are often left indistinguishable from each other when culture is discussed. On the one hand, culture is a suprapersonal (collectively shared) entity. On the other hand, however, culture has something to do with the development of highly idiosyncratic psychological functions of every individual person who can be said to "belong" to the given culture. How can these two sides of culture be reconciled?

Culture as a Collective Entity

Culture has been a term with many implied meanings in anthropology (Schweder & LeVine, 1984) as well as in psychology (Jahoda, 1984; Rohner, 1984). Therefore, a brief overview of two different kinds of views on culture as a collective phenomenon is necessary in order to prepare the reader for the use of this term in our present context.

Culture viewed as a "variable." In psychology, it has often been used as a "variable" in investigators' statistically flavored thinking in cross-cultural comparisons (e.g., Whiting & Whiting, 1975). As such a "variable," culture is practically used as a *synchronic* index that marks a person's formal membership in an assumedly homogeneous social unit (similarly to "social class," "sex," and other frequently used index variables). This way of utilizing "culture" in psychological discourse capitalizes on the detectable differences between different social conglomerates. For example, a comparison of "the American culture" with "the German culture" overlooks the heterogeneity within both of the cultures. Such a comparison of "typical" features of cultures does not penetrate into the essence of "culture" as the reason for some similarity (on a background of formidable dissimilarities) between persons who are ascribed to the given "culture." For instance, the majority of so-called "effects of culture" that have surfaced in cross-cultural psychology where different samples of subjects "from" different cultures are compared with the help of widely popular statistical techniques of the analysis of variance. Inductive generalizations from such studies, claiming the "effect of culture" on particular psychological parameters, are of no explanatory relevance, since they first of all eliminate interpersonal variability from consideration (by interpreting the results averaged for the given "culture" sample), and subsequently arrive at "effects of culture" by comparing the averages for different "cultural samples." In essence, such comparisons provide us with some knowledge about differences in average results between samples drawn from different "cultures," and can be interpreted only within the interindividual metatheoretical frame of reference. As is demonstrated elsewhere (Valsiner, 1987), that frame of reference is rather unproductive for the use in social sciences. Treatment of "culture" as psychological "index variable" is therefore leading the investigator towards replacing the fundamental research question (what is culture and how does it function?) by a totally different issue: as long as we classify human beings into supposedly homegenous classes (and label those "cultures"), what are the differences between these classes in some responses of their average representatives to the administration of psychological instruments of our choice to them? Empirical data that are produced to answer some particular version of this displaced research question will be inconsequential as to the basic question of how culture functions in the process of child development.

Culture as a structured causal system. An alternative view on the "culture" makes use of that term in reference to the structural organization of social norms, rituals, conduct rules, and meaning systems that are shared by persons belonging to a certain ethnically homogeneous group. That perspective treats "culture" as a self-organized system, which can be studied either in its static (or homeostatic) form (e.g., Levi-Strauss, 1963), or as undergoing constant structural transformation in the course of its history. It is that latter—structural dynamic—view of culture that is implicated when we try to make sense of children's development within culturally structured environments. This view has been present in the "cultural-historical" perspective in psychology (Luria, 1974; Vygotsky, 1929, 1986). Nevertheless, it has usually remained an implicit theoretical idea behind investigators' empirical description of their anthropological research materials. Anthropologists, like psychologists, have found it difficult to conceptualize change, especially as it occurs in the form of transformation of structures of cultural processes.

It is the structural-dynamic view of culture that can be used in the theoretical endeavors of the co-constructivist perspective on child development. Undoubtedly, such use will increase the theoretical complexity of the task understanding child development. The "culture" as a structured context of child development can no longer be taken for granted in its static form, but has to be viewed as undergoing constant change itself. However, that aspect of culture is essential, since the co-constructivist perspective on child development has to include *culture change* as one of the by-products of adults' and children's joint construction of *novel* psychological and social phenomena. This, in its turn, makes it necessary to explicate in which ways individuals' innovations can lead to culture change, and to elaborate the ways in which individual persons become interdependent with their culture as a collective entity.

Personal Culture

Culture as a collective (i.e., interpersonally shared) entity has its counterpart in the psychological domains of individual persons—*as a result of internalization of experiences first provided in the sphere of social transaction.* The system of culture as a structured social entity provides the basis for a myriad of individually unique forms of internalized "personal cultures"—the personal versions of the "social culture" that fit the developmental life history of the particular persons.

The relevance of personal internalization of social expectations and experiences is no news in social sciences. It emerged in the context of efforts to make sense of "imitation" (see Danziger, 1985; Scheerer, 1985) in nature, and of "social hypnotism" or "suggestion" in the society (Janet, 1889; Tarde, 1884). It led into the establishment of the "sociogenetic perspective" in psychology by James Mark Baldwin and Josiah Royce in the 1890s, from which both the "social interactionism" of George Herbert Mead and the "cultural-historical perspective" of Lev Vygotsky emerged (Valsiner & Van der Veer, 1988; Van der Veer & Valsiner, 1988). Internalization is viewed as the basic mechanism that unites every person's psychological processes with the phenomena of his or her social environment in which the person acts and interacts (Baldwin, 1898; Mead, 1934; Royce, 1903; Vygotsky, 1982; Wertsch & Stone, 1985).

Internalization and externalization. Internalization is a general process that takes place in individual-specific forms over the development of persons over their idiosyncratic life courses. As a result, each person's "personal culture" is unique in what it includes (in the form of personal senses as reflections of cultural meanings—see Vygotsky, 1986, Chap.

7), as well as in the ways by which content of "personal culture" becomes related with the environment of the person. The latter relation takes the form of *externalization* of one's "personal culture"—organization of one's environment and external appearance in ways that fit the person's internalized psychological "needs." The externalization of the person's (previously) internalized psychological processes reintroduces the products of internalization into the sphere of social transaction. Mati Heidmets, one of the few theoretically-oriented thinkers among contemporary environmental psychologists, has argued that it is the externalized part of "personal culture," located in the person's environment, which could serve as the unit of analysis in environmental psychology:

> The unit of analysis of the inclusion of the physical environment in a person's psychological sphere can be found in the *personalized environment,* that is, the part of the environment that is controlled by the subject who regulates others' access to it, or which serves the purpose to expose the self to others. The subject identifies oneself with that part of the environment, which functions as a means of regulating his or her social relationships. Different objects and places can perform that mediating function: for instance, personal things, the person's room, or hospital room or place in school classroom, and so forth. The goal of environmental mediation of social relation can be in the *reduction of uncertainty* in these relations. Through personalization of one's immediate environment, the person largely determines the range of possible behavior by others towards him or her: Who can enter the personalized territory, what may one do on that territory, and so forth. Personalization gives stable, material form to the social relationships, which are made explicit through their projection into the surrounding environment. (Heidmets, 1985, p. 223)

Heidmets's functional view on the use of environment by persons for psychological purposes makes it possible to study "personal culture" in explicit ways. A study of that kind would involve a careful scrutiny of subjects' personal belongings, environments that they have organized for themselves (e.g., preferred places for private "leisure") or for their children (e.g., children's rooms in the home). The psychological roles that these objects and places play in the system of their "owner's" and "creator's" personality needs to be studied through explication of the personal "senses" (in Paulhan's and Vygotsky's use of the term—as the personal counterpart of socially shared "meanings") that are inseparable from them. Only rarely has that angle of research been seriously used in contemporary psychology. Its best contemporary example is the work by Csikszentmihalyi and Rochberg-Halton (1981), which nevertheless lacks an explicit developmental orientation.

The internalizing and externalizing person: active or passive? The internalization and externalization processes can be elaborated from two irreconcilably opposite perspectives that differ in their axiomatic treatment of the role of the person in these processes. First, the internalizing (externalizing) person may be viewed as a passive "carrier"— first, of the external social experience into the internal psychological sphere, and secondly, in a similarly passive externalization of the internal psychological content. If the internalizing/externalizing person is axiomatically assumed to play a passive role, then the internalized "picture" of the external experiences of people should accurately mimic the latter, perhaps with some "signal loss" detectable in the process. Such a view of internalization is a kin to strict environmental determinism—persons exposed to certain social "input" would transpose it into their internal-psychological sphere, thus becoming "internal copies" of the social "input." In other terms—everything present in the person's mind is a direct reflection of the social environment. That reflection is seen as only slightly altered by some "internalization error" (an analogue of the "measurement error" in classical physics). The person, according to that perspective, is *not* expected to restructure the internalized content material and turn it into a reflection of the social experiences that possesses *new features that were not part of the "social input."* The second perspective on internalization differs from the first one exactly by making the latter assumption. In every instance of internalization (or externalization), the person is active in the sense of transforming the social "input" (or "personal output") into a new structural form that goes beyond "the information given." In this respect, any idea or emotion that a person has internalized from social experience can be transformed into novel form as a result. The internal "picture" of the "social input" does not passively imitate that input, but goes actively beyond it in some, personally idiosyncratic, ways.

The distinction between the active and passive roles of the internalizing/externalizing person is theoretically crucial for the co-constructivist viewpoint, shared by the majority of contributors to this volume. *It is impossible in principle to build a co-constructivist theory of child development on the basis of the idea that the child is a mere passive "target" of the "social input" provided by socially organized environments.* In any co-constructivist theory, the child necessarily is included as an active partner (even if a *de facto* "novice"—see Chapter 1, by Winegar) in the social process that guides his or her own development. That active role is observed in the child's opportunity for modifying his relations with the environment, in ways that do not follow the goals set by his "socializers"—adults or older siblings.

The active role of the young in the co-construction process makes it natural that individuals' personal cultures are idiosyncratically created, in ways that bear some basic similarity to the communally shared collective "culture." A developing child is surrounded with many adults and older siblings, all of whom share the "collective culture" by way of idiosyncratically generated unique "personal cultures." The child develops within an environment that is being organized by "social others" who are bearers of different "personal cultures" (by way of externalization of those into the environment). He is not "confronted" by a "monolithic" and strictly structured "social culture" that guides the child's development. This rearrangement of the emphasis from what is common for the persons in the child's social environment (i.e., the culture as a collective entity), to the multiplicity of "personal cultures" that organize child–environment relationships, sets the theoretical issue of cultural transmission up in a novel way.

CHILD DEVELOPMENT AND CULTURAL TRANSMISSION

A widespread idea accepted in cultural (social) anthropology is that culture is learned in the course of children's growing up, and that it superimposes constraints on the biological maturation of developing individuals. This view of children's socialization is based on a limited set of culturally axiomatic assumptions that have been used by anthropologists over decades.

Cultural Transmission Viewed as Passive Reception

Anthropological literature on culture transmission is full of examples that are given to prove that culture (in its "social" form—as described above) "influences" or "determines" the outcomes of child socialization (Benedict, 1949, 1953; Middleton, 1970; Mead, 1963; Whiting, 1963; Whiting & Child, 1953; and others). The unidirectional (from adults to children) flow of information was the axiom used by social anthropologists in the past to explain cultural transmission from generation to generation. Bronislaw Malinowski outlined that perspective emphatically in 1936:

> The integral process of education in every society consists in the *formation of mind, character and a sense of citizenship*. This process exists at the lowest level of development, among the Bushmen, Australian aborigines, or Firelanders, as well as in Chicago, Cape Town, or London. In the more highly differentiated societies we also find schooling, in which the child learns from professional teachers such skills as reading and writing,

natural philosophy. In no community, however highly differentiated, does the school alone teach future citizenship. The earliest *molding of mind and character* must be given at home. The *influence* of playmates may be incalculable for good or evil. Apprenticeship to a particular craft or profession, as well as apprenticeship to life, is not *given* at school, but in actual contact with the future work to be done. (Malinowski, 1976, p. 42; emphasis added)

Malinowski's emphasis on the child as the recipient of cultural transmission, whose mind and character are "molded," first at home and then through schooling, and who may further be "influenced" by peers, represents the tradition of social anthropology in which the passive nature of the socialized person is an a priori given. Such assumption of the passive role of the recipient of teaching follows from the history of education, where this idea can be seen to be accepted by different religious contexts of adults' educational endeavours (see Sommerville, 1983; Wagner, 1983). In contemporary anthropological literature, it has survived with some modifications that cater to inter-individual variability between children (e.g., Dobbert, 1976). Although a transactional approach to culture transmission that emphasizes the active role of the "recipient" has emerged in anthropology over the recent decade (see Gearing, 1976), and anthropologists have begun to take interest in the analysis of the education as a process (Kimball, 1974; Spindler, 1974, 1976), the crucial overlook of the active role of the recipient in cultural transmission lingers on in that discipline. Only infrequently have anthropologists conceptualized children as coproducers of cultural meanings, thus viewing cultural transmission as bi-directional in nature (Holland & Eisenhart, 1983).

The reasons for the perseverance of unidirectional models of cultural transmission are quite obvious. Overwhelmingly, anthropology has been nondevelopmental in its emphasis, and has demonstrated particular difficulties when faced with cultural phenomena that are undergoing rapid change (Srivastava, 1986). Children's culture acquisition is a similar phenomenon of change, only in the ontogenetic sphere. The limits of anthropologists' views on culture have been noted by some leading investigators of the past:

It is strange how little ethnology has concerned itself with the intimate genetic problem of the acquirement of culture by the child. In the current language of ethnology culture dynamics seems to be almost entirely a matter of adult definition and adult transmission from generation to generation and from group to group. The humble child, who is laboriously orienting himself in the world of his society, yet is not, in the normal case, sacrificing his forthright psychological status as a significant ego, is somehow left out of account. This strange omission is obviously due to the fact that anthropology has allowed itself to be victimized by a convenient but dangerous metaphor. This metaphor is always persuading us that culture is a neatly packed-up assemblage of forms of behavior handed over piece-meal, but without serious breakage, to the passively inquiring child. I have come to feel that it is precisely the supposed "givenness" of culture that is the most serious obstacle to our real understanding of the nature of culture and cultural change and of their relationship to individual personality. Culture is not, as a matter of sober fact, a "given" at all. It is so only by a polite convention of speech. (Sapir, 1934, pp. 413–414)

The "obstacle" that Edward Sapir so vividly saw to limit the theoretical sphere of anthropology in the 1930s remains in place five decades later. Its metatheoretical basis is the traditional lack of interest on behalf of anthropologists in the psychological processes of child development. Instead, cultural transmission and its analogue in the form of mass communication theories since late 1940s (e.g., Lasswell, 1949) follow the heuristic model provided by Shannon's information theory which is appropriate to technical communication systems. In those systems, the possibility that the receiving device actively restructures the "messages" is ruled out. In contrast to that, in communication between active human beings processes that lead to restructuring of the "messages" by their recipients prevail.

A Co-constructivist Perspective on Cultural Transmission

At least in one respect, there is no need to disagree with traditional anthropologists' view of socialization. Culture—in the sense of collective entity—is undoubtedly learned by the children in the context of their *whole* experience within their environments, rather than merely in settings where adults explicitly teach the children (Williams, 1958). However, it is in respect to the ways of *how the learning takes place in the context of implicit and explicit teaching* that contributors to this book part ways with traditions of anthropology. The co-constructivist perspective, as it can be applied to the issue of cultural transmission, implies that *children transcend the culture of their parents in the process of learning it.* Our perspective may promise to give a developmental answer to the paradoxical issue of cultural transmission that was captured by Gregory Bateson in his metalogue 'How much do you know?':

Daughter: . . . Do you know more than I do?
Father: Hmm—I once knew a little boy in England who asked his father, "Do fathers always know more than sons?" and the father said, "Yes."

The next question was, "Daddy, who invented the steam engine?" and the father said, "James Watt." And then the son came back with "—but why didn't James Watt's father invent it?" (Bateson, 1971, p. 21)

Bateson's playful paradox leads us straight into the crucial question—how is inventiveness among the young generation possible if the cultural transmission process is aimed at the unidirectional transfer of the culture from parents to their children? The co-constructivist view deals with child development *within* the context where adults try their best to transmit their culture to the children, but never succeed *in the exact way* as they contemplate it. The *active* role that the child plays in cultural transmission guarantees that the culture that the children's generation shares goes necessarily beyond that of their parents. The parents organize the life environments of children in ways that promote the cultural transmission in their ways. However, the promoted cultural messages are actively assimilated into the children's internalized knowledge structures *in novel ways*. Children's knowledge structures are simultaneously accommodated to the kind of cultural messages that are assimilated by the child. As a result, the child internalizes cultural input in his or her personally unique ways, which nevertheless come to be similar in the children's age cohort, by way of being shared collectively. The process of collective sharing, in way of discourse, leads to negotiated commonalities in individuals' knowledge that are socially (interpersonally) meaningful. That process is similar to any collective construction of "social norms" that has been described in social psychology (Sherif, 1936). The stucture of the process of collective construction was analyzed in Chapter 5 by Robinson, in a framework that fits Baldwin's and Vygotsky's lines of theorizing in psychology. Furthermore, the co-constructivist perspective builds upon the traditions of work of those anthropologists who have emphasized the relevance of active symbolization in psychological functioning of persons within their cultural environments (Hallowell, 1950; Obeyesekere, 1981). It is at the intersection of the activities of persons and their surrounding (communal) culture that symbolization takes place within the socially constructed "personal cultures" of individuals.

CHILDREN'S DEVELOPMENT WITHIN SOCIO-CULTURALLY STRUCTURED ENVIRONMENTS

The two perspectives on culture—one viewing it as communally shared, and the other as a personally internalized psychological entity—connect the psychological traditions of the study of child development with the psychological traditions of the study of child development with those of anthropologists and sociologists. All child development that necessarily occurs within structured environmental contexts is guided by the culture as a collective entity. That guidance leads to the internalization of the shared culture by the developing child, which is evidenced in the emergence of his or her "personal culture." In the course of social life, the person externalizes his or her "personal culture" in ways that meaningfully organize the physical environment. Thus, a person's "personal culture" becomes accessible to others, including developing children. The great variety of "personal cultures" that we can observe within any social or ethnic group serves as a resource for the next generation, the members of which develop as future full-fledged members of that group. That resource, however, is made use of by the developing child, who is active so that his or her activity in respect to his or her environment necessarily involves constructing "personal culture" as a means for future encounters with novel environments. It is the personal construction of culture that serves as the major tool in the hands of *Homo sapiens* in the constant quest for changing oneself with the help of the environment.

REFERENCES

Baldwin, J.M. (1898). On selective thinking. *Psychological Review, 5,* 1–24.
Bateson, G. (1971). *Steps to an ecology of mind.* New York: Ballantine Books.
Bell, R.Q. (1979). Parent, child, and reciprocal influences. *American Psychologist, 34,* 821–826.
Bell, R.Q., & Harper, L. (1977). *Child effects on adults.* Hillsdale, NJ: Erlbaum.
Benedict, R. (1949). Child rearing in certain European countries. *American Journal of Orthopsychiatry, 19,* 342–350.
Benedict, R. (1953). Continuities and discontinuities in cultural conditioning. In C. Kluckhohn & H.A. Murray (Eds.), *Personality in nature, society, and culture* (pp. 522–531). New York: A. Knopf.
Bronfenbrenner, U. (1979). *The ecology of human development.* Cambridge, MA: Harvard University Press.
Bronfenbrenner, U. (1986). Ecology of the family as a context for human development: research perspectives. *Developmental Psychology, 22,* 6, 723–742.
Cairns, R.B. (1979). *Social development.* San Francisco, CA: W.H. Freeman.
Csikszentmihalyi, M., & Rochberg-Halton, E. (1981). *The meaning of things: Domestic symbols and the self.* Cambridge, England: Cambridge University Press.
Danziger, K. (1985). The problem of imitation and explanatory models in early developmental psychology. In G. Eckardt, W.G. Bringmann, & L. Sprung

(Eds.), *Contributions to a history of developmental psychology* (pp. 319–328). Berlin: Mouton.

Dobbert, M.L. (1976). Another route to a general theory of cultural transmission: A systems model. In J.I. Roberts & S.K. Akinsanya (Eds.), *Educational patterns and cultural configurations* (pp. 205–212). New York: David McKay.

Gearing, F.O. (1976). Steps toward a general theory of cultural transmission. In J.I. Roberts & S.K. Akinsanya (Eds.), *Educational patterns and cultural configurations* (pp. 183–194). New York: David McKay.

Hallowell, A.I. (1950). Personality structure and the evolution of man. *American Anthropologist, 52,* 2, 159–173.

Heidmets, M. (1985). Environment as the mediator of human relationships: Historical and ontogenetic aspects. In T. Gärling & J. Valsiner (Eds.), *Children within environments: Toward a psychology of accident prevention* (pp. 217–227). New York: Plenum.

Holland, D.C., & Eisenhart, M. (1983). *Peer groups and the metaphor of cultural transmission.* Paper presented at the meeting of the American Anthropological Association, Chicago, August.

Jahoda, G. (1984). Do we need a concept of culture? *Journal of Cross-Cultural Psychology, 15,* 2, 139–151.

Janet, P. (1889). *L'Automatisme psycholoqique.* Paris: F. Alcan.

Kimball, S. (1974). *Culture and the educative process.* New York: Teachers College Press.

Lasswell, H.D. (1949). The structure and function of communication in society. In W. Schramm (Eds.), *Mass communications* (pp. 102–115). Urbana, IL: University of Illinois Press.

Levi-Strauss, C. (1963). *Structural anthropology.* New York: Harper & Row.

Luria, A.R. (1974). *Istoricheskoe razvitie poznavatel'nykh protsessov.* [Historical development of cognitive processes]. Moscow: Nauka

Malinowski, B. (1976). Native education and culture contact. In J.I. Roberts & S.K. Akinsanya (Eds.), *Educational patterns and cultural configurations* (pp. 42–61). New York: David McKay.

Mead, G.H. (1934). *Mind, self, and society.* Chicago, IL: University of Chicago Press.

Mead, M. (1963). Socialization and enculturation. *Current Anthropology, 4,* 2, 184–188.

Middleton, J. (Ed.) (1970). *From child to adult.* Austin, TX: University of Texas Press.

Obeyesekere, G. (1981). *Medusa's hair: An essay on personal symbols and religious experience.* Chicago, IL: University of Chicago Press.

Rohner, R.P. (1984). Toward a conception of culture for cross-cultural psychology. *Journal of Cross-Cultural Psychology, 156,* 2, 111–138.

Royce, J. (1903). *Outlines of psychology.* London: MacMillan.

Sameroff, A. (1975). Early influences on development: fact or fancy? *Merrill-Palmer Quarterly, 21,* 267–294.

Sameroff, A. (1982). Development and the dialectic: The need for a systems approach. In W.A. Collins (Ed.), *The concept of development. Vol. 15. The Minnesota Symposia on Child Psychology* (pp. 83–103). Hillsdale, NJ: Erlbaum.

Sapir, E. (1934). The emergence of the concept of personality in a study of cultures. *Journal of Social Psychology, 5,* 408–415.

Scheerer, E. (1985). Pre-evolutionary conceptions of imitation. In G. Eckardt, W. Bringmann, & L. Sprung (Eds.), *Contributions to a history of developmental psychology* (pp. 27–53). Berlin: Mouton.

Sears, R.R. (1951). A theoretical framework for personality and social behavior. *American Psychologist, 6,* 476–483.

Sherif, M. (1936). *The psychology of social norms.* New York: Harper & Brothers.

Shweder, R.A., & LeVine, R.L. (Eds.). (1984). *Culture theory: Essays on mind, self, and emotion.* Cambridge, England: Cambridge University Press.

Sommerville, C.J. (1983). The distinction between indoctrination and education in England, 1549–1719. *Journal of the History of Ideas, 44,* 3, 387–406.

Spindler, G.D. (1974). *Education and cultural process: Toward an anthropology of education.* New York: Holt, Rinehardt, & Winston.

Spindler, G.D. (1976). From omnibus to linkages: Cultural transmission models. In J.I. Roberts & S.K. Akinsanya (Eds.), *Educational patterns and cultural configurations* (pp. 177–183). New York: David McKay.

Srivastava, V.K. (1986). Culture and development. *Man in India, 66,* 1, 67–80.

Tarde, G. (1884.) Qu'est-ce qu'une societe? *Revue Philosophique, 18,* 489–510.

Valsiner, J. (1987). *Culture and the development of children's action.* Chichester: Wiley.

Valsiner, J., & Van der Veer (1988). On the social nature of human cognition: An analysis of the shared intellectual roots of George Herbert Mead and Lev Vygotsky. *Journal for the Theory of Social Behaviour, 18,* 117–136.

Van der Veer, R., & Valsiner, J. (in press). *On the origin of Vygotsky's concept of sociogenesis. Developmental Review.*

Vygotski, L.S. (1929). The problem of the cultural development of the child. *Journal of Genetic Psychology, 36,* 415–434.

Vygotsky, L.S. (1982). *Sobranie sochinenii. Vol. 1. Voprosy teorii i istorii psikhologii [Collection of writings. Vol. 1 Problems of theory and history of psychology].* Moscow: Pedagogika.

Vygotsky, L.S. (1986). *Thought and language* (2nd rev. ed.). Cambridge, MA: MIT Press

Wagner, D.A. (1983). Rediscovering "rote": Some cognitive and pedagogical preliminaries. In S. Irvine & J. Berry (Eds.), *Human assessment and cultural factors.* New York: Plenum.

Wertsch, J., & Stone, C.A. (1985). The concept of internalization in Vygotsky's account of the genesis of higher mental functions. In J. Wertsch (Ed.), *Culture, communication, and cognition* (pp. 162–179). Cambridge, England: Cambridge University Press.

Whiting, B. (Ed.). (1963). *Six cultures: Studies in child-rearing.* New York: Wiley.

Whiting, B., & Child, I. (1953). *Child training and personality: A cross-cultural study.* New Haven, CT: Yale University Press.

Whiting, B., & Whiting, J. (1975). *Children of six cultures.* Cambridge, MA: Harvard University Press.

Williams, T.R. (1958). The structure of the socialization process in Papago Indian society. *Social Forces, 36,* 251–256.

Wozniak, R.H. (1986). Notes toward a co-constructive theory of the emotion-cognition relationship. In D.J. Bearison & H. Zimiles (Eds.), *Thought and emotion: Developmental perspectives* (pp. 39–64). Hillsdale, NJ: Erlbaum.

Author Index

Subject Index

A
Action
  aspiration in, 42
  economy of, 39
  goals in, 22, 42–43
    hierarchy of, 22–23
    structure of, 56–62
  intentional, 37
  "primary" and "secondary" (Janet), 38
Adolescence
  initiation rituals, 225, 245–249,
    254–256, 260–262
Affect
  and intelligence, 33–42, 53

B
Behavior
  contingencies in, 82–91
  dependence supportive, 77, 79
  dependent, 78, 79
  "fossilized" (Vygotsky), 109
  independence supportive, 77, 79
  independent, 78, 79

C
Caregivers
  interaction with children, 77–91
  perception of children by, 75–77
  sensitivity of, 67–69
Cognition (see also Conflict)
  and coping, 204–205
  challenges in, 111–116, 132–133
    case studies of, 121–132
    dialectical perspective on, 116–121
  information processing, 113–116
  socialized and nonsocialized, 37
Communication

attempts at, 149–151
listener feedback in, 151, 156
role of shared knowledge in, 144–149
signals of noncomprehension, 139–144,
  152–153
speaker response, 154–157
Competence, 70, 92
Conflict, 29–33, 54–55
Constraints (constraining), 1, 4, 9, 18,
  126–129, 142
Contradiction, 31
Coping, 109, 199–201
  in children, 206–216
  and control, 205–206, 221
  emotional vs. problem-focused, 201
  interactionist perspective on, 203–204,
    216–221
  stage theories of, 202–203
Creeping
  development of, 29, 55–62
Culture
  as a collective entity, 285–287
    as a "variable", 285–286
    as a "causal system", 286–287
  material
    ideology in, 227
  personal, 287–290, 294
  transmission of, 290–293

D
Development
  canalization of, 46–48, 62–63
  cognitive, 3
  sensori-motor, 3, 41–42
Dialectical synthesis, 120

304